LEGAL
AFFAIRS
. . . . .

FREDERICK HERTZ

LEGAL AFFAIRS

· · · · ·

Essential Advice
for Same-Sex Couples

Foreword by
FRANK BROWNING

An Owl Book

Henry Holt and Company / New York

Henry Holt and Company, Inc. / *Publishers since 1866*
115 West 18th Street / New York, New York 10011

Henry Holt® is a registered
trademark of Henry Holt and Company, Inc.

Published in Canada by Fritzhenry & Whiteside Ltd.,
195 Allstate Parkway, Markham, Ontario L3R 4T8.

Library of Congress Cataloging-in-Publication Data
Hertz, Frederick.
Legal affairs : essential advice for same-sex couples /
Frederick Hertz ; foreword by Frank Browning.—1st ed.
p.   cm.
"An Owl book."
Includes bibliographical references and index.
ISBN 0-8050-5224-0 (pbk. : alk paper)
1. Gay couples—Legal status, laws, etc.—United States.
2. Unmarried couples—Legal status, laws, etc.—United States. I. Title.
KF539.H47   1998
346.7301'3—dc21   97-41750

Henry Holt books are available for special promotions and premiums.
For details contact: Director, Special Markets.

First Edition 1998

Designed by Victoria Hartman

Printed in the United States of America
All first editions are printed on acid-free paper.∞

1   3   5   7   9   10   8   6   4   2

To Ran,
for all he has done for me,
for so many years

Contents

Acknowledgments

This book never would have existed without the inspiration and dedication of my agent, Lisa Swayne, formerly of Adler & Robin Books in Washington, D.C. It is every author's fantasy to get a phone call out of nowhere from an agent offering to pitch an idea, and Lisa did just that.

Many of the ideas in this book were inspired by my discussions with other gay and lesbian attorneys in the San Francisco Bay Area who handle same-sex dissolutions. This is one sector of the legal community that truly works cooperatively, even when we find ourselves on opposite sides of a case. Over the last several years I have spoken often with Paige Wickland, Paul Melbostad, Cheryl Sena, and Meriel Lindley of San Francisco and Rachel Ginsburg, Elizabeth Hendrickson, Linda Scaparotti, and Emily Doskow of Oakland, California and I truly appreciate their ideas and collegiality. I also have benefited from conversations with Ann Viitala of Minneapolis, Debra Guston of New Jersey, and Peggy Brady of New York City.

Nonlawyers also have enlightened my effort to make sense of same-sex relationships. My thanks to Eric Marcus, John D'Emilio, Frank Browning, Joyce Lindenbaum, Merle Yost, Stewart Levine, Greg Merrill, Chris Kollaja, Barbara and Dennis Hendrickson, Martina Reaves, Professor Laurent Mayali, Professor Julie Shapiro, and Barbara Raboy for taking the time to share their views and insights with me.

Many others helped keep me organized and efficient as I kept my law practice running while writing this book. Ken Wright and Tracy Sherrod of Henry Holt were perfect editors, there when I needed them, offering encouragement and clear thinking whenever I had doubts, and knowing where to cut and paste. My office staff and the two lawyers I work with, Sanford Margolin and Joel Biatch, have always been ready to pitch in.

I also must express my true appreciation for all that I have learned from my clients. Helping people in the midst of a breakup is not an easy task, but it is far less onerous than being the one enduring the dissolution. Many of my clients have been able to take the time to share their insights and to work with me as a team, and this is part of what makes it all worthwhile.

And finally, my deepest thanks to my partner, Randolph Langenbach, for his continual love and support, for his careful reading of the manuscript, and for his wise suggestions. Randolph has always seen the bigger potentials of life and then helped transform them into actualities. Because of the steadiness of his support and the strength of our relationship, I was able to focus on the needs of my clients knowing our partnership was solid—which is truly what relationships are all about.

Foreword

BY FRANK BROWNING

Marriage, most of us grew up believing, is what our parents did in order to make a family and have children. Mom chose a lacy white dress, trimmed in silk and taffeta. Dad fitted himself for a, well, dull rental tux. And the parents, most likely her parents, coughed up four or five thousand dollars for The Wedding. Then there was the bounty: Silver. China. Useless serving plates. Ugly glasses and overpriced knickknacks that eventually rose to the dark corners of the attic or descended to a yard sale two moves later.

Sometime in our middle adolescence, however, we began to have doubts. Half of us saw the wedding vows turn into alimony checks. Almost all of us began to realize that our eyes were wandering toward hips, breasts, eyebrows, and haircuts that would never fit into those photo spreads in *Brides* magazine. When my brother got married in a fancy Connecticut wedding, it seemed like a grand, frothy party. As best man I drove the newlyweds to their hidden getaway car, where a somewhat tattered "Just Married" tag had been attached. "You're next for this one," they assured me, not knowing that I was far more taken with the sharp-jawed head usher than any of the dewy-eyed bridesmaids.

I can't rule out the possibility that I might sometime head off to Hawaii or Copenhagen, sign a paper, have a party, and find such a sign taped to my rental car. But it doesn't seem likely. Even if it were legally available, I retain severe doubts about the value or the resilience of conventional marriage for queer people in the modern world. As currently organized, the institution doesn't seem to be serving even the heterosexuals particularly well.

Frederick Hertz, however, has not written a brief for the pro-marriage campaigners. He has done something much more valuable. He has examined the general legal principles underlying most marriage contracts, looked at the personal, social, legal, and economic interests governed by marriage laws, and constructed a handbook that those of us who do not marry can use to organize and protect our family relationships.

The key word here is *family*. Married or not, most of us do live in some sort of family. There is the biological one into which we were born. In most states those family members—brothers, sisters, parents, aunts and uncles, sometimes children—do have some rights over our lives and properties which, if we are not careful, can preempt the rights and expectations of our actual mates, partners, and loved ones. While it may happen less frequently now than two decades ago, resentful parents and siblings are still keeping some of us apart from our mates at times of illness or death. Courts in some jurisdictions, as well, are removing the children from queer parents or ordering homosexual partners out of the house where a child is being raised. Those "traditional" families, which we all have, affect everything we do in the unconventional families we have built. Odds are that those influences will continue for a very long time, even if the courts or legislatures should begin to recognize some sort of gay marriage.

Families exist, however, outside of marriage. They always have. Only since the dawn of the Industrial Revolution and the rise of the middle class has modern, legalistic marriage been widely available to ordinary people. Mating rules to prevent too much inbreeding date well into prehistory, but ritual, legal marriage has for the most part existed primarily for the preservation and transfer of property. Until recently, very few of the world's human beings owned anything more than a few household chattels, a goat, a pig, or a donkey. Even so, people fell in love, raised children, fed themselves, and, all too often, abandoned or murdered each other when aggravation or inconvenience grew too burdensome. For better or worse, it is within this sort of family tradition that gay and lesbian people exist. Excluded from the prevailing rules of property conveyance and child rearing, we have fabricated our own pragmatic arrangements.

We like to say that love, or at least passion, forms the foundation of queer families. Well, maybe. Certainly it often requires great love or untold reserves of endurance to overcome the fiercesome barriers and bigotries that queer people face in an often hostile, homophobic society. But before we overcelebrate ourselves, we might also want to undress our motivations more carefully. Gay people can be just as venal as straight people. Lesbians look for material security just as straight women do. Queer men put up with sexual bed death about as often as the husbands of *Peyton Place*. Middle-aged partners often seek out nubile playmates regardless of which genitalia most inspire them. Since we don't live in a state of nature, and since we do live in a society where personal disappointments and resentments are the mother's milk of the legal profession, it would be foolish not to teach ourselves something about the laws that do affect our fluid and ever-evolving homo-families.

Legal Affairs does not provide us boiler-plate forms to settle all the possible contests surrounding love, endurance, and disappointment. Instead, Frederick Hertz asks us to think practically, concretely, about the legal issues our family arrangements raise and then to sit down with our partners to construct legally sound relationships reflecting our own needs and values. Like any good lawyer—and he has handled a great many spousal agreements and dissolutions—Hertz offers no blanket rules or solutions. Rather, he urges us to spend thoughtful hours reflecting on just what sort of husband-wife-partner-mate-lover-fling-or-longtime-companion(s) we would like to have in our homemade families.

Naifs may accuse him of cynicism in suggesting that lovers imagine the terms of "divorce" even as they tie the bonds of passionate commitment. Heterosexuals who marry, however, do exactly that by signing onto a government marriage that has already established for them the ground rules for divorce. Those of us who live in queer families in fact possess a greater freedom, for, incrementally and collectively, we can construct new rules of family life that will not only serve us in the course of our private legal affairs but may one day revolutionize the laws of marriage for all people.

A Personal Prologue

Feeling a little gutsy and quite a bit curious, I ventured into my first gay liberation gathering in the fall of 1970 while living in Ann Arbor as a college freshman. I went with my girlfriend—I'd had a few furtive and rather confusing sexual experiences with men, but both she and I considered ourselves bisexual. The scene was everything I hoped it would be. A hundred or so wonderfully animated men and women sat in a circle and argued over social change, sexual freedom, and breaking down gender roles. Some of the women speakers wore denim coveralls—a radical act in those days—and many of the men sported earrings. The room teemed with people hugging and touching each other, openly and affectionately.

I felt I had truly broken free of all possible social constraints.

More than twenty-five years later I find myself living on a tree-lined residential street, sharing a rambling Victorian home with my partner of fifteen years. From a distance there is little that distinguishes us from our married heterosexual neighbors other than the simple fact that we are both men. Like the families next door, we worry about the security of our jobs and the cost of roof repairs, we look after our ill friends and relatives, we join community organizations hoping to make some incremental improvements in society as we experience it, and we delight in the love and affection of our friends, our families, and each other.

At times I look critically at my own life and wonder, skeptically, whether our struggle for gay rights and sexual liberation has taken us where we thought we wanted to go. Our success feels so very conventional, despite the decades of theorizing, meeting, and marching. I recently heard gay marriage described as "civilized commitment," and the term "commitment" struck me as more like a punishment than a reward. Last year I was handed a political flyer calling for a more radical kind of gay politics that ended with the stinging slogan "Assimilation Is Not Liberation." It brought home to me that when I joined the gay movement nearly thirty years ago, one of its strongest selling points was the prospect of *not* getting married and *not* having to join the military.

How times have changed.

Not that these changes have all been for the worse. On most days I fervently believe that our progression from sexual liberation to—let us say more positively—"social community" is of enormous emotional and practical benefit to everyone who is lesbian or gay—and to their friends, family, and neighbors as well. In creating stable families we are forming new and valuable varieties of social and sexual partnerships. We *are* breaking through those rigid gender barriers and, at the same time, avoiding the terrible condemnation of having to live as isolated and, all too often, unhappy and socially marginalized individuals. Many of us are discovering that in very different ways and following far different norms than those of our parents, long-term relationships can strengthen us and help build our communities.

From this vantage point, a well-kept house surrounded by a picket fence—even one with two smiling children standing on the porch—can be an emblem of liberty and not a sign of acquiescence. If it is authentic and well built, this "neotraditional" family structure can evolve into something more desirable than the confining and constraining homes so many of us left behind. Assimilation, it appears, may indeed be one of the paths of liberation.

My own life has shown me the value of creating a home and a long-term relationship, on my own nonheterosexual and nonmarried terms. And it is not just the gender of my partner that is different. The liberationist goals we articulated at those early meetings have not been totally lost. Set free from the models of our parents and forced by the law to build new sorts of relationships from the foundation up, we end up viewing ourselves and our families on wholly different terms. A great many lesbians and gay men have had similarly wonderful relationship experiences, and this is clearly the positive side of our new reality.

•   •   •

My work as an attorney, however, has exposed me to some of the darker corners of our otherwise innovative and liberated lives. As I struggle to advise and counsel my clients, many of them refugees from failed same-sex relationships, I have witnessed close up the cracks and ruptures in many of our community's much-touted long-term relationships.

I have spent much of the past ten years of my legal career representing lesbians and gay men who are forming or dissolving their relationships, and though it may be politically incorrect to say this, the scene is not always a pretty one. Yes, it is absolutely true that millions of same-sex couples take good care of each other, support each other, and flourish in each other's care and company. AIDS, breast cancer, and simply growing older have taught us all about the need to form lasting and nurturing bonds of support, and there are inspirational models of happy long-term homosexual relationships around nearly every corner in America. And, when circumstances require it, a great many of these couples are able to part company with mutual respect and kindness.

But quite often things don't work out so well. We have limited knowledge about *how* to form such bonds in the first place, and many of us find our relationships as problematic and conflicting as they are liberating. Mimicking the traditional marriage model of our parents rarely makes much sense for us: most of us don't have kids, and not all of us will follow the "one partner for life" regimen or the dependent spouse arrangement that comes with the marriage package. And, *all* of us differ from our parents in two absolutely crucial respects: we are the same gender as our partners, and most critically, at least as of today, we are not allowed legally to marry the partner of our choice. Thus, we inhabit a totally different legal world from those who are married, a difference that has profound social significance.

Our lack of relationship skills and our exclusion from the laws of marriage permeate the spring of our courtships as much as the autumn of our dissolutions. Few of us know how to discuss the terms of financial interdependence, make legal commitments, or negotiate fair domestic arrangements. The law provides us with little assistance, let alone protection, for those in need of it. Unlike our straight counterparts, we have no preordained set of marriage rules ready to fall into place as we walk down the aisle. To make matters worse, many of us are afraid to confront our fear of abandonment and our need for security, perhaps, because we are afflicted with an irrational suspicion that talking about such obligations will jinx our fragile family ventures.

And if these matters are left unaddressed during the formation of our relationships, you can bet it will be rocky in a dissolution. People are people, and so the gay divorce rate is probably just as high as the straight one, which in itself is not necessarily bad. Some relationships don't work out, and, especially if no kids are involved, engineering a congenial breakup may be far more preferable than sticking with an unhappy marriage.

Hard as it may be to admit, the fluidity and informality of our relationships can create havoc in a dissolution. Lovers who were generous during the romantic phase may suddenly want to be reimbursed for their "gifts," promises of long-term support can dissolve in a morass of "he said-he said" or "she said-she said," and echoing accusations of blame and denial can, given the lack of court supervision over the breakup, erupt even more hurtfully than is usually allowed in a heterosexual divorce. The law is of little use, and our community has not developed any enlightened means of accommodating and facilitating a rational dissolution. Amid all the righteous struggle for gay marriage, little attention has been focused on the equally important need for equitable forms of gay divorce.

But the outlook need not be so bleak. I strongly believe that if couples face their fears and share their love openly, and if they build some structure into their relationship during the happy times, it's more than likely they will be able to form a partnership that is genuine, appropriate to their particular needs, and able to accommodate life's conflicts and stresses. As a result, these couples will be able to create a relationship that fosters their mutual growth and individual happiness and, if things don't work out well, a calmer and fairer dissolution.

And for those who are not able to overcome their conflicts during the formation stage, the discussion process will illuminate the limits of the partnership, which is not such a bad result. This realization should encourage a more cautious approach, with less dependency, fewer financial involvements, and less ambiguous arrangements—and yet allow the partners to remain friends or even lovers. One of the best features of the traditional marriage protocol is that it provides an opportunity for either partner to say "no," and even if old-fashioned engagement rituals are shunned in our community, there's a great benefit to having similar decision points on the way to the nonmarital equivalent of the altar.

THE PURPOSE OF THIS BOOK

The purpose of this book is to explain, from a lawyer's perspective, how to seize the challenges and opportunities of forming a legally sound long-term unmarried relationship with the same-sex partner of your choice. Then even if things don't work out, you should be able to separate sanely, equitably, and, believe it or not, with a modicum of kindness.

The book also explains how the law treats these new forms of relationship in comparison to the rules for married couples and shows you how to mesh your personal needs and goals with the daunting and inhospitable world of law. My hope is that these teachings will provide you with the skills, the courage, and, indeed, the motivation to tackle these difficult issues with your partner directly so as to avoid or resolve the conflicts that may otherwise plague your relationship. Doing so may actually enable the two of you to avoid the need for the courts—and even lawyers.

The first half of the book ("The Happy Times") focuses on the relationship-formation process. After the introductory histories of marriage and the gay movement, it moves into a survey of the law that applies to married and unmarried couples (Chapter 1) and then on to a review of the commitment process (Chapter 2) and the details of making agreements (Chapters 3 and 4). Part One closes with a discussion of issues connected to having or raising children (Chapter 5) and the interaction between the couple and the larger world (Chapter 6). Part Two ("The Hard Times") focuses on separation issues, including the process of breaking up (Chapter 7), home and property divisions (Chapters 8 and 9), and a discussion of "external" matters such as taxes and the role of the extended family (Chapter 10).

While each part of the book is complete in itself, the two halves are inextricably interrelated. Building a solid foundation is the best way to avoid many of the worst separation conflicts, and, conversely, acknowledging the realities of a potential separation and understanding the laws of dissolution will greatly assist you in establishing your partnership. Both parts are essential reading. The policy discussions at the beginning and end of the book are designed to get you thinking more creatively about the political and social implications of your lives, and they should help you make better sense of the convoluted legal system you are going to have to deal with.

A few words about terminology. In the good old days when I attended my first gay gathering, gay meant anyone who wasn't 100 percent straight. Over time this word has grown rather narrow in its usage, referring mostly to homosexual men. Without question the issues raised in this book are of equal importance to the women in our community. Indeed, because so many lesbian families are having children and because of the historic exclusion of women from financial and legal decision making, the need for education and encouragement is perhaps even greater in the women's community. Bisexuals, transgendered persons, and all those who call themselves queer are equally in need of the advice presented in this book.

I propose to resolve the terminology issue by using the words lesbian, gay, and homosexual almost interchangeably in this book, informally, without intending to exclude *anyone* from the discussion. If one term rather than another is used in one particular context, it is usually done for variety or efficiency, except in the few instances where the gender is of obvious importance. *Anyone* involved in a same-sex (or is it same-gender?) relationship should benefit from these lessons and everyone in such a relationship or considering being in one—or even hoping to be in one—is included in my audience.

I'm equally informal in my use of the terms divorce, dissolution, separation, and breakup, all of which refer to the ending of the relationship. For straight couples who can receive a document declaring an official end to their marriage, the separation is an event as well as a process, whereas since same-sex couples can't yet get married they can't get divorced. But the different terms used for these different experiences are not in themselves of great consequence.

By the way, unmarried heterosexual couples will benefit from most of this book, as the law these days treats all unmarried couples equally, even though the real-life experiences for different-gender couples can be dramatically different. Unmarried heterosexuals are more than welcome to listen to my suggestions and ideas. In fact, I suspect that most married heterosexual couples could also benefit from this book, but that's not really for me to say. At least not for now.

A FEW CAUTIONARY WORDS

First, this book is written in general terms, discussing the law as it exists commonly throughout the United States. Each state, however, has its own particular laws, and each couple faces particular legal situations. If you are facing a major decision in your life, you should obtain advice from a local attorney before taking action. That advice will be based on the unique facts of your own situation as they relate to the specific laws of your city or state. Such advice is essential, so *please*, do not rely on anything in this book as a substitute for good legal advice.

Rather, consider the book as required background reading. It will help you along the way and assist you in framing your life in legal terms, and thus it should ease your decision-making process. It can help you become an informed client, which can only improve the quality of the advice you receive. But no book, even the most thorough one, can replace the focused personal counsel of a well-trained and attentive attorney.

Second, even though this book is written in optimistic terms, by no means am I so naive as to believe that handling these issues is going to be easy for anyone. Every issue mentioned in this book has the potential of bringing up deep and painful feelings and desires. We are dealing with matters of commitment, caretaking, and trust, and for everyone—especially lesbians and gay men—these are not simple topics for discussion. You and your partner are bound to disagree, strenuously, in many of these discussions. Building up the courage even to initiate these discussions is going to be an enormous challenge for many of you. The key is to trust that you are capable of dealing with these sensitive matters and to admit that if you don't deal with them straightaway, you are bound to face serious troubles later on. Avoiding the heavy stuff can cause you to drift aimlessly into imbalanced, unrealistic, and unexpressed agendas, with harmful results.

Third, while many of the legal dilemmas facing same-sex couples can be resolved through careful planning and clear agreements between the two parties alone, many of them cannot. The rules of the tax and the immigration authorities cannot be altered by your agreements, not even with the help of the most expensive attorney. Redressing many of the legal problems facing same-sex couples requires political change, and those of you in long-term relationships are in the best position to make that change. You have the support of a loving partner, you are most likely to win the sympathy of the powers that be, and you know firsthand how discrimination works. Seize control of the arenas that are within your grasp, and then use the resulting empowerment to tackle some of the larger legal inequities. You and everyone you care about will surely benefit from the effort!

Introduction

Looking Back
and Moving Forward

"What made marriages to be so long honored and so secure in Rome was the liberty to break them off at will. [Roman men] loved their wives the better as long as there was the chance of losing them."

—Michel de Montaigne, *Essays II*, 1580

"One of the things [homosexuals] are forced to re-examine is relationships. . . . Our relationships have little social or legal reality. As a result, we must invent love all over again. . . . Today more and more straight couples are deciding that traditional marriage doesn't work. . . . Straight people might well learn something from us, since we have already sorted out the issues, even if we haven't arrived at solutions that will suit everyone."

—Edmund White, from *The Joys of Gay Life*, a talk given in 1977, as published in *The Burning Library*, 1994

"If the rest of us could only 'get used to it,' the experiments and experiences of gay families might serve as instructional models of postmodern family challenges, ingenuity, variety and courage—ones from which all contemporary families and communities could learn and benefit. Perhaps their example could inspire others to accept the burdens, the paradoxes and the possibilities of 'what our families are like now.' "

—Judith Stacey, *In the Name of the Family*, 1996

Whether we realize it or not, anyone in a long-term same-sex relationship (or considering one) is engaged in a social experiment of enormous importance. The critics are right about one thing: we are at the crossroads of a social revolution. Heterosexual marriage is confronting homosexual liberation as we move into the previously sacred and rapidly evolving territories of "the family."

Having reached this monumental crossroads, we know what direction *we* want to proceed in. After centuries of oppression, fear, and self-loathing, lesbians and gay men are standing proudly, declaring to the world that they are entitled to *all* the bounties of family life, including public and private financial benefits. As so many of us now realize, the struggle for sexual freedom was only a prelude for an equally important achievement: acceptance of the families of our own making.

But we know very little about our own history and even less about the social territory we are struggling to enter. We cling to—or react against—memories of our own parents' marriage, and we are surrounded by stereotypes of marriage enshrined by others. We are beginning to learn our own needs and wants, but if we are going to make our way through the confusing and often unfriendly legal terrain of long-term relationships, it is incumbent upon us to pay some attention to the history that has shaped existing family structures.

This is especially true nowadays, when the battle for moral correctness is so fierce. A bit of historical reflection will reveal insights that should make our enterprise much more manageable and help us understand that our struggles for inclusion are taking place just as the traditional systems of marriage and family are evolving—and, to some minds, unraveling. In the old days, traditional marriage couldn't possibly incorporate homosexual families of any variety. It has taken generations to dismantle the sexist marriage hierarchy of yesteryear and replace it with a more equitable kind of partnership—a prerequisite to the acceptance of our less-traditional varieties of relationships.

So before you sit down to design your own same-sex relationship, spend a bit of time reviewing the brief social history that follows. Doing so will help you understand how our revolution intersects the ways of traditional society and will greatly assist you in constructing your own little corner of the universe.

A CONDENSED VERSION
OF THE HISTORY OF MARRIAGE

We begin with a brief history of marriage. First of all, forget what the Christian Coalition has been proclaiming—the story is *not* a simple one, and the rules you grew up with are *not* the ways things have always been. Marriage has mostly been a rather informal arrangement, with only limited church or state involvement. For centuries it was an economic relationship, only secondarily imbued with any sacred connotations. The needs of families, property, and propagation were the dominant forces, not the exhortations of the Bible.

In the Days Before Christ

Who knows whether "in the beginning" God created Adam and Eve. One thing is certain: they weren't legally married, nor was any other character in the Bible. Most religious zealots forget that no one got married in the Old Testament—the institution as we know it hadn't been invented yet! There is little available evidence of how sexual unions were formalized in earliest times, but we know that men and women met, formed bonds, and produced children. Myths of pre-Biblical Western cultures are replete with stories of captured women, seduced men, and extended noble families, but the details of the social and legal arrangements are far from clear.

"Marriages" in premodern times generally fell into one of two categories. For the rich and powerful families, formal liaisons were established primarily by the making of deals between families who arranged the couplings of their children. Property and lineage were the most important elements, and the matching of the blessed "newlyweds" served primarily as a vehicle for consolidation of wealth and the procreation of heirs.

For most other folk there were no formal ceremonies, no rigid rules, and no laws of marital property. Ordinary men "took" their wives, who were thereafter considered their property simply by means of the power exerted over them. Sexual union and domestic functionality were all that counted; when the man sexually conquered a woman and she moved into his house, the two were bonded as a couple. When children were born, they were family.

According to most historians, Roman society marked a dramatic intensification of the social organization of family life. Rules were promulgated for every aspect of family interaction, and even though the law still treated wives as the property of their husbands, in other ways the Romans were truly modern. Marriages were viewed as contracts between individuals that could be terminated if either partner breached his or her marital obligations. There were rules governing when a marriage could be consummated or dissolved, and for those with extensive property holdings, a contract specified the monetary obligations of each party, both at time of engagement and time of divorce.

Early Jewish tradition was modeled in many respects on Roman law. Marriage was a contract between two individuals, initiated by an informal engagement agreement and the negotiations over the family dowry. A formal contract soon followed, and then, a year later, the nuptial ceremonies took place. The written marriage contract delineated the husband's promises to care for his wife, including specific details of food and clothing to be provided and for fixed payments to the wife in case of dissolution.

The Rise of the Gospels

And then came Jesus. Sexual relations were intensely important to the early Christians, and the New Testament is filled with severe proscriptions on the subject. In passages that remain the subject of debate and discussion to this day, sexual unions were no longer viewed as functional arrangements between men and women and their families but as promises made in front of God—and thus involving God as well. As such, marriage slowly began to evolve into a sacrament, a religious ritual, not just a secular arrangement between mortals.

Sexual desire was increasingly viewed as an evil force, a moral failing that could only be cleansed by a sanctified marriage. Sex outside of marriage was viewed as immoral, and producing children was increasingly considered the *only* purpose of sex. Marriage was something ordained by God as the sole remedy against wrongful fornication and the only context in which children should be conceived.

Christian notions of marriage as a sacrament that transformed an otherwise horrible sin have dominated much of our culture for the past two thousand years. Even though there were few formal church marriages during the first millennium and current laws of marriage are officially secular, these Christian doctrines have held sway for centuries, whether or not priests actually participated in weddings and regardless of whether the doctrines had any legally binding effects.

Church and State in Early European Society

The Christian rules were not, in fact, very easy to implement. For centuries the Church struggled to define a "valid" (and therefore sacred) marriage, even though it was rare for a priest to officiate or for any kind of ceremony to take place. For centuries the solution was to anoint the notion of consent, by itself, as sufficient to validate a marriage—and it was the consent of the parties themselves, not their parents. Marriages were recognized where consent appeared to have occurred and where a couple shared their daily lives and functioned as "man and wife." Poor people continued to "marry" without benefit of clergy, while the Church's campaign for tighter control of the process pressed on. Apparently, the gap between the informal realities of daily life and the rigid regulations of the authorities continued to be an annoyance. As a result of steady pressure by the Church, by the tenth century a priest's benediction was essential for marriages of the propertied and high-status class, and by the sixteenth century the Church's blessing had become, in most European countries, a legal necessity.

The English tradition—probably the most dominant force in our own laws and culture—is especially instructive. Until the mid-eighteenth century most couples simply cohabited, much like the "common-law marriages" still allowed in about thirteen states in this country. Children were baptized, the terms husband and wife were regularly used, and churches readily accepted these couples as married, but only the ruling elite partook in public and clerically supervised marriages, in a church with widely published notices and with formal licenses issued by the clergy. Almost everyone else simply uttered their verbal promises, perhaps celebrating the union with a folk ritual or a party.

In the late sixteenth century religious leaders tried to give greater certainty to marriage by encouraging public ceremonies before a priest and two witnesses and a written entry in a parish register, but still there remained a wide gap between this religious ideal and the common realities of life. As a result, sorting out marital disputes was not easily. Protestant authorities in England tried to follow the Catholic law, but when property disputes arose these informal "contract" marriages were vulnerable to dispute and misinterpretation. The rights of children to their parents' property was uncertain, one spouse's liability for her or his partner's debts was in doubt, and control over a wife's property was forever in disagreement.

For a time the English courts agreed to honor all types of church marriages, but conflicts over marital status continued to arise. Finally, in 1753, informal "contract" marriages were abolished, and henceforth formal marriage ceremonies were required throughout society. Only then were the casual folk traditions of marriage displaced by the more legalistic formal ceremonies.

The Return of Civil Marriage

For reasons that are not clearly understood, habits quickly changed and formal marriage grew increasingly common across all class lines. But interestingly, it was civil rather than religious marriage that emerged as the dominant model. Governments grew in ascendance and Protestant resistance to Catholic dominance took hold in northern Europe, and while religious ceremonies continued to be performed and spiritual overtones often lingered below the surface, the notion of marriage as a secular contract—as in Roman days—began to re-emerge. As part of a broader secularization of the culture, governments rather than churches began to regulate marriage.

The nineteenth century was marked by major shifts in the social and economic function of the family as a whole. It is important to recall that in the days before corporations and consumer culture, marriage wasn't just a source of sexual satisfaction and children. Extended families raised crops, ran shops, made crafts, and served as the social hearth for the education and subsistence of its members. Consistent with this societal context, marital choices were part of an integrated fabric of kin and community. Only when the family's responsibilities diminished over time and the household no longer served as the center of social activity or the source of economic survival were grown children free to move to the exciting new urban centers and to form individuated liaisons with partners of their choosing.

By the twentieth century marriage had become a fully civil legal matter, with religious ceremonies serving as an optional added dimension for those who—sentimentally or spiritually—valued sanctification. Each state and country proffered its own rules about who was allowed to marry (no siblings or first cousins, for the most part), the minimum age for marriage, the health requirements and minimum mental capacity for marriage, as well as the property and economic rules for married life. In this setting, it was the legal vows that mattered, not the sacred ones.

Of course, the transition from religious to secular marriage has never been an absolute one. Many of the legal rules of marriage contain residues of religion, and few participants are aware of how secular this institution really is. Most Americans blend a religious and a civil ceremony in their weddings, with priests vested with "the power" to perform the civil rites of marriage. But the essential rules—from the heterosexual bias to the details of spousal support upon divorce—are wholly secular in their design and enforcement.

A Look at Contemporary Arrangements

Marriage today is an amalgam of social conventions whose purposes and structures have changed over time. Traditional marriage reflects economic strategies intrinsically linked to the status of women, it recalls religious conventions that only have symbolic value, and it embodies rituals of long-since-forgotten meaning. Viewed mostly broadly, marriage in modern Western society has come to embody a multifaceted cluster of social, spiritual, and economic needs. Marriage isn't a "natural" way for men and women to mate but a culturally defined and historically evolving set of strategies for organizing society.

According to most observers, the four needs that marriage attempts to serve are:

1. The provision of sustenance by a partnership. While often only one person (traditionally the man) is expected (or allowed) to earn money, both partners are expected to participate in the maintenance of the household—a "risk pooling" or buffer against the uncertainties and difficulties of life.
2. Sexual fulfillment, which, in most societies, includes a commitment to sexual exclusivity.
3. Long-term assurances of affection, friendship, and passionate love—and, in some instances, a deeply felt sense of spiritual connection between the spouses.
4. A stable and supportive social connection with extended families, including parents, children, siblings, and the surrounding community

Food and shelter, sexual pleasure, companionship, and community. This is what families—all of our families—are about.

And where are we now? The second half of the twentieth century has witnessed a dramatic change in the marital landscape, fueled by the independence of women and everyone's heightened emotional expectations. Far beyond what was ever the case in rational Rome or other "enlightened" societies, women are free to live outside of marriage—and to leave a marriage when it no longer meets their needs. During the course of the marriage—at least on paper—women are equal to their husbands. Property is controlled by both partners, women are free to earn their own salaries (even if lower than men's) and decisions are equally the domain of the wife and the husband. In fact, this growing gender equality has, in effect, reduced the significance of a partner's gender in the structure of the marriage.

Marriage has also changed in its emotional and social functions. No longer is the family primarily a matter of extended social relations, where married men and women solidify their identities and their sense of social purpose through their relationships with others—the wife, mother, husband, father—or in compliance with perceived social duties. Marital obligations used to be derived from a web of interdependence and by expectations imposed by extended social networks, and from a larger sense of what society expected of each player. Marriage was a social contract, not a personal one, in which parents, children, and the rest of society were the major determinants of how the contract was formed and how it was enforced.

In the past fifty years marriage and family arrangements have become, to a very great degree, vehicles for individual achievement, emotional satisfaction, and individual economic protection. Obligations between partners are viewed as the product of individual conscious choices, where loyalty is earned and commitment conditioned on assurances of reciprocity. We live in a world of emotional exchange, and old-fashioned notions of societal duty and social rank are no longer the central determinants of marital satisfaction.

Concurrent with this change in attitudes has come a shift in the laws of marriage. Being married is no longer a matter of establishing a "status" with fixed social obligations; it is a private contract that can be individually negotiated—and terminated if its terms are breached. Despite the lingering powerful influence of archaic social conventions in the rituals of marriage, to a great degree today's laws allow married couples to form intimate relationships of their own design.

Marriage has thus become the province of two individuals, contracting privately between themselves to establish a relationship that meets their economic, social, sexual, and domestic needs. The needs of society or of extended families are of diminished importance, multigenerational economic consequences are secondary, production of children is increasingly viewed as optional (and designed primarily to meet the emotional needs of the parents), gender roles are increasingly seen as archaic remnants of an outdated social system, and divorce is, unquestionably, an equal right available to either party if the long-term expectations of the parties are not met.

Lesbians and gay men take note: it is a structure that is remarkably close to how we organize our lives.

A SHORT HISTORY OF DIVORCE

Divorce was officially allowed in most pre-Christian cultures, though it is difficult to cite many examples of its actual occurrence. Roman law granted divorces primarily at the instigation of men and primarily as the solution to a wrongdoing by a wife. Husbands were offered fifteen possible grounds of divorce to choose from, including, of course, adulterous activity by the wife—and also such trivial breaches as frequenting the circus or theater after being forbidden to do so by the husband.

The Romans had a knack for organizing family life. Property issues were initially handled by family councils, not by courts, and only when that didn't work were disputes adjudicated by judges. Decisions were based on principles of practical fairness, not moral condemnation. In ways that we are only today beginning to value, Roman divorce was based on a view of marriage as a civil contract for mutual benefit and pleasure. As the Emperor Justinian is said to have written, "If marriages are made by mutual affection, it is only right that when that mutual affection no longer exists they should be dissoluble by mutual consent."

But Christianity changed everything. Marriage was no longer viewed as a civil contract between two human beings; it was a sacrament with God and thus something that only God could tear asunder—through the death of one of the parties. "Till death do us part," remember? As stated in the New Testament: "Let not the wife depart from her husband, but if she does depart, let her remain unmarried or be reconciled to her husband, and let not the husband put away his wife." And so divorce was to be banished from early Christian society. One God, one Church, and only one marriage.

But the ban against divorce always allowed exceptions. Since marriage between relatives was prohibited, belatedly discovering a family connection between spouses could nullify the marriage. The Catholics even banned marriages between people who were related "by sacrament"—in other words, baptized by the same priest. In most small towns, therefore, it was nearly impossible to find anyone who *wasn't* related to you in some way. But solutions were found: for a fee one could purchase a "dispensation" allowing a marriage despite the close connection. Then, if the marriage went sour, one could pay the Church another fee for official nullification of the unlawful marriage and thus be free to remarry.

Maneuvering oneself through these canonical mazes was neither easy nor cheap, and so, not surprisingly, divorce was a luxury only the rich and powerful could enjoy. Everyone else had to resort to abandonment, de facto separation, or death—indeed, a short life expectancy rescued many unfortunate marriages. For most couples, though, marriage meant forever, a holy union of a man and woman, with divorce reserved for only the very sinful or the very rich.

The Protestant Reformation took the marital regulations out of the hands of the Catholic Church but did not loosen up the divorce procedures. One marriage per lifetime continued to be the norm, and marital dissolution remained primarily a matter of crime and punishment. If one partner was "guilty" of a breach of the marriage vows by committing adultery or abandonment, he or she would never be allowed to remarry and was denied any of the marital property. However, since desertion and adultery left the "innocent" party without a spouse, he or she would eventually be allowed to remarry.

And so, even while the nominal control of the marital law system shifted into secular hands, the sacred foundations of marriage and the draconian restrictions on divorce were for the most part left undisturbed. Only the morally righteous victim of a desertion was allowed to proceed with his or her life, and without such wrongdoing neither partner had any right to terminate the marriage—not unlike the "covenant marriages" of recent discussion. In England it took an act of Parliament followed by a lengthy civil lawsuit to obtain a divorce, a wildly expensive venture of little use to most people. Most just moved out of the house and lived with their new partners, happily ever after, in sin.

The French Revolution of 1789 was founded, in part, in an effort to liberate society from the dominance of judges and clergy. As such, it provided a dramatic opportunity to reform the divorce laws—or, rather, to revolutionize them. In the subsequent decade divorce became available to everyone, without any requirement of attribution of fault. Both parties could petition for dissolution, and incompatibility was sufficient grounds for divorce. Even more novel, disputes arising in a divorce were resolved not by judges, but by a "family court." If either party wanted to prove that someone was at fault, each party would appoint two members of his or her family as arbitrators, and the four of them would listen to the disputing spouses, take evidence from witnesses, and decide whether to grant the petition. A local judge would affirm the order to ensure that it was legally valid, and the entire procedure was completed in as little as a week. If neither spouse was interested in a finding of fault, each party would nominate three family members (or neighbors), and the six of them would meet to grant the divorce and divide up the property. No lawyers, no fees, no judges, and no delay.

As is well recognized, divorce rules have loosened up dramatically in the past fifty years. Before World War II in most countries of North America and Western Europe, divorce was still very difficult to obtain—it was even banned in many states of this country. In most jurisdictions there had to be a "guilty" party and an "innocent" one, so much so that some petitioners for divorce were forced to stage adulterous acts to be able to prove to the court that they deserved a divorce. Men and women had unequal access to divorce, and the right of guilty women to remarry was strictly limited.

As society became more mobile, these traditional doctrines were eventually discredited. The first steps toward liberation involved an expansion of available justifications of divorce. By the late nineteenth century in Germany, for example, a divorce could be granted based upon allegations of impotence, sexual refusal, madness, syphilis, defamation of character, chronic disorderly conduct, or failure to provide economic support. At the same time, economic protections were eventually provided to the victims of divorce, usually women.

Slowly at first and soon at near breakneck speed, a few states in this country became havens where divorces could be liberally obtained—but only by residents of that state. Americans have always been mobile and in Nevada one could become a resident in only a few months, and so the "Road to Reno" was soon flooded with well-to-do couples in search of a quick divorce. Ultimately, as women became more independent and increasing numbers of judges, attorneys, and academics realized the absurdity of requiring proof of fault prior to divorce, the rules began to loosen.

Shedding the notion that divorce was only to provide relief to the victims of a spouse's wrongdoing, liberal doctrines similar to those of the French Revolution eventually began to take hold.

No-fault divorce meant two revolutionary changes: neither spouse had to prove that the other one had committed a "sin" in order for the couple to obtain a divorce, and the couple's property was no longer divided based on which one was the wrongful party. The simple breakdown of the marriage—usually characterized as an "irretrievable" breakdown—by itself was sufficient to justify divorce.

What Does This Mean for Us?

Once marriage is viewed as a voluntary contract designed to meet a couple's emotional needs, divorce emerges logically as a morally acceptable consequence of emotional dissatisfaction—without fault or punishment in the distribution of the couple's financial assets. And so, contemporary family structures are more like the lives of same-sex couples than ever before—apart from the gender of those involved. It shouldn't surprise us, therefore, that lesbian and gay men feel so comfortable setting up households and creating families in ways so similar to straight married couples. The law may not have caught up with the convergence of these two worlds, but the social conventions are certainly pointing the way!

THE IMPORTANCE OF THE
GAY LIBERATION MOVEMENT

Looking in the direction away from the current social crossroads, we face an equally compelling imperative: to comprehend how the gay rights movement has brought us to this important juncture. A bit of humility is in order here, as none of us has reached this place alone. Anyone who is open about his or her sexuality or is considering living with a lover is, without question, standing on the shoulders of valiant lesbian and gay pioneers who had the courage to step out of the darkness, proclaim the legitimacy of their desire, and struggle to express their desires. But to be sure, making babies and buying real estate was not the first on the list of demands in the campaign for sexual freedom.

The islands of safety for lesbians and gay men have been few and far between. Yes, in some traditional Native American societies there are transvestites (mostly men) celebrated as sacred oddities or spiritual messengers. Ancient Greece had a tradition of older man/younger boy friendships, where sexual fulfillment and ennobled instruction drew the two men together for joy and comfort—but only until the younger one reached adulthood. Roman poets celebrated the beauties of young homosexual lovers, occasionally a political figure would take a same-sex partner, and, yes, stories of passionate love between women appeared from time to time.

But long-term familylike relationships of lesbian or gay men were rare, and until recently there was little awareness or recognition of such unions. A few Roman poets took note of same-sex partnerships, including a renowned ceremony between the Emperor Nero and a man—with a dowry and a veil, no less! In the first century such ceremonies were commonplace enough to warrant some disparaging comments in a satire by the Roman writer Juvenal, but established homosexual couples and families were hard to find in historic times.

Recent studies by the late John Boswell have documented what can rightly be called same-sex "unions" in Roman and early Christian life, though there is debate as to whether these were sexual relationships. While recognizing that marriage can be a social arrangement, a financial partnership, or a compassionate bonding as well as a sexual romance, Boswell interprets certain religious ceremonial texts as proving the existence of an early variety of same-sex marriage. An eighth-century manual recites nuptial prayers dating back from the earliest of Christian times and notes a remarkable parallel between heterosexual ceremonies and the less-common celebration of same-sex unions. The "prayer for marriage" gives credence to the belief that such unions existed, legitimized under the aegis of the Catholic Church. Like heterosexual marriages, these unions sanctified a permanent commitment between two people and were witnessed and supported by their community.

Throughout modern history, however, our community's focus was, necessarily, a fight for sexual freedom free from criminal prosecution, social ostracism, physical violence, and religious condemnation. Formalized relationships were beyond the horizon. Even today, gay bashing remains a regular occurrence, gay teenagers are hounded and often driven to suicide, and job discrimination against lesbian and gay men remains rampant and often legal. Homosexual conduct remains illegal in more than twenty states, and while such laws are rarely enforced, they have been sanctioned by the United States Supreme Court, reflecting the bigoted and hostile attitudes of many in this country.

Given this situation, it is not surprising that legal protection for our relationships has not been our highest political priority. Moreover, in the early years of our movement being gay also meant being free of family: free from the disapproval of traditional families, free from the obligation to be parents, and free from serving as members of a traditional community. Being gay meant living happily on the edge, liberated from the bonds and expectations of straight culture. Romantic affairs were certainly welcome, and, in the lesbian community, long-term relationships were quite common, but it was sexual expression that dominated our political agenda, not families.

But over the past fifteen years, something began to change. A growing number of lesbians realized that while much of traditional society was not to their liking, certain things (like having children and raising families) were things they wanted. At the same time, many gay men were confronted with the onslaught of AIDS, realizing that life on the edge could be quite risky, impoverishing, and lonely.

Matured by these trends, we began to discover something many had already known but had not really focused on: the importance of creating family on our own terms. Just like anyone who seeks the shelter of marriage in a turbulent world, we began to sense that pooling risks and sharing a search for sustenance, establishing stable emotional and sexual connections, and creating community was just as important as winning sexual freedom. We began to recognize the enormity of the financial discrimination we were suffering as a result of the disenfranchisement and delegitimization of our families, and our priorities began to change.

And so we find ourselves today in search of family, looking for that perfect mate to join us in the enterprise of creating a relationship of mutual satisfaction. Just as the traditional marriage has increasingly evolved into a bond of equality and a contract designed to serve the parties' individual needs, we are moving beyond sexual exploration in a search for family. Both the straight and the gay communities have moved great distances to meet at today's crossroads.

The current debate over legalization of same-sex marriage is of critical importance to anyone in a relationship for two reasons. If marriage is legalized for lesbians and gay men, you will need to decide whether to get married, and this decision will have enormous ramifications. It will put you on the same footing as your straight friends and relatives, it may eliminate the need for many of the special arrangements described in this book, and it will provide critical areas of legal protection for you and your partner. You will still need to talk about money and property, and you will need to understand the laws of marriage even more clearly, though many of the rules will be pre-set for you.

The second important impact benefits you immediately, in that the debate by itself is transforming the public image of same-sex relationships. Marriage isn't just about the private relations between two people; it is also a social institution around which a vast array of expectations, perceptions, and images are formed. The very notion that lesbians and gay men could—and should—participate in this institution has forever changed the public image of homosexuality. Gay men are no longer seen solely as sex-crazed

John D'Emilio, a historian and former policy analyst for the National Gay and Lesbian Task Force, articulates this change succinctly: "Because the public representation of gay life in the 1970s and early 1980s emphasized freestanding adult males in an urban sexual subculture, it preserved the stereotypical—and oppressive—boundary between homosexuality and a heterosexual world of children and families. Gay freedom, in other words, was a sharply constricted one. Asserting a claim to family ties, with or without children, pushes the struggle for equality and justice forward on to new and broader grounds."

carriers of HIV, and lesbians are no longer stigmatized as angry women. We are family, and as the politicians, the media, and the general public grow increasingly aware of that reality, our strength as couples soars.

HONORING OUR DIFFERENCES, MAKING OUR CHOICES

As similar as gays and straights can be these days, many important differences remain—and it's essential that we not try to conceal or eradicate these differences. As each of us knows in our heart, our experiences as adolescents and adults as well as the fabric of the communities in which we now live—not to mention our ways of experiencing our sexualities and our personae—*are* different. It is imperative that we incorporate the best features of these differences into our relationships. Volumes could be written on this subject, and the closer these two worlds grow, the more significant it is, in a sense, to be mindful of the remaining differences. Consider these comments as topics for reflection as you ponder the legal discussions that comprise this book. As you take mental note of how fundamentally different we really are, you will better understand the challenge that awaits you.

We were raised to believe we could never get married, and until recently we have had few role models of long-term relationships. Envisioning a long-term relationship isn't natural to us. It will take serious re-orientation for us to feel at home in these relationships, and it will take serious education for others—including those who run the legal system—to get used to our families.

We were raised to believe we would never have children, and few of our homosexual friends have kids. In parenting, more than in any other area, homosexuals face enormous discrimination. It isn't always easy for us—especially gay men—to acknowledge that we may want to include children in our families.

Many of us have survived in a hostile world as single people, fighting off discrimination and constructing our lives as individuals, and we rarely expect that there will be someone else around to help us. Time and time again I am struck by how courageous and self-reliant so many of my gay friends and clients are. Courage and self-reliance are wonderful attributes and we couldn't survive without them, but at times they can become handicaps. Learning to work as a team and sharing risks and benefits is often contrary to our instincts, and so it can be hard for us to form lasting bonds.

Society is convinced our relationships won't last, and the law reinforces that sentiment. One thing about traditional marriage: getting into a relationship is easy, but getting out of it can take years. Homosexuals confront a reverse arrangement. Legalizing our relationships requires hours with attorneys, whereas breaking up can be as simple as packing our bags and driving away. Add the lack of social support or community recognition, and it's no surprise our relationships feel so fragile.

The legal and economic rules for our lives establish a reign of separateness, and if we want to merge our property we have to set things up ourselves. If every married couple had to forge individually the legal links that hold their families together, few of them would work things out. We're not so different as human beings, and these tasks are just as hard for us as for heterosexuals.

Sexual freedom and sexual openness have been integral to our liberation, and the traditional family structure and its rules of monogamy may be foreign to our core beliefs. One of the most striking facets of our relationships is the way in which they may conflict with social expectations. "Settling down" may be popular these days, but face it, ours has been a sexually liberated culture and that is part of why it is so wonderful. Squaring sexual openness with a desire to create families can be hard.

Immediate satisfaction is often the primary basis of our relationships, and rarely are there financial, legal, or community justifications for lingering in an unsatisfying relationship. Ask your unhappily married straight friends how long they would stick with marriage if it offered no financial benefits. There's a lack of social incentive for us to stick together through the unhappy times.

We live in communities that include other lesbians and gay men with unique priorities, models, and values. Unlike those who reside in communities made up of parents, church members, and neighbors with congruent values, we often inhabit a variety of social environments. In addition to our parents and siblings and our ethnic and racial communities, same-gender couples live in communities with differing priorities and perceptions. Depending on where we live, whether we socialize with older or younger friends, or are members of a political community, these groups can influence our sense of who we are and what we value.

We are both the same gender, and none of the psychological and social dynamics of our relationships arise from gender differences. If one person is more caring, more successful, more withdrawn, or more social, it is because of that person's individual being and not because of gender differences. To most of us gender roles are like prisons—cold and restrictive—but they sure make life easy to organize. Few of us would want to return to the world of rigid gender roles, even though many heterosexual marriages still preserve gender-based divisions. In our lives, by contrast, roles are based on who each of us is as a person. While this can make our relationships more egalitarian, it also can make for some painful emotional dynamics. When income differentials are based on background, skill, or motivation rather than gender, the partner who earns less can feel even more inferior—and without a sexist sense of a husband's duty, there is no assurance the higher-earning partner will feel any duty of support if the love declines.

There are no wives in same-sex relationships. Few of us would ever admit to wanting to play the traditional-wife role, but in our overstressed world, every one of us knows how wonderful life would be if we had such a person around the house. The absence of a "domestic spouse" is a problem that plagues many straight dual-career relationships, but it's frequently compounded by the economic limitations facing lesbian couples and gay men.

Each of these differences has an impact on the way we structure our lives together. When you sit down to decide whether incomes are going to be shared, when you decide whether to raise a child together, and when you decide whether to buy or rent a home together, these unique features of same-sex relationships are bound to shape the questions you ask and the decisions you make.

Perhaps the *best* feature of living outside the world of the traditional marriage system is that we truly have choices. We can take the best of both worlds and combine arrangements that honor our own needs and wants. Setting up customized agreements between you and your partner will enable you to fashion a relationship that incorporates your own identities and allows you the emotional freedom *and* sense of commitment you desire.

And what are our choices? Here are five general approaches, and in this book you will learn what each includes and how you can customize it. Once you have a grasp of what is involved in each option, you will discern what choices you want to make, what direction you want to move in, and what timetable you want to take.

Girlfriend/Boyfriend

The place to start is as boyfriends or girlfriends. You live apart, your finances are separate, there is no commitment for the long term, and each person is free to move on at any time. Your basic decisions are emotional ones, and the legal and financial interaction is minimal. Feel free to linger here for a while, and *don't* let yourself get forced into moving further too quickly. But don't feel that you are doomed to live here the rest of your life. Unlike straight folks, you can advance to a more intimate level *without* getting married, so don't be too scared to take the next step.

The Atomic Model

Atomic relationships are marked by a separation of spheres: you have made a commitment to each other and you may live together, but each person's money is kept in a separate account, property is owned individually, and each person remains self-supporting. The love may be intense, bolstered by spiritual and emotional commitments that are long-term and sincere. It's just that you've decided to keep your possessions, your savings accounts, and maybe even your housing separate.

Some couples prefer to stick with this model for decades. Older couples or those in their second or third relationship may prefer this model, as will those who wish to stay closeted. But such separation will inevitably limit the emotional connection, and even if this approach works for one it probably won't work for both of you forever. So if you prefer to stick with this kind of arrangement, be attentive to the isolation it can generate and be open to shifting gears after a few years.

The Fusion Model

Fusion is marked by a blending of the more extreme approaches: certain realms of your lives are fused in partnership, whereas other areas are left separate and individuated. Most typically, the domestic realms are merged: the residence is co-owned, funds necessary to maintain the house are pooled, and perhaps the vacation, car, and clothing budgets are combined. But other areas, such as savings accounts or businesses, are kept separate, and each of you may have particular assets or debts that are kept separate.

With this approach you will need to set the boundaries of the joint territory and manage the joint arenas. The boundaries separating joint from separate realms will change over time, and it is critical that you recognize the implications of living in this kind of divided universe. If one of you is saving money and the other is accumulating debt, anxieties may not be shared, and this can create serious emotional rifts. Creating well-defined arenas that are solely the domain of one of you alone can preserve an independence that addresses many real needs, needs the traditional marriage model doesn't really address.

The Nuclear Model

For some of you the nuclear model—modeled on the traditional nuclear family—may be just right. Even without marriage you can establish agreements that re-create such a structure within the confines of your partnership. You can pool all of your resources, agree to support each other while you are together, and even agree to provide "spousal support" in the event of a dissolution. If you are raising children you will want to provide for your children as well, and even if you can't both be legal parents, you can set up your life very close to that model.

Generally, this option requires a lifetime commitment—financially if not emotionally. Thus, it is essential that both of you be really ready before taking the big plunge, and it may take a while to reach a sufficiently deep level of understanding and trust to know this is what you want. Unwinding a nuclear-model relationship is not easy, and you shouldn't select this option until you both are ready for it.

Marriage

Legal marriage is much like the nuclear model, with two big differences. First, bonds are formed simply by saying "I do," whether or not you know what you are getting into or actually enter into an express agreement. There's no negotiation over the details or a trip to the lawyer unless you want to limit the sharing of assets the law will provide. Second, you are not only married in the eyes of each other and your spiritual counselor, you are also married in the eyes of the law. As a result, all the benefits and burdens of marriage, as well as the courtroom procedures of divorce, will apply.

We are similar to straight folks in many ways and different in so many others. But, most important, we have choices. Capitalize on them as opportunities, and use your freedom responsibly.

PART I

The Happy Times

1

The Legal Landscape
for Same-Sex Relations

Well before you begin to negotiate your agreement, it is crucial to learn the lay of the legal landscape. In fact, scoping out how life is lived in the land of the marrieds is as important as knowing the law that applies to those who are unmarried.

Sobering as it sounds, weaving together a life with your lover isn't just a matter of romance and domesticity. Without access to legal marriage, solidifying your affair and creating a fair relationship demands that you come to terms with the legal rules that govern your relationship and mesh your personal needs with the real-world structure of the law. If this integration is lacking and anything goes awry, sorting out your legal affairs can be very difficult.

Few betrothed straight couples give these matters much thought. Many move along the paths set before them, unaware of what they are undertaking by becoming husband and wife. By the time they realize what being married means legally, many are on their way to divorce court. Unmarried couples have no such well-trod paths to follow, no prepackaged arrangements to subscribe to en route to a church ceremony. We are on our own, and if we want to avoid the messiness of an ugly gay divorce, we must be conscious of the legal consequences of what we are doing.

THE RULES OF MARRIAGE

Despite all the valiant efforts, it is unlikely that marriage—in the strict legal sense of the word—is in the cards for you and your loved one anytime soon. Anyone with a rational mind should agree that the ban against same-sex marriage is wrong—legally, morally, and politically. But put those concerns aside for now, as this isn't the time or place for arguing constitutional law or sexual politics.

This *is* the time and the place, however, for you to learn how to construct your not-quite-legally-married life in the here and now. And even though legal marriage may not be an option for you at this time, it is vital that you have a grasp on how the legal marriage system works for several reasons.

First, it is downright empowering for every homosexual to understand how our society structures its most favored relationships. Traditional marriage remains *the* model that nearly everyone lives with and aspires to, and knowing how this system operates will teach you how our social and legal worlds work.

Second, understanding how marriage operates will help you decide whether you want to incorporate any of its features into your own unmarried relationship. While most of the public perks of marriage remain off limits to same-sex couples, many of its private features can be agreed to privately.

Third, viewing traditional marriage from the outside will help you sort out your own goals and needs. It may whet your appetite for a degree of social security you've probably never dreamed possible, or it may dissuade you from offering long-term assurances. The exploration will bring to the emotional surface your deepest wishes and dreams, as well as your worst fears and doubts.

And, fourth, if legal marriage ever becomes an option for gay couples, you will be better equipped to decide whether marriage is the right choice for the two of you.

Family law is a funny business, in which millions voluntarily enter into binding agreements without knowing what they are agreeing to. I once said to an experienced divorce attorney that traditional marriage laws make little sense for same-sex couples, who rarely see themselves as taking on *lifetime* obligations such as spousal support, especially for a rejected ex-lover. Her response was immediate and to the point: "Neither do most husbands, which is why we need a legal system to enforce these laws!"

And that is precisely what family law systems are about: structuring people's lives according to a code of conduct under threat of state enforcement, placing obligations on husbands (and occasionally wives) they would never take on if left to their own volition. Like a well-meaning but overbearing parent, the rules of marriage descend upon the irrational, often self-centered, and volatile emotions of romantic love, family conflict, sexual pleasure, and financial dependency and impose on the participants a moral framework of legally binding obligations.

The rules derive from a plethora of well-founded human concerns: the protection of women in a sexist culture, the financial needs of children, and the emotional value of continuity and stability. In a mysterious and rarely studied way, marriage and divorce laws have evolved out of our social and cultural practices about how we humans bond, and, then, the rules themselves shape our behavior.

Let us begin with a survey of the four *general* features of the family law system. Once we've surveyed the general realm we will explore the nitty-gritty details.

Marriage Laws Are Local but the Principles Are National

As revealed by the debate over recognition of same-sex marriage, marriage laws are primarily the domain of state legislatures. Each state has its own laws. Some have a lower minimum age for marriage, some used to allow first cousins to marry each other, and one or two states, such as Hawaii, may be brave enough to legalize gay marriage long before any other state does. Procedures at the breakup stage also differ from state to state.

Despite such local differences, the general principles remain strikingly similar. And in order to avoid the potential calamity of incompatible state laws in a highly mobile society, there is a national rule that generally compels every state to recognize the validity of marriages and divorces performed in other states. The "full faith and credit" provision of the United States Constitution guarantees—except where crucial local policies are thought to be jeopardized—that so long as a marriage or divorce was performed according to the laws of the state the parties were living in at the time, anyone can safely venture across state lines and retain her or his same status.

Marriage Laws Are Both Procedural and Substantive
The second key concept is that the laws are both procedural and substantive. The procedural ones are easy to spot, as they dominate both the courtship and the dissolution phases of a marriage. In the courtship phase, for example, the rules establish what it takes procedurally to be married (i.e., whether living together is good enough to bind you legally—a process called common-law marriage—or whether you need to pronounce your vows in front of a justice of the peace), who gets to officiate at your vows, and how old each of you has to be to get married. At the end of a marriage the procedural rules determine how long you must live in a particular state to get divorced there, what methods the courts will follow when they rule on divorce disputes, how child-support obligations are calculated, and when a couple is merely separated and when the divorce is final.

Substantive rules include the allocation of financial burdens and how property is divided upon divorce. Many substantive codes are based squarely on long-standing cultural beliefs about marriage. For example, husbands (and working wives) have a duty to pay the living expenses of their spouses, even after a divorce; married people generally are jointly responsible for each other's debts; and if a married person dies without a will his or her spouse will inherit the decedent's possessions. Other rules regulate the custody and care of children. Custody, visitation rights, and support disputes are resolved according to strict standards of legal parentage, along with subjective judgments about who would make the best parent "in the best interests of the child."

Marriage Is a Lifetime Partnership

Third, marriage is presumed to be a lifetime partnership of two people, and divorce is viewed as a breach of the marriage. In the western states, where Spanish and Mexican law historically was dominant, the partnership is structured as a community property framework. Everything acquired during marriage other than by gift or inheritance is owned equally by the couple, whereas everything acquired before the marriage or as a gift is retained by its owner. Earnings and debts are owned equally, and upon divorce the court distributes everything between the partners and can order the richer one to pay alimony to the poorer one.

In the central and eastern states the history is different and different terms are used, but similar doctrines are in effect and the financial results differ only slightly. Assets and debts accumulated during marriage are available to meet the needs of either partner, and if there's a divorce, the judge can distribute the accumulated assets to *either* partner, depending on each one's particular needs. Spousal support in the form of alimony also can be awarded however the judge sees fit.

Marital Laws, Inside and Outside the Marriage

Fourth, marriage laws say a lot about how the married couple is treated by the rest of the world. There are evidence rules determining who can testify against whom in a trial, property laws that establish who needs to sign documents for sale of a home, and well-entrenched guidelines governing access by married couples to insurance, government benefits, and employee perks. The guiding principle is that a married couple is viewed by the outside world as a single legal and financial unit.

THE FINE-PRINT RULES OF MARRIED LIFE

Having surveyed the four basic principles of marriage, it is worth examining the specific laws that regulate the lives of married couples. Keep in mind that rules like these apply to *everyone* who gets married or divorced, unless a private agreement negating these provisions is drawn up and signed by the parties.

Premarital and Postmarital Assets

Assets and debts accumulated before the marriage by either partner generally remain the sole and separate property of the person who owned them beforehand, unless the owner of the asset expressly conveys it to her or his spouse. Recognizing that many married couples don't keep their lives so tidily organized, each state has its own rules for resolving conflicts that arise when assets are commingled and a financial dispute subsequently occurs.

Commingling takes place when a husband or wife spends his or her own premarital savings renovating a house that was newly bought with the couple's joint assets or when joint savings are spent redecorating a house that one of the partners owned before the marriage. Commingling also occurs when one person's premarital funds are pooled with postmarital joint funds in a single stock account and the funds are then diversified without earmarking precisely where each portion of the account originally came from.

If there is a divorce and there has been a commingling of separate and joint assets, it may not be easy to ascertain whose money went where and how the commingled assets should be distributed. As a result, each court will apply that state's statutory presumptions (i.e., ruling that the money is yours alone so long as you can identify it versus declaring it a joint asset unless you can prove an agreement to the contrary), and each partner will try to trace the funds back to whatever source is in her or his best financial interest. There won't be much argument in court about which legal principles to apply, only about how those well-established principles are to be applied to the particular facts of the case.

Bear in mind that assets for married persons include not only savings accounts and home equity but also retirement plans and government and private pensions—and even the value of a private business such as a law practice or medical office. The goodwill of a private business may be hard to evaluate, but in a hotly contested divorce, business evaluation experts will come to court armed with their appraisals and professional opinions, ready to defend their opinions. If your savings are mostly in the form of ownership of a well-respected business or professional practice, the value of that business will be fair game.

The Partnership Paradigm

All postmarriage assets and debts (including real estate, furniture, and bank accounts) are the joint property of the married couple, regardless of which partner earned the money or incurred the debt. Either partner is free to spend the asset during the marriage, although the other partner's consent may be needed to sell property such as real estate. Each partner also will be liable for her or his partner's debts.

These rules derive from the partnership principle of marriage, and it is worth noting what a radical concept this rule really is. You may be slaving away in corporate America while your partner gardens and cooks (and, in the traditional marriage model, takes care of the kids), but in the eyes of the law you are each contributing *equally* to the accumulation of the marital assets. Many married couples are quite surprised to learn that the legal system gives equal value to the contributions of the stay-at-home spouse—a recognition many married partners haven't yet acknowledged!

If there's a divorce, the court has the power to distribute *everything* the couple has acquired, be it bank accounts or credit card debts, regardless of who earned what or spent what or whose name is on the account. In community-property states (the western United States), assets are divided on a fifty-fifty basis, whereas in most other states they will be divided equitably, based on what the judge concludes each partner needs and can afford to contribute. What is critical to understand is that who earned the money or racked up the debt is irrelevant.

The Duties of Marital Life

Partners in a marriage aren't just bound by emotional, sexual, and domestic obligations. They are each legally responsible for each other, which means that one person's wealth can be tapped to pay for the other's hospital visits and either spouse's wealth will disqualify his or her partner from welfare benefits. Debts incurred for household expenses are the burden of both partners. You may be able to shift the burden for some of these obligations between yourselves as you see fit, but if a crisis arises and a creditor is knocking on your door, the state's laws allow the creditor to seize any marital property, no matter what kind of private agreement you may have negotiated between yourselves.

The Divorce Court Rules

Whenever there is a divorce (called a "dissolution" in most states), the family law division of the local court will have control over the distribution of the marital assets, unless the parties reach an amicable settlement prior to trial. In community property states the parties are restricted to fighting over relative values of assets and methods of distribution, a system that reduces potential court arguments.

In noncommunity property states the court has greater discretion to distribute the jointly owned property to *either* party, based upon the economic needs and the financial capacity of the parties, the family duties regarding children, and in a few states even the fault of the parties during the divorce. Since the allocation process is much more subjective, the needs of each party—and the sympathy factor—can sway the judge. Each state establishes its own set of factors to be used by the judge in dividing up the goods, and the list of relevant factors is a long one.

The rules in Illinois are typical, instructing courts to divide the marital property "in just proportions," taking into consideration twelve factors: what each contributed to its purchase, the spending of marital assets by each party, the property's value, the length of the marriage, each spouse's economic circumstances, financial duties arising out of former marriages, any prenuptial agreement, the age, the health, and the occupation of each party, the child care needs, the need for alimony, each spouse's likely future assets, and the tax consequences of the divorce for each party.

Most families haven't accumulated enough wealth to support either spouse on interest income alone, so in addition to distributing the assets and debts of the marital partnership, most family courts also have the right to compel a higher-earning spouse to provide for a dependent or lesser-earning spouse. California courts, for example, award spousal support based on a list of factors similar to the Illinois marital property division list. If the couple has children, each state also authorizes judges to order one parent to pay child support to the other.

The California provision on spousal support looks at the extent to which the party's future income will be sufficient to sustain the standard of living he or she had during marriage, the marketable skills of each party, the possibility of retraining, the extent to which the previously supported party contributed to the training of her or his spouse, the needs and the separate assets of each party, the duration of the marriage, child care needs, the health and age of the parties, the tax consequences of the divorce, and "any other facts the court determines are just and equitable."

In some states, like California, spousal support will be provided only for a few years if the marriage lasted less than ten years, but it can be imposed for the duration of the partner's life if the marriage lasted longer than that. Support awards are not always obeyed, but the court can issue support orders, and a failure to pay can land even the richest of ex-husbands directly in jail.

A couple can renounce these rules with a "prenuptial" (signed before the marriage begins) or "marital settlement" agreement (made during the course of the marriage). Doing so requires the couple to be in touch with their preferences, be willing to confront these delicate issues, and devote the time and money needed to reach an agreement. Every state establishes standards for such agreements, and each partner's assets must be fully disclosed to the other, and each partner must hire an attorney to advise her or him before the agreement will be considered valid.

Not surprisingly, few couples make this effort. The more complicated the couple's lives are the more elaborate the prenuptial agreements can get, extending not only to who owns the house or the stocks but to who gets the pets, the jewels, or the rights to that best-selling novel. Thus, the right of a married couple to opt out of the marital laws is, in fact, a luxury that only the very rich usually can afford.

Compare this "call-in-the-lawyers" approach to the far simpler French system, which allows married partners to "choose" between two alternative marital law systems from the start. The different property systems are "prefabricated," and nothing needs to be worked out in detail by the parties; they simply go to a *notaire*, a legal professional equivalent to a paralegal, and select their preference on a preprinted form. One option declares all property accumulated during the marriage to be jointly owned, and the other system, equally valid in French law, allows each partner to retain separate ownership of anything he or she earns or acquires during the marriage.

CHANGES IN CONTEMPORARY MARRIAGE AND DIVORCE PRACTICE

It is not just our social ideas about marriage that have evolved over the years; the legal canons of married life have changed as well. Some of these changes, especially the increasing equalization of the marital partnership, are of great relevance to same-sex students of the marital law system.

Marriage as a Contractual Partnership, Not a Property Relation

In sync with the evolution of the legal rights of women, the historic concept of marriage as "ownership" of women by men has been replaced by an equal partnership between husband and wife, reinforced by the emergence of marriage as a voluntary contract rather than the establishment of a fixed social status. Under the laws of most states, women are now equal partners in their marriage, and their consent is required for disposition of marital property.

Equal Rights Under Law

The codes also have changed regarding the way married women function in the public realms. For centuries women, whether married or single, had little economic or legal power. Men controlled the property, and women had little to say about anything in their lives. Married women didn't own businesses and couldn't deal with family property, let alone exercise dominance in the public realms. In a change that has improved the lives of all women (lesbians included), women have emerged as powerful players in the political and economic worlds. The growing economic strength of the lesbian community is a reflection of this process.

Whose Fault Versus No Fault

In a global shift of the post–World War II social discourse, divorce has become a "no-fault" option available to either party on demand. Either spouse can initiate the dissolution without having to prove a breach of the marriage contract. Under the nearly universal no-fault rules, courts look only to statutory provisions and the economic needs of the parties, and rarely is anyone allowed to make any mention of the fault of the other in asking for the divorce or demanding a greater share of the assets. Those who leave their spouses for a younger lover and even those who are abusive and cruel are, legally speaking, just as equally entitled to alimony and to a fair share of the savings account as are better-behaved spouses.

Simpler Rules for Simpler Lives

Another trend—which has been increasingly questioned of late—is the simplification of divorce proceedings. Few questions are asked of the separated couple, neither is allowed to prove the marriage can't be saved, and there is little if any effort to save the marriage. More and more often quick and simple settlements without the need for attorneys are encouraged. Equal division of the property regardless of fault reinforces this simplification process as well. As a direct result of the simplification process, the costs and the strain of getting divorced have been significantly reduced.

THE RULES OF UNMARRIED LIFE

Take a deep breath and bid farewell to the tightly woven tapestry of marriage. Put aside the finely wrought rules, say good-bye to the presumptions of a lifetime partnership, and let go of that fantasy of alimony. You are now entering a *true* twilight zone of the law, as the legal environment for nonmarital relationships is completely different from that for marriages. The chasm between these two worlds runs deep and wide, and the landscapes differ on both the substantive as well as the procedural planes. They also differ in how the coming-together times are treated as well as, if things go awry, how the separation phase is treated.

While the specific laws for unmarried couples differ somewhat from state to state, the underlying doctrines for the rules of nonmarital relationships are nearly the same nationwide. Indeed, because the rules for unmarried couples tend to be stated more generally than the detailed codes that apply to married couples, rules for unmarrieds tend to be quite consistent from state to state. But watch out: because these rules can be so vague, the outcomes in cases that end up in court may be very difficult to predict.

There are three main reasons why our corner of the legal world is so amorphous and confusing.

First, unlike the comprehensive codes that apply to married couples, the rules for unmarrieds are so general and abstract that they leave unresolved most of the sticky problems that real-life unmarried couples—straight or gay—confront.

Second, there are very few statutes, few published precedents, few experts in this field, and, until recently, few same-sex couples with property worth fighting over. Few couples have had the courage to fight their battles publicly, so it is difficult for anyone to give clear guidance on the likely outcome of a particular case.

Third, disputes involving unmarried couples are almost always handled in the same civil courts that decide all other personal and business disputes, rather than in specialized family courts. Thus, a "domestic" dispute is unlikely to get the kind of judicial reception and assistance it needs—and deserves.

The Root Cause of the Problems
The single cause of all these problems can be found in one bottom-line fact: the legal doctrine that regulates nonmarital relations is contract law. All homosexual couples and almost every unmarried heterosexual couple (except in states where heterosexual couples may be allowed to form a common-law marriage) are viewed by the law as an unusual species of a business partnership. As such, unless the individuals voluntarily enter into legally binding agreements they each remain separate legal and financial entities. No agreement? Then no obligations. Good sex and a lifetime of emotional dependency might make for joyous celebrations, sentimental anecdotes, and intense crises of the heart, but without a legal marriage these events, by themselves, have no legal effect.

In theory this should not be such a problem, but in fact it is—and for many of us it can become a *really* big problem. The problems come in all different sizes, and understanding them is vital to avoiding a major legal dispute. But before we begin our comprehensive review of the law for unmarrieds, let's first look at some of the broader consequences of using a partnership model for an unmarried relationship.

Consideration Considered

The first problem should be more anecdotal than debilitating, but it isn't. As in any other kind of legal partnership, a contract must be based on *consideration*. Consideration is defined as "bargained for exchange," which means that in order for a contract to be legally enforceable each party must give something of value to the other person. Otherwise, the law will consider the promise as a gift that is not, in general, legally enforceable. For example, a lover's promise to pay for your vacation generally isn't legally enforceable unless you've given him something of value in exchange or done something like painting his office or paying his car insurance bill.

Not only must there be consideration for every contract, the consideration must be valid, which means the contract cannot be based on an agreement to provide sexual services. Those kinds of deals are considered illegal contracts that will not be enforced by a court—the same fate that prostitutes demanding payment must endure. But only a few state courts have invalidated cohabitation contracts on such grounds, and nowadays few judges worry about this issue so long as something other than sex is being exchanged. Unless you live in one of these ultramoralistic states (be careful if you live in Mississippi!) or have a written contract that specifically proclaims that the *sole* reason the house or bank account is being shared is because one of you agrees to provide sex, chances are your contract will be enforced just like any other. Love and affection alone probably will not suffice as consideration nor will being a "confidante" or social hostess. Unlike the contract of a legal marriage, some kind of financial contribution or some real work on your part is necessary.

The Dangers of the Implied Assurance

The second major problem for unmarried couples can be a potential landmine—a terrible trap for the legally unwary. In most states, relationships between unmarried couples are distinguished from "arm's length" business arrangements in one important respect: because unmarried partners are in a "quasi-marital" relationship, there are special bonds of love and commitment that the court can impose on the parties. As a result, the law generally declares that the two of you owe each other a fiduciary duty (in some instances this is called a confidential duty). Once a relationship is labeled as such, the courts will give greater validity to oral or implied contracts. Courts also can conclude that if your partner has relied on your assurances, you can be prevented (estopped) from going back on your word.

This special rule even applies to contracts that are supposed to be in writing, such as those involving real estate, and can lead courts to impose duties of fairness upon the angriest of ex-lovers. As a result, the lack of a written contract may still make it hard to prove your argument, but generally it won't prevent you from coming into court to try to establish your case.

Don't make light of this fancy-sounding concept of a fiduciary duty. In the soap opera–like case of a heterosexual unmarried couple who have been fighting in the Los Angeles courts for years, a jury ruled that Mr. Maglica breached his fiduciary duties by only giving his girlfriend a salary of several hundred thousand dollars per year when she worked for his company, whereas, she claimed, he could have given her something far more valuable: some stock in the company. The jury's verdict: a whopping $63 million owed to the girlfriend. Don't you wish *you'd* taken a job like that and been so cruelly underpaid?

So What's a Homosexual to Do?

At first glance it may seem that given these uncertainties, an unmarried life must be a terrible thing. The law of contracts is not in sync with the way we think or act when dealing with our significant other. Combine the clash between these legal doctrines and the way we actually live our lives with the vagueness of the rules and the cumbersome nature of the legal procedures for resolving domestic conflicts, and it may seem difficult to organize our relation-ships. But saying the task will be difficult does not make it *impos-sible*, and this is where the challenge lies and where the solutions will be found. If you read on, spend some time talking with your partner and with an attorney, and then proceed to sign a few simple documents, you *can* prevent the world of contract law from ruining your romance.

So put aside your fears of living your life according to the law of unmarried couples, and proceed. Armed with a solid knowledge of the basics of nonmarital law and the courage to deal openly and fairly with your partner, you can create a partnership that is every bit as legal and, chances are, a lot more equitable, than that of most married couples.

THE LEGAL BASICS OF UNMARRIED LIFE

Family Law Rules Are Irrelevant

Until same-sex couples are allowed to marry legally, the family law rules that apply to your married siblings and your parents probably are going to be inapplicable to you. Hold on to your knowledge of the marital codes of conduct, but only for your own edification and possible future reference. Unless you reside in one of the very few places that have recently begun to apply family law rules to gay couples (Seattle is one such exception), don't expect your local court to apply them to your disputes.

Contract Law Principles Arise Out of the Business Context

As we've learned, the law treats us as though we were business partners, albeit intimate ones. Most of the procedures and doc-trines are based on the cold and calculating world of business law. A deal is a deal, and no one automatically owes his or her partner anything just because they are sleeping and living together. The procedures for dividing up property tend to be rather mechanical and expensive, more appropriate for dividing up ownership of an apartment building between investors than dealing with the separation of the home of a formerly loving couple.

A Deed Creates a Presumption

As a result of the businesslike origins of contract law, property in dispute that has a title or a deed is legally presumed to be owned by the person named on the deed. For any object that lacks a title and is portable, the person possessing the thing will be presumed to be its owner. This rule applies to houses, cars, savings accounts, and credit card debts, as well as art objects, furniture, and jewelry. The law also will presume that unless there is something in writing that specifies the percentage of ownership of a jointly owned property, the object in question is owned fifty-fifty by those listed on the title.

If either of you wants to assert an ownership interest *different* from what the title says or possession implies, you must prove there was an agreement contrary to the language of the deed or the fact of possession. Wishes and hopes aren't sufficient; unless you can prove a genuine agreement to the satisfaction of the judge or jury deciding the dispute, the property will be distributed to whosever name is on the title or whoever is in possession.

No Presumption of Joint Ownership

As a direct corollary of these presumptions, anything solely in the name or possession of just one person is going to be under the legal control of that person, unless one of you can prove an agreement to share ownership. No matter how long you've shared a bed and dinner table with your lover, his bank account remains his and your debts remain yours. Following your girlfriend from town to town as she climbs up the corporate ladder will not give you any rights to her pension fund, either while you are together or if you split up, unless you can prove that the two of you *agreed* it was going to be shared.

Agreements Can Be Enforced if They Can Be Proven

At the same time, agreements between unmarried couples *will* be enforced by the courts if they can be proven, just like any other private contract. An agreement can cover the ownership of a house or furniture, sharing a bank account or a retirement account, or allocating the obligations of a bank loan. Because of the fiduciary duty rule, oral and implied agreements between unmarried couples in many states—even those affecting real estate—also can be enforced, if proven. The legislatures and courts of a few states (Texas and New York, for example) recently enacted laws invalidating unwritten contracts between unmarried couples, but in most states the problem isn't the validity of an oral agreement in principle, it's the difficulty of proving what was agreed to in the first place.

The burden of proof is on the shoulders of the person making the claim, so if there's any conflicting testimony about the alleged agreement, it can be very hard to win such claims—and yet it can be equally difficult to *disprove* these claims. We all know from our own experience that even when people love each other their words can be ambiguous and their memories can differ, and this is all the more so when the love has disappeared and a lot of money is at stake.

Here's a classic situation. Ken and Allen buy a house together and each pays half the costs, but then Ken wants a fancier kitchen. He's just received a bonus, so he offers to pay for the kitchen renovations out of his own pocket. The couple owns the house as tenants-in-common, but they have never written up any agreement about their shares of ownership. They talk at length about the situation, and Allen actually agrees, but in vague terms, that Ken should be reimbursed for his contribution to the new kitchen. But what should they do if they break up a few years later and real estate values have dropped? Does Ken get 100 percent of his remodeling expenses before the sales proceeds are split, or only an amount that is equal to the increased value of the house? Chances are their oral conversation never dealt with these specifics, and chances are equally great they will each have a different memory of the conversation and conflicting opinions of what it all means.

There is a further consequence of the fiduciary duty doctrine that makes matters so amorphous, so as to make these conflicts all the harder to resolve. This is the problem of the implied agreement. Legally speaking, an implied agreement occurs when the actions of one party lead the other one, thinking reasonably, to believe an agreement has been struck. An implied agreement exists when conduct rather than words are used to express the agreement, in the eyes of the law.

If one partner appears to be taking advantage of the lack of a written agreement and the other one will suffer if the implied agreement is not acknowledged, most courts will be quite willing to enforce an implied agreement. The judge will insist on hearing clear and convincing evidence of the conduct that allegedly constitutes the agreement, which usually means having a very credible witness tell a very believable story. But if your story is truly convincing, in most states the lack of a written agreement and even the lack of a face-to-face oral conversation will not prevent you from winning your claim.

Take our example of Ken and Allen's new kitchen. Imagine if they never took the time to discuss whether Ken was going to be reimbursed for his contribution, and, again, by the time they broke up real estate values had dropped. There's no question but that Ken has invested additional money in the residence, but there was no oral or written agreement regarding a possible reimbursement. Ken may feel that Allen's acquiescence to the project implied that he would be reimbursed, whereas Allen may feel that the lack of an agreement and Ken's spirit of generosity at the time meant that the kitchen remodeling was simply a bountiful gift, never to be repaid. A judge is likely to want to know a lot more about the general conduct of the couple to decide whose interpretation of the story is more persuasive and may be inclined to award Ken only a portion of what he spent.

Ex-Lovers Can Be Litigants

Ex-lovers can also sue each other on a wide variety of other types of legal claims. Breach of contract is the simplest kind of lawsuit, for an unpaid debt or a broken promise to pay for household work, but there can also be claims of emotional distress (like AIDS transmission), breach of fiduciary duty (resulting from an alleged mishandling of a joint asset), or claims for payment for services rendered (for help with the family business or restoring a partner's home). If two people really want to be nasty to each other, there are dozens of allegations that can be launched in court.

Claims can be made on the grounds of constructive trusts or joint venture, in which one person asserts she contributed skills or money to a project set up solely in the name of one partner alone or where joint funds have been invested in property held in only one person's name. As long as the underlying reason for the one-party ownership isn't illegal (such as avoiding taxes or child support), the courts generally will try to honor the intent of the parties and look beyond the literal language of the written documents to protect an innocent victim.

There's No "Unmarried Couples" Divorce Court

Because claims of unmarried couples in nearly every state are resolved in the same courtrooms and use the same rules as business disputes, we have no counseling services, no simple petitions for divorce, no rapid-action procedures to get the job done quickly, and no specially trained judges familiar with the emotional terrain of domestic relations. We follow the same rules and time lines as business partnerships, and the deadlines for filing legal claims (called statutes of limitation) apply. In most states you must file your claim within a year or two of breaking up, no matter how many hours of mediation you've endured trying to resolve things amicably.

In addition, there are no easily accessed forums for deciding who gets to live in the house, no special means of adjudicating the value of one person's labor, and no binding appraisal process for resolving conflicts of the property's value. It's a matter of filing a complaint, hiring experts, waiting for a trial date, and watching helplessly as the court sells your property at auction and distributes the proceeds of the sale.

Unmarried Couples Are Strangers in the Law

As a result of these principles of contract law, unmarried partners are considered "strangers" in almost every aspect of the legal world unless they have agreed to share their financial and legal lives in a manner approved by the codes and courts of their state. If one partner dies, the other one gets nothing by inheritance unless there's been a valid will signed by the deceased. If one gets sick, the other one has no say about the appropriate medical treatment unless a valid power of attorney has been executed ahead of time. If a couple is raising kids and a conflict arises between the two partners, the nonlegal parent generally has no rights to seek custody unless there has been a court-approved second-parent adoption.

Domestic Partnership Registration Is of Little Help Here

In the late 1970s in Berkeley, California, Tom Brougham and his lover, Barry, grew tired of being denied spousal benefits from Tom's civil service job. After extensive discussion between themselves and their friends, they coined the term "domestic partner" and pressured the city of Berkeley to change its rules about employee benefits. Over the course of the past twenty years, dozens of cities and hundreds of private corporations have expanded domestic partnership coverage for insurance and retirement benefits.

As vital as this effort has been politically and as equitable as the extension of insurance coverage certainly is, the legal benefits of this system are quite limited. Even if you've signed up as domestic partners in your local jurisdiction, in most respects the law won't treat you as a couple. Except for the specified benefits of the domestic partnership provisions in your particular town or your particular company, your legal life remains otherwise unchanged.

Thus, if your city has decided to grant hospital visitation rights in public hospitals to domestic partners you can exercise that right, but it will be of no effect in another city. Your employer may grant insurance benefits to your partner—but they will be irrelevant if you try to claim parallel benefits from your partner's social security account. Even though most domestic partnership forms include a statement that you agree to care of your partner's basic financial and personal needs, that burden only remains in effect while you remain partners. If there's a breakup such provisions are largely irrelevant, and rarely will the domestic partnership promises carry any weight in a dissolution battle.

THE BENEFITS AND BURDENS OF UNMARRIED LIFE

While being unmarried deprives same-sex couples of many important public benefits (i.e., immigration rights, tax privileges, and pension benefits), it also protects you from some nasty burdens (i.e., other tax obligations or alimony obligations). Political change is the only cure for the governmental deprivations, but most of the deficiencies in the private realm can be remedied by private agreement.

Apart from the very real public sector impacts, therefore, being unmarried in the private realm is *different* legally than being married, *but the differences are not always that terrible*. Marriage has its good and its bad sides, but depending upon what kind of personal arrangement you and your partner want to establish, being excluded from its preordained legal umbrella may not make a dramatic difference in your financial and legal arrangements. The main difference may be that you must walk down a different sort of aisle to establish your particular brand of commitment. Instead of going to the chapel, you may have to see a lawyer. Not quite as romantic, but often just as effective.

To help you form a clearer picture of your options, here is a summary of the burdens and benefits of being unmarried in the eyes of the law.

A Burden: The Absence of Landmarks. One of the oddest features of being unmarried is that there is no date of marriage or divorce. This fluidity may be fine when all is going well, but it can wreak havoc for the legal system. If a couple dates for a few months, shares financial obligations for a while and an apartment for a while longer, then buys a house, and a few years later has a commitment ceremony, when did the affair become a legal union? The law has no clear answer.

A Burden and an Occasional Benefit: The Absence of the "I do" Ritual. The absence of the rituals of proposal, engagement, and marriage can allow one person to proceed naively for years, believing that he or she is in a quasi-marital relationship while the partner thinks otherwise. If emotions run high and there's economic disparity between the parties, resolving these ambiguities can be fraught with anxiety and apprehension—with devastating economic consequences for the dependent partner.

On the other hand, for those who find it hard to make big decisions, *not* having such landmarks means you can avoid that potential landmine: the rejected proposal. The absence of benchmarks allows relationships to flow more loosely, as people can move apart and drift back together, often without any bright-line certainty as to where they stand legally. It's a bit confusing from a legal perspective, but from a human vantage point it may be just what the two of you need.

A Burden: The Vagueness of the Rules. In contrast to the tightly woven fabric of rules for married folks, unmarrieds dwell in a landscape of vague rules and few legal precedents. Since the outcomes of our disputes depend on such nebulous concepts as implied agreements, it's hard for anyone—lay people or lawyers alike—to resolve our legal disputes.

A Possible Burden, a Possible Benefit: The Absence of Special Dissolution Procedures. One of the nicest features of being unmarried is that you don't have to go through any legal hassle to break up. Even though the procedures grow simpler each decade, *every* divorcing couple has to go to court, file papers, usually see an attorney, and await the court's issuance of a divorce decree before remarrying. By contrast, if we act reasonably we can simply divide up our belongings and call it a day, without the need for lawyers or courts. If you are facing a major property battle, however, you may suffer from bouts of "divorce court" envy, wishing you had access to a clear set of rules and a bevy of attorneys who understand your concerns.

A Possible Burden: The Lack of Any Presumption of Partnership. Unmarried couples can write private contracts to pool in-

---

As Katha Pollitt said so succinctly in *The Nation* magazine in April 1996: "Why should straights be the only ones to have their unenforceable promise to love, honor and cherish trap them like houseflies in the web of law? Marriage will not only open up to gay men and lesbians whole new vistas of guilt, frustration, claustrophobia, bewilderment, declining self-esteem, unfairness and sorrow, it will offer them the opportunity to prolong this misery by tormenting each other in court. I know one pair of exes who spent in legal fees the entire value of the property in dispute, and another who took five years and six lawyers to untie the knot. Had these couples merely lived together they would have thrown each other's record collections out the window and called it a day. Clearly something about marriage drives a lot of people round the bend. Why shouldn't some of these people be gay?"

comes and liabilities and provide for each other if the relationship falls apart. But unless they go through the process, neither partner will have any rights to the other person's assets. This legal presumption of independence is reinforced by the way we are socialized, and, as a result, few same-sex couples are brave enough to make long-term investments in their relationships. This is not just a question of splurging on cars or homes; it is, far more profoundly, a matter of deciding whether to invest one's time, energy, and spirit in the creation of a shared future. In many same-sex relationships the supportive role rotates, but for some couples one partner may play a more consistently traditional wifelike role. There's nothing objectively wrong with this arrangement, so long as each person recognizes that his or her contribution is an essential ingredient for the other person's economic well-being.

And that is where the lack of marriagelike protections can severely hamper a same-sex relationship. If you have to negotiate every agreement—rather than simply follow the traditional path and say "I do"—it is far less certain that you are going to establish the kind of mutual protections you quite rightly want before you give it your all. Therefore, it is no surprise that you will feel a bit uncomfortable making those long-term investments.

A Major Burden and Occasionally a Benefit: The Limits of the Private Agreement. Perhaps worst of all, for some same-sex couples no amount of negotiating and agreement writing will provide the protections they need and are entitled to receive. A private agreement cannot overcome the regulations of the Immigration and Naturalization Service, and it won't enable your foreign lover to live with you. A private agreement won't get you the Social Security benefits you may need, and, in most places, it won't get you the health insurance you deserve. On the other hand, being unmarried can, in some instances, provide financial protections married couples rightly envy. Without an agreement neither of you has any duty to pay spousal support upon a separation, and you can organize your tax liabilities more creatively.

And, Finally, a Really Big Benefit: The Freedom to Create Your Own Kind of Marriage. Most profoundly, being excluded from marriage forces each of us to create our own personal arrangements. We are free of the culturally imposed rules of coupledness and thus free to shape our lives on our own terms. We can choose to be independent or we can elect to pool our resources, we can choose to provide each other assurances of long-term support or we can decline to do so, and we can choose to function as a unified financial entity in the public realm or we can each retain our private financial independence.

This freedom can open up tremendous opportunities. The one who cooks the dinner also can be the one who earns a higher salary. The one who cares for the dog or the newborn baby can also be the one who makes the final decisions about home renovations. And the one who does the most caretaking one year need not be banished to that role forever. Just as we are free to design our own legal and financial arrangements, we also can set our own parameters for the emotionally charged all-too-often gender-aligned obligations of the domestic sphere.

We are free to listen to our own inner needs and build a relationship based not on what our parents think is proper or how the state mandates life ought to be lived, but, rather, on what we ourselves want and need. It's a daunting challenge, but if seized upon with the right combination of self-knowledge and a willingness to talk about our needs and fears, the process can result in a far healthier, more honest, and more equitable relationship.

2

Tying the Knot:
Navigating Commitment in
a World Without Marriage

Without the rituals of betrothal and marriage it's often hard to know where we stand in our relationships. In order to better manage your same-sex affair, new forms of ritual and commitment may be needed.

TYING THE KNOT IN THE ABSENCE OF MARRIAGE

In the heady lore of pulp fiction—as in the intricate dramas of nineteenth-century novels—the incremental march from first date to courtship and on to engagement, marriage, and sexual consummation was rigidly choreographed. Extended families established the matrimonial script, and most likely the boy took the overt steps while the girl manipulated and seduced her husband-to-be. Every society had its own patterns, and bountiful opportunities remained for strategy and surprise, but the path of romance was clearly mapped.

Life is no longer so mechanically predetermined for heterosexuals, as sexual exploration occurs well before the marriage and women assert increasing control in the process—and at least in the *style* of relationships an air of mutuality wafts through the fields of courtship. But the underlying patterns of love and engagement remain. Statistics tell us what our "modern" self-image attempts to mask: of those over twenty years of age, nearly everyone gets married by the time he or she is twenty-five, and those whose marriages end in divorce usually remarry promptly. Styles may have changed, and, most certainly, sexual mores have loosened, but the ritualized trajectory toward the altar remains remarkably unaltered.

As homosexuals we haven't been allowed to marry legally and so we follow far less predictable romantic paths. We forge our own routes to pleasure and romantic love, and contrary to the heterosexual norms sexual fulfillment need not lead to domestic partnership, domesticity need not mandate sexual exclusivity, and a dissolution may even result in a long-lasting friendship between former partners.

From an interpersonal vantage point this lack of pre-set patterns can generate a wondrous repertoire of exploration and self-discovery, as each person finds her or his way through uncharted territory. But as bracing and as character building as this unscripted approach may be at times, from a legal perspective this informality creates confusion and uncertainty on a major scale. In a world devoid of well-demarcated boundaries characterized by unclear signals and unwritten scripts, it is hard to know when the actions of two loving people create legally binding commitments. Without the institution of marriage to set the rules, how do we signal to each other what we want, what we need, and what we intend to do?

The Unrealistic Romantic Promise

How many of you have made grandiose promises in the midst of a seduction? Have any of you *not*? Chances are you've made some fairly far-reaching offers, hoping, as the words fly from your mouth, that the object of your affection knows you didn't *really* mean it. Some people offer to move across the country, others across town, despite the horrible commute that may result. Some promise to pay all the bills until the loved one lands a new job, others plunk down their credit card to pay for a plane ticket to meet in Provincetown, Key West, or San Francisco. Many of us make such promises frequently.

Are any of these promises legally enforceable? Probably not. Can any of these promises create legal problems for the promise maker? Absolutely yes. Why? The answer lies in the murky realms of implied agreements and promissory estoppel. Implied contracts between fiduciaries often can be enforced if proven, whereas those between casual acquaintances cannot. Depending on the depth of your relationship, some of these late-night assurances can be construed as implied agreements. It's a hard case to win but not hard to file, and hence the confusion and the conflicts.

Beyond the uncertainties created by such implied contracts, oral promises regarding small financial matters (less than $500 in most states) that don't involve real estate are generally enforceable, even between strangers. As hard as they are to prove (and how many people are really going to file a lawsuit over a canceled vacation?), in theory your partner could try to hold you to your commitments. The law's vagueness coincides with the ambiguities of our actions to create confusing predicaments.

Making matters even messier, the law in most states follows the rule of promissory estoppel. The legal context is that one-sided promises, like promises of gifts, aren't enforceable as contracts because the intended recipient hasn't paid or done anything in exchange (in legal terms, there's no consideration). Each of us has the right to withdraw our promises of gifts. Hurt feelings may result, but no one will show up at your house with a summons and no judge will ever find you liable.

But there's a mammoth exception to this legal principle when a listener (1) has reasonably relied (2) to his detriment (3) on a promise. When this happens, the person making the promise can be prevented (in old-fashioned French that's called estopped) from backing out. Take careful note of the terms "reasonably relied," "to his detriment," and "on a promise," and you'll see how hard it is to make use of this argument. Wishful thinking based on a whimsical comment probably isn't reasonable reliance, and hurt feelings don't constitute the kind of detriment required by law.

When do passionate utterances create an enforceable contract on the grounds of promissory estoppel? Hardly ever—but not never—and that is why this situation is so confounding. If the lovers (1) have been together for a while, (2) have repeatedly made and honored such promises in the past, and (3) make promises that are clear and specific, and if (4) one person acts on the promises such that they would be harmed if the promises weren't enforced, a credible legal claim actually can be made. The classic examples of promises that create trouble for the promise maker are those that directly induce a lover to leave a job, move across the country, sell a car, or take some similarly bold action that has major financial consequences.

The Not-So-Temporary Arrangement

Another dilemma for those excluded from the world of ritualized marriage arises from temporary arrangements that extend beyond their anticipated duration, often for years. Like the character in *The Man Who Came To Dinner* (who, after having an accident, stuck around for years), many of us make loans, rent an apartment, or move into a house only one of us owns, believing the arrangement will last only a short while. We act impulsively, without ever sitting down to talk about the precise nature of the financial and legal agreements that these actions may imply.

The motivations for such actions are usually noble and good. Legal problems arise when these right-for-the-moment actions overstate one person's true feelings or, even more frequently, when they outlast their intended duration and aren't followed up with serious discussions or more formal arrangements.

The key to handling these situations is to try to be aware of the consequences of what you are doing, and if the legal consequences are contrary to what you really intend, modify your actions ASAP or generate a formal agreement with your partner to clarify your intentions. For example, if one partner agrees to buy a car for her lover whose credit is bad, with the intention of straightening out the finances later on, it's very simple to write up a promissory note (an IOU) that states how much has been borrowed and when it will be paid back. No lawyer or notary is needed. As long as the note states the amount owed, the interest to be charged (if any), and the due date—and is signed by the borrower—it's enforceable.

Similarly, if you sign a deed adding your name to the title to your boyfriend's new house to help him get a loan but aren't responsible for the payments and don't expect any share of the equity, don't rely on good intentions to change the deed later on. Both of you should sign a letter of agreement stating the terms clearly before you sign on the dotted line. It's advisable in this situation to see a lawyer to formalize the terms, but there's nothing wrong with drafting and signing an informal letter agreement until you have time to see the lawyer.

If your partner balks at being "formal" or accuses you of lacking trust, then you'll be forced into a serious discussion about legal relationships and trust, which is exactly what you should be doing. Depending on the outcome of the discussion, one of you may change your behavior, either holding back a bit on your generosity or acknowledging to yourself that you *are* relying solely on your partner's trust without any legally enforceable agreement. Neither of these alternatives is particularly attractive, but either of them is better than proceeding blindly. Remember, if someone isn't willing to sign an IOU when you ask for one, then he or she is the one who is creating the lack of trust, not you.

The One-Sided Marriage

One of the most important features of marriage is that it's not something you can do by yourself, and one of the most pernicious tendencies in many same-sex relationships is the one-sided commitment. It's amazing how many folks consider themselves totally committed to a relationship, willing to share their every resource, only to discover much later that their lover felt quite to the contrary. In some instances the generosity was always one-sided and the generous one never wanted to admit the imbalance; in other situations there were glimmers of mutuality that never materialized.

While many relationships work fine with one person acting as the prime initiator—though it's better when both of you are doing some initiating—it's essential that neither partner overextend his commitment unilaterally, in an unconscious fashion, year after year. It's fine if one person keeps a savings account while both partners pool their incomes for house payments—spouses have retained earnings as pin money for decades. Similarly, it's okay if one partner uses her truck solely for business while both use her partner's Lexus for domestic errands. What's *not* okay is a situation in which one person shares all her assets while the other shares nothing or where one person covers all the debts while the other goes on spending, day after day, never acknowledging the consequences of this pattern.

You don't need to get down on your knees to learn what your partner thinks about your proposal: just sit down together in a comfortable setting and talk. If your emotions are in sync the outcome should be positive, but don't be blind to the potential negative complications of opening a dialogue. As you listen to what your partner is saying it's possible you may hear some painful words, and you may need to put off the caterer or even the house purchase for a month or two. But that is far better than moving full speed ahead when your partner is having second thoughts.

THE FIVE GIANT STEPS TOWARD COMMITMENT

Navigating this romantic landscape demands that you pay close attention to the stepping-stones that lie along the road to commitment, acknowledge what you are doing, and adjust to the legal consequences at each stage. Becoming familiar with the landmarks—as well as the landmines—allows you to stop along the road and rest where you feel comfortable.

And if trepidations well up from the deep, creating emotional doubts about your partner's or your own needs and your willingness to make a commitment to this particular soul, or if you find that those loving assurances of the night melt away in the harsh light of day, don't call a lawyer to talk about partnership agreements; deal with the inner needs of the soul—yours and your partner's. Nonlegal problems demand extralegal solutions. It's essential that you be conscious of the way the legal structure shapes your relationship, but don't expect a legal agreement to overcome the nonlegal obstacles.

Once you are ready emotionally, the five giant steps toward commitment are:

1. Moving into a rented residence together
2. Buying a home to live in together
3. Pooling your finances and debts to a significant degree
4. Choosing to have or adopt children
5. Having a commitment ceremony, signing legal documents, or, if allowed, getting married

Renting Together

Whether you are sharing a house or apartment or living jointly in a place just one of you rents or owns, sharing a home has legal consequences. If you are crashing with your lover for a few months it should be simple: all you have to decide is who is going to pay for what and who has control over the place. Base your decisions on your immediate needs, and be sure to revisit these discussions if the stay lasts more than a few months. The only likely sources of conflict for renters are who pays what expenses and who gets the place if the relationship goes sour.

Sharing a rental apartment for a longer period of time doesn't bind you to any significant financial commitments, other than how much each of you contributes to the rent, and it's a great way to experiment with living together. But make it clear in writing what those costs are and whether you have any other joint obligations. You don't need an elaborate lawyer-drafted agreement—a letter signed by the two of you will suffice.

Buying Together

Buying a place together can mean as much to a gay couple as a marriage does to a straight couple, and there are a fair number of heady issues to tackle when making this purchase. You definitely should sign a detailed co-ownership agreement, even if the place is owned equally. At the very least, you should sign a letter describing who has paid what and who is going to own what percentage of the property. You're putting a lot of money into the house and probably incurring more debt than you ever thought possible, and the costs of not having a well-thought-out agreement can be enormous.

Consider this: if your down payment is $10,000 and you spend six months arguing over a house dispute while one of you rents elsewhere and both of you have to pay lawyers, you'll spend more than your down payment resolving the problem. By comparison, a few afternoons talking about the issues and $500 on an attorney's time is one of the best bargains around. Because of the practical and symbolic importance of moving in together, you need to talk out the possible financial and legal arrangements.

The details on how to reach such an agreement and what needs to be included in this agreement can be found just ahead, in chapters 3 and 4.

A Lender or a Borrower Be, Perhaps?

An equally big step—and one that certainly has legal consequences—is the sharing of financial assets or debts. This can take many forms. The simplest occurs when one lover lends money to the other. A variant of this involves spending one person's money on something that both of you own or on something that is owned solely by the one who is not paying anything. More complicated ways of sharing assets include investing in your partner's business or having one person obtain credit, either by a loan or credit card, while the other receives the proceeds.

There is nothing wrong with being generous to a loved one. Talk to people who have succeeded in business, and chances are someone helped them along in their climb to the top. Many of us don't have the support from our parents and extended family that our straight relatives receive, and many have faced some very difficult times getting through the educational and career process. Friendly support can be absolutely vital.

The crunch arises when one party to the transaction doesn't make it clear if the money is a loan or a gift and then tries to demand repayment from an ex-lover. The person who does this may delude himself into thinking that keeping things vague allows him to exercise control, believing that if he has his partner sign an IOU, he will know it isn't a gift and therefore won't feel so grateful, or the lender may even intend to forgive the loan if all goes well—but not if it doesn't. Make your expectations clear from the start, and be willing to live with the consequences!

The law in most states presumes that money passing between partners is a gift unless there's a written agreement signed by the *receiver* that states the amount lent, deadline for repayment, and what interest, if any, is to be paid. If you feel guilty about demanding repayment, then admit that it's a gift—or if it was originally labeled a loan, tear up the promissory note on your next anniversary. If one of you is willing and able to help out the other, don't be afraid to acknowledge this up front—but don't pretend to be more generous than you really feel.

A Child Is Born

The fourth big step is the birth or adoption of a child. Whether you share in the raising of a child one of you has brought into the relationship from a past marriage, or choose to have or adopt a child jointly, this is serious stuff. Raising a child requires some very clear thinking about the legal aspects of your relationship, including such practical matters as finances, housing, estate planning, and support for the primary child rearer.

If you plan to include children in your family, take a close look at chapter 5.

Promises, Registrations, and Rituals

The fifth step is having a commitment ceremony, signing binding legal documents, registering as domestic partners, and/or getting married if the opportunity arises. Remember, you can solemnize your relationship regardless of the precise financial arrangements you intend to make. Your vows can take various forms, and you needn't get hung up on any legal ramifications. Private ceremonial promises rarely have any legal significance by themselves, although they should and will create emotional expectations that may give rise to legal claims in conjunction with other actions the two of you may take later on.

In many cities you can sign up as domestic partners, which may enable you to obtain benefits such as health insurance for city employees or equal treatment at public hospitals, and, increasingly these days, similar benefits from enlightened private employers. Read the rules carefully, though, as buried within most domestic partnership registration forms is an economic commitment that you need to understand. In most cities domestic partners agree to be responsible for each other's expenses by agreeing to "share the common necessities of life." While there haven't been any court cases of lovers enforcing the provisions of these forms in a lawsuit against each other years later, it could happen, so you should take the document's language seriously. If it says that you promise to support each other until you terminate your partnership, don't sign on the dotted line unless you really mean it.

If your emotional commitments or your practical involvements are getting serious, take yourselves seriously. As described in detail in chapters 3 and 4, talk out these issues, make a formal agreement, and follow it—or if things change and following it no longer makes sense, change it. You can do this with or without an attorney, but don't ignore the need for an agreement—and be fully conscious about its legal consequences.

In nearly every state you also may signify the importance of your commitment by taking each other's last names, as married couples have done for centuries. You can take a new name in most states simply by using it—as long as you don't try to defraud any creditors—or by court order. In a few states, however, judges have denied such applications to gay couples, and if this happens you may need to pursue an appeal to secure this privilege.

Since there isn't a "wife" in the traditional sense, you may prefer to use a hyphenated name or even to create a last name that belongs to neither of your families. A name change is primarily a matter of public image, which by itself doesn't have any legal consequences. But it will change the way you view yourself and how others perceive you, and it could be cited in a subsequent legal dispute as evidence of how you structured your relationship. While this sort of inference is not likely to be as determinative with a same-sex couple as has been the case with straight unmarried couples who take the same last name, it is something that everyone—including a jury and a judge—is bound to notice.

As you thread your way along these paths, you will definitely face some moments of crisis. One of you may find yourself ready to move up to a new level of commitment while your partner is holding back. What felt right during the good times can suddenly feel all too scary during an economic or medical crisis. When these dilemmas occur please remember that you aren't married and therefore you can shift the operating rules of your partnership without having to get divorced. Each of these changes will take time to negotiate and resolve, and if some degree of distance is required to get through a stressful time, either or both of you may experience a sense of rejection as a result of the partial separation. But flexibility is necessary for the survival of any relationship, so be prepared to accommodate some changes.

THE RIGHT OPTION FOR YOU

One of the secrets of having a successful relationship is knowing its apparent limits, but it is also equally important to know when to push beyond these limits to establish its *real* potential. The reluctance that can show up during the early stages of any relationship may be just be a hurdle that cries out to be overcome. Every relationship faces such hurdles, and the key to ensuring a genuinely healthy relationship is knowing when to honor the limitations and when to push on past them.

The Opening Chapters

The beginning of any relationship is characterized by a minimum of ties, an absence of binding financial and legal connections, a phase I designate as the Atomic Model. Both partners should stay alert as to how long this obligation-free phase should last. Nothing kills new passion quicker than talking about opening a joint checking account too early or asking your new lover to cosign a car loan after only a month of dating.

For some couples this initial "free-range" period will last months or even a year or more. Being truly loved yet retaining a sense of independence and freedom can be exhilarating. If the emotional bond feels good and you keep dating, let it be—at least for a while—but don't overreach or overoffer. Pay for dinner and maybe even a vacation, but hold off on buying a car or opening a business together. Keep your legal involvements to a minimum, and avoid falling into the not-so-temporary temporary situation that creates a long-term obligation too early on.

Key to surviving the early phases of a relationship is being able to distinguish expressions of love from financial commitments. We have all experienced the phenomenon of substituting practical promises for genuine emotions, only to discover that the actual sentiment was not so deep. If a new lover asks you to lend her money, cosign a lease, or share your car for a month, you may be inclined to say yes, even though your heart may be quietly uttering "Wait a while." Agreeing is not a good idea. The financial or material bind can all too quickly overtake the depth of the emotional commitment, and when you try to enforce the deal your underlying doubts can create some mighty messy conflicts.

Another reason for taking things slowly at the outset is to get to know each other in the nonromantic sense. We forget how rigorous premarital investigations used to be. In Junichiro Tanizaki's classic novel *The Makioka Sisters*, which concerns the tensions between traditional Japanese values and modern society (circa 1930), the marriage broker rigorously investigates the mental and financial health of a prospective partner, examining everything from grade-school attendance records to X-rays, to see if the designated bride's chronic colds and pale complexion result from congenitally weak lungs. A brother with manic episodes or an uncle with unpaid debts could cast a serious shadow on a budding romance, and an impropriety by the groom himself would instantly doom an otherwise serious prospect.

While such in-depth investigations are probably not warranted, take note of whether your partner has a string of unpaid bills before you cosign on that loan, and learn a bit about your lover's employment history before cosigning a lease. Paying attention to these details and asking direct questions at the right time are legitimate means of getting to know your partner. Find out why things didn't work out in the last job, and show concern about why the car got repossessed.

Moving Toward Commitment

The next stage, which may last a few months or even more than a year, involves the creation of a limited realm of financial and legal connections as you test the strength of your new bond. One of the special features of the same-sex relationship is that these linkages can be built up organically, rather than emerging fully formed with a formal "I do" after an impulsive proposal of marriage.

The secret to mastering the mysteries of the incremental linkage is knowing when to move forward, where to take the first steps, and how extensive the early interactions should be. The *best* first step is to take a vacation together. If you can agree on how fancy your hotel should be, decide who the better driver is, make the right plane reservations, and apportion the costs of the trip satisfactorily, you may even be able to handle renting an apartment together. If the first weekend trip goes well, try a week together and you'll really know what living together may be like.

If you can swing some kind of living-together experiment for a few months without making a long-term commitment, try that. Experts often say that living together without commitment is not a good idea, on the theory that you are so busy testing each other and questioning the effort that you fail to throw yourself fully into the relationship and thus never make the leap of faith necessary for any good partnership. There is some truth to this maxim, but you can avoid its negative consequences by limiting your experiment to a fairly short time period.

Another mode of entry into the high-stakes world of commitment is sharing responsibility for one major item, perhaps a car, pet, or computer. See if you can negotiate paying for it, work through the shared "custody" issues, and see if he, she, or it gets the proper care and feeding. If you can't work out who is supposed to bathe the dog, it's questionable how you are going to handle a house full of kids. If sharing a car means one of you ends up handling all the repairs and maintenance, it doesn't bode well for divvying up the burdens of home ownership. This approach is in effect a limited version of the Fusion Model described earlier, by combining the autonomy of separation of the major assets with the formation of a partnership for a set of specific assets, as small as a computer or as big as a house.

While there are times to be cautious and careful, there are also opportunities that suddenly appear, and those of you with confident and courageous hearts should be open to grabbing them with gusto. The perfect house suddenly comes on the market and neither of you can afford it alone, one of you gets a job offer you cannot refuse but it means moving to a new city, or one of you suddenly faces a terrible personal crisis and the other one is there, ready to help. These are always scary moments, so be sure to document what you are agreeing to financially and work out the legal components of the adventure as best you can.

About That Domestic Partnership

Between the free realm of passion and the legally structured partnership is the option of domestic partnership. Initiated as an end run around the ban against same-sex marriage, domestic partnership was created as a mechanism to document our relationships in a formal way so that employers and cities could bestow benefits such as health insurance on our nontraditional relationships.

In many cities you can register as domestic partners by going to a government office where you fill out a one-page form, pay a small fee, and become domestic partners. The typical form states that you are living together, sharing your basic expenses, and have formed an emotional bond that is generally much like a marriage. In San Francisco, domestic partner registrations can be accompanied by a solemn ceremony performed by the city clerk.

For the most part, the only consequences are those that led to the creation of domestic partnership: obtaining private and public benefits. Your domestic partner may be entitled to health insurance, and you may be allowed hospital visits and bereavement leave. You may obtain some nominal private benefits like discount air tickets or lower tuition through your employer's educational programs, and you may be able to add your partner as a beneficiary to your life insurance policy at no extra charge. But if you are receiving Social Security benefits, don't ignore the provision that affirms that the two of you are responsible for the expenses of your daily life together, as this could be pointed to by a government agency seeking to deny you Social Security benefits.

Going to the Chapel

Every few months now I receive an invitation to a "union ceremony." At first, I was confused by this trend. My own partner immediately complained of having to get dressed up for yet another fancy event, and we both began to wonder how many nonmarital wedding presents we were going to have to buy. My sixties-era informality and memories of too many artificial-feeling weddings made me wonder whether this was what the sexual revolution really had in mind.

Then, during a recent summer I attended the ceremony of two dear friends, and suddenly I got it. The week before Terry and Carole's event I had dinner with the bridal couple, and Carole told me a story I will never forget:

> I was only eleven when my older sister got married, and I remember how everyone in the house was eagerly getting prepared for weeks. Relatives came from all over the country, there were parties for days, and my parents beamed with the joy of their daughter's marriage. During the reception I found myself sitting in the garden in tears, knowing on some level that I was different and fearing that as a result of this difference I would never bring my family such joy or experience it for myself. My own wedding is a chance to finally heal that long-buried and very deep wound.

A second such event was for Bruce and John. John had lost a lover of more than a decade to AIDS, and with Bruce he had found a new source of love, an emotional connection he thought he'd never again experience. As they stood in the fragrant flower garden pledging their dedication to each other in front of a few dozen close friends, and as John spoke openly of how Bruce had showed him that he truly could love again, their lives were forever changed, as were the hearts of everyone standing before them. Their public proclamations and the formality of the ceremony imprinted on all of our hearts and minds the significance of their commitment and demarcated their bond in a way no informal dinner party or brief champagne toast alone ever could.

A commitment ceremony is a public statement, and the impact is incredibly powerful. There are months of preparation and discussion between your friends and family about your ceremony and daily demands on both of you to clarify your intentions and declare your expectations. As the day approaches there may be moments when you want to back out—and every once in a while someone does—but as you move through your anxieties and go forward with the event, you will have forever changed the way you experience your relationship.

You also will forever alter how others treat you, especially those present at the event. You are stating very publicly that whether or not gay marriage is legalized, you consider yourselves married in your own eyes. Every couple who goes through such an event reports that it has had an enormously positive impact on the way others treat them and how they treat each other.

Having a ceremony without any legal agreements doesn't bestow legal duties, although I have considered introducing testimony on the vows in a particularly nasty dissolution to show the judge the context of my client's actions. A ceremony is, however, often accompanied by a visit to a lawyer to establish a legal relationship, and even when it isn't, the ceremony can change the actions of the couple, and this can have significance. If you are ready to make the commitment that a public utterance of vows symbolizes, seize the occasion as an opportunity to resolve your practical and financial issues—just as legal marriage should do for heterosexual couples.

MARRIAGE: IF YOU CAN, SHOULD YOU?

If same-sex marriage ever is allowed, you will need to think about whether marriage is right for the two of you, not just whether it's politically correct. Here are a few general points to help you make your big decision.

Children First

If you are going to share custody of children, marriage should be a top priority. Married couples have equal rights to raise their children, and, in turn, the children have the right to demand support from both their parents. If the couple breaks up both parents can seek visitation and custody, and if one parent dies the other one steps right in as the primary legal parent. Just as important, your children are guaranteed a full platter of inheritance and government benefits rights.

As you will learn in chapter 5, unmarried parents face enormous problems. The child is usually connected legally to only one parent. Some states (New York, for example) allow lesbian and gay parents to adopt a child jointly, but even where that's allowed it's not a simple process. Many states deny unmarried couples the right to coparent children—even *straight* unmarried couples—and if the relationship breaks up, the nonlegal parent has no rights of custody and no duties of support. Domestic partnership legislation does not solve this problem, and private contracts about children's rights generally are not enforceable.

Homeward Bound

Whether or not you are married you can always share ownership of a house, a bank account, and rooms full of furniture. Marriage simply changes the rules of ownership. If you get married your property will be jointly owned regardless of who pays for it, the reverse of the independence presumption that applies to unmarried couples. You can write up a private contract assigning ownership to just one of you, but unless you do that the law will probably consider the property "marital" property.

Incoming Assets

In most states a married person's income is marital property, which means one's earnings are owned by the two of you—a big change from the way you probably think about your money now. If the marriage breaks up—regardless of who is at fault—your ex generally gets half the bank account and half of everything else you've accumulated. If you are unmarried, property is co-owned only if you have signed a co-ownership agreement. While unmarried couples have to create a partnership if they want to own things jointly, the law presumes married couples are a partnership throughout the life of the marriage.

The same goes for debts and obligations. If your spouse has an appetite for fancy cars and exquisite remodeling, chances are your savings will be tapped to pay the bills, even if you haven't signed up for the loan. Marriage has always been as much a financial partnership as a romantic one, and for those couples who are used to keeping their money separate, this can be a sea change.

Receiving or having to pay spousal support should also be a factor in your decision making. Since marriage is supposed to last a lifetime, divorcing couples are entitled to demand alimony if the marriage doesn't last. As we have seen, the level of support usually depends on the length of the marriage, the economic status of each spouse, the standard of living during the marriage, and the abilities of either spouse to work after the divorce. It's impossible to predict what any judge will order, but if one of you is supporting the other, be prepared for this arrangement to continue even if the relationship falls apart. If anything makes you think long and hard before signing up for marriage, the prospect of spousal support should. Remember that you can write a premarital agreement keeping your finances separate and waiving any rights to postseparation support. This may cost you some lawyer time and trigger some testy moments, but it is an option that many married couples wisely select.

And remember, while legalities can arise for some unmarried couples in a dissolution, *every* marital separation requires some kind of formal court action and quite often the help of a lawyer.

Until Death Do Us Part

As we age and, all too often, confront the terrible fate of losing loved ones to AIDS and cancer, we have come face-to-face with some of the most painful penalties of being unmarried. The law provides a bountiful package of financial benefits for widows and widowers. Without a legal marriage a couple needs to sign legal agreements to create even a partial framework of protections, and certain tax benefits are forever denied to unmarried couples. Some have considered having one partner adopt the other one to ensure inheritance and other benefits. Some states do not allow adults to adopt each other, and to many of us this feels downright weird. But if you have significant assets and are worried about a will challenge, by all means speak with an attorney about this option.

In a marriage without children, the surviving spouse generally inherits all the property if the partner dies without a will, and when there is a will chances are other relatives won't contest a bequest. We've all heard of long-term companions being cut out of the estate by distant blood relatives, and same-gender marriage could eliminate most of these disasters. The same goes for powers of attorney and handling medical decisions. Unmarried couples are never "next of kin," regardless of the length of the relationship. Marriage makes *you* the decision maker if your spouse becomes ill.

The tax code similarly smiles favorably on wealthy married couples—at least upon death. Bequests between spouses are free of inheritance taxes, which could mean an enormous difference in what you owe to Uncle Sam. Marriage solves a lot of problems for surviving spouses, so getting married may be the easiest way to take care of your partner upon your death.

The Benefits of Benefits

Finally, marriage can bestow a cornucopia of important benefits that your married friends have long taken for granted. On top of the inheritance rights and tax benefits, government programs can be extremely useful to married couples. If your spouse is in the military or entitled to Social Security benefits, you may be eligible for education, health care, and nursing home care.

Marriage could also qualify you for unpaid leave from your job under the Family Leave Act if you need to take care of a sick partner, knowing you'll be able to return to your job in a few months. Watch out, though, as your income could *disqualify* your spouse from receiving social or medical benefits that he would probably receive if he were unmarried. For those of you with lovers with foreign citizenship, marriage is probably *essential*.

The value of the potential private benefits depends, of course, on your immediate situation. If your employer honors domestic partnerships or if you are both fully employed, the private benefits of marriage may be quite limited. But if one of you works free-lance or is unemployed and the other's employer only recognizes a legal marriage in doling out health insurance, a wedding may solve those crucial problems. Life insurance, bereavement leave, and employment-based discounts for your spouse can really add up.

Nonemployment-based benefits, while of lesser financial consequence, can create powerful emotional impacts for the unmarried couple. Think about the last time the two of you tried to rent a car together and were denied the family discount or tried to use a companion-fare certificate on an airline.

Making the Decision

If you are ever allowed to make this difficult decision, first decide whether you fall into one of the got-to-marry or better-not-to-marry situations. Raising kids, courting a foreign lover, or facing a serious illness, for example, generally favors a wedding (unless marriage disqualifies you for Medicaid), whereas getting saddled with your partner's debts or losing Social Security benefits probably indicates a no vote.

If you don't fall into either extreme, take a close look at the marital property rules for your particular state. Evaluate the benefits outcomes of your personal situation and get a good sense of what being married would do for you financially, during the marriage, and if there is a divorce. And reflect on whether the image of being maritally merged feels right for both of you emotionally. If the answers come back positive for *both* of you, then proceed, but consider creating a prenuptial agreement if any aspect of the traditional marriage structure doesn't meet your needs. If the impacts of marriage feel unduly negative for one or both of you, hold off a bit. The push for legalizing same-gender marriage hasn't made marriage mandatory—at least for now.

THE ROLE OF PROFESSIONALS

As you proceed along the road toward commitment in your relationship, give serious consideration to seeking help from one of an assortment of professionals. The three most likely sources are therapists, attorneys, and accountants and/or financial planners.

The first thing to consider is *when* you need skilled assistance. The basic rule is that if you don't know the answers to a critical question or can't get past a dispute despite weeks of trying, you need help. If you fear that what you are doing is going to cost you a lot of money in taxes, or if you want to avoid negative tax consequences, don't be afraid to ask an accountant for advice. If you have never before faced the legal questions involved in buying a house with someone, call a lawyer. And if the two of you are constantly hitting roadblocks in your efforts to make a major decision; a few sessions with a therapist can be of enormous benefit.

How do you find and select the help you need? Start by asking your friends and relatives, or ask another professional in a related field. Don't limit yourself to lesbian or gay professionals, though make sure you are working with someone who is comfortable with who you are. Interview at least one or two potential experts before making a selection, and ask for references to vouch for their skills. When you first speak with the prospective expert, summarize your situation succinctly, ask her or him how such problems are generally resolved, ascertain the professional's hourly rate, and inquire into the professional's expertise in your particular areas of concern.

When do you need separate counsel, either therapist or attorney, instead of only one professional? As long as you are committed to staying together and are able to talk about your disputes openly, you can share just one expert. But if one of you wants to keep your plans secret for a while or if you are battling terribly, separate counsel probably is necessary.

How much will counsel cost, and how can you keep costs to a minimum? If you can focus your questions, read up ahead of time, and are willing to work out the details of implementing the advice on your own time, you should need only two or three hours of a professional's help in most instances. The total cost should be less than $500, which you should split equally. Be prepared to spend a fair amount of time afterward processing and acting on the professional's advice.

How do you make the best use of a professional's time and expertise? Look to your expert as a consultant and a source of information rather than a counselor who will work with you on every detail of your situation. Start by admitting that you are entering uncharted territory, so don't be angry if the explanations seem a bit vague, and stay focused on the practical problems that need to be resolved.

How do you best deal with conflicting advice or with questions that not even the wisest professional can answer? Listen to the reasons behind the explanation, and probably you will soon understand the issues that result in the conflicting advice. Be cautious, and, when in doubt, be especially certain that you and your partner understand what you are doing and what your priorities are. If you can respect the unavoidable uncertainties in these uncharted waters and keep the channels of communication clear, you can avoid legal disputes and the consequences of following uncertain legal doctrines.

Partnership By Agreement:
Negotiating Fairly
In an Uncharted World

Reaching agreement is the way to clarify your relationship, and it isn't simply a matter of filling out a form. It requires serious thought and a willingness to confront a plethora of difficult issues. But the effort is worth it.

Now that you understand how the legal system frames your partnership, you are prepared to initiate the agreement process. This chapter sets forth the eight basic steps which make up the agreement process. They will serve as a map, keeping you on a steady course as you navigate the road to agreement.

Eight Basic Steps of Reaching Agreement

1. Recognize the need to reach an agreement.
2. Agree on a safe structure for living your lives in the meantime.
3. Take stock of what issues really need to be dealt with.
4. Figure out where you and your partner stand on each issue.
5. Sort out the controversial from the noncontroversial issues.
6. Tackle the controversial issues thoroughly.
7. Reach an agreement, as specific as it needs to be.
8. Document your agreement.

Knowing that reaching agreement is necessary does not guarantee that it will get done, as the obstacles to reaching agreement are manifold and complex. The most important points to master are (1) what a legal agreement is, (2) what the best methods of reaching an agreement are, and (3) how to overcome the obstacles that most frequently arise in attempting to reach an agreement.

A MEETING OF THE MINDS

Under the provisions of the common law in just about every state in the United States, a contract is defined as a "bargained-for exchange" resulting from "a meeting of the minds." An agreement, which is a less legalistic term for a contract, is *really* a very simple concept. A contract exists whenever two or more people (or two business entities) come to a consensus (the meeting of the minds) that one of them will do something specific (the bargain) in exchange for the other's promise to do something else (the exchange).

Contracts don't need to be written to be legal. Contractual agreements exist when we get into a taxi and implicitly agree to pay the fare if the driver takes us to our destination. They exist when we sign up with a phone company, which expects us to pay our bill. On the home front, we pick up the groceries in exchange for our roommate's promise to drop off our dry cleaning. All these arrangements are contracts, agreed-upon bargained-for exchanges between two human beings whose minds "meet" in agreement.

The same rules apply, in much the same manner, to both intimate relationships and arm's length commitments. When property owners sell a house, for example, the parties enter into a detailed written contract covering the terms of the purchase. They agree on a price for the property, the buyers figure out how to come up with the down payment, and once everything is documented everyone moves forward and implements the agreement. The agreement is the process of reaching consensus; implementing an agreement occurs when you take the actions you have promised to take.

So don't be intimidated by the prospect of reaching a "legal" agreement. The law of contracts follows this very familiar framework, and the basic rules of contract law are neither strange nor disquieting. It's a world you've been living in for years.

The Three Kinds of Agreement

Contracts are of three types: written, oral, and implied. Fortunately for you, the rules are much the same in just about every state of the union.

Written agreements are written documents, either prepared by laypeople or attorneys or produced in preprinted forms, containing words that express the terms of the agreement. In order for a written agreement to be legally valid, it must include all of the key points, be clear and understandable to a neutral reader, and be signed by the party who is obligated to act (or by both parties if each one is supposed to take some kind of action). The agreement need not be written by an attorney, typewritten, notarized, or witnessed. A handwritten, one-page letter signed by the parties is just as valid as a ten-page formal contract notarized in a lawyer's office.

A written agreement is always the most reliable form of contract. Indeed, even if it is incomplete, partially inaccurate, or somewhat ambiguous, a written document will stand as the best evidence of what the parties really meant at the time. Some areas of law, such as real estate deals between strangers, require written contracts, and written agreements always carry the most clout if a subsequent dispute arises. For these reasons most lawyers will advise you to "get it in writing."

Creating a written agreement also forces everyone to focus on the critical issues, talk about what is really on his or her mind, and confront the uncertainties and doubts that will inevitably surface. Putting things in writing, as we all know, also tells the world you are serious, and that alone can be tremendously clarifying and reassuring for both parties. While asking for a written contract can suggest a lack of trust, if your partner refuses to put anything in writing your lack of trust may be well founded.

If you think that having a written agreement avoids every possible legal dispute, bear in mind that buried within the most eloquently written agreement there are bound to be some dicey interpretation problems. The most common disputes arise when the agreement is incomplete, either because an unanticipated problem arises or the parties simply forgot to include part of what was on their minds when they wrote it down. Other conflicts arise when the writing misstates what was really meant. The problems of interpreting written agreements are legion, but the *scale* of conflict will be diminished when there is a written contract. Each party will also feel far more confident insisting on enforcing an agreement, knowing that the judge or jury will be able to read the agreement and can compel the parties' compliance.

Oral agreements are a lot like written agreements in their content, except very little if anything gets written down. In theory they are binding in most every state. But because there may be inconsistencies in each party's memories, a judge or jury will have to decide whose version is true. Moreover, some courts won't honor oral agreements involving assets such as real estate. But in *most* instances in *most* (but not all) states, oral contracts between unmarried partners can be enforced, so long as the basic components of the oral agreement can be proven to the jury or judge making the final decision.

Keep in mind that an oral agreement still requires an agreement, not merely a statement of your personal desire or intent. Telling your partner that you expect her to contribute half the cost of maintaining the jointly used sportcar you recently bought is *not* the same as reaching an agreement, unless she turns to you and says, "Yes, I will do that." Similarly, offering to pay the cost of a bathroom renovation and announcing that you think it is only fair that in exchange your partner pay for the roof repair will *not* constitute an oral contract unless your partner agrees, loud and clear, to cover those payments.

The need for oral confirmation is hard to deal with, as no one feels comfortable pressing a loved one for a firm proclamation of legally binding intent. But it is essential that you be direct. The truth has a way of emerging out of the recesses of memory, so you should not count on your own personal belief about what you *meant* to say or *hoped* to hear as a substitute for a clear agreement.

Oral agreements also need to be fairly detailed to be honored by a court of law. If you are sharing ownership of a house or a car, your conversation has got to cover the key financial terms of the deal. If one of you is going to contribute a significant amount of labor in exchange for a share of the property, the nature and extent of your contribution needs to be spelled out in detail and out loud.

Make sure you know how the law treats oral contracts in your particular locale, though, as in many states oral agreements about real estate generally are *not* valid. In most states, however, oral agreements about real property between unmarried couples *are* valid, even when they wouldn't be between nonlovers. So long as you are living together and sharing your lives, an oral agreement about the ownership of your house may be enforceable—*if it can be proven.*

Oral agreements are easiest to prove when there is supporting documentation or partial performance. If you and your partner have agreed that you will be reimbursed for contributions you make toward the repair of a house owned solely by your partner, it will help a lot if you keep a detailed ledger of your contributions or if your partner adds your name to the deed, even if you don't take the time to itemize the detailed percentages of ownership. Similarly, if your payments for renovations are going to be considered equivalent to your partner's coming up with the down payment, you will have a much stronger case if you've kept all your receipts and your partner has initialed each of them. By contrast, if the written documentation directly conflicts with your version of the agreement or if you have nothing on paper at all, proving your case is going to be difficult.

Partial performance also can help prove an oral agreement. If one of you religiously makes monthly payments on a house you don't own, it will be pretty convincing to an outsider that making payments was part of your agreement. If one of you handles all the repairs to your partner's car in excess of the value of your use of it and you go on to cover half the payments and arrange for the insurance, that is fairly solid evidence of an oral agreement to share ownership. Splitting all costs equally on a car titled in one person's name alone, by contrast, by itself puts into serious question the owner's claim that the nontitled partner has no ownership interest in the car whatsoever.

Implied agreements are actions that reasonably give rise in one person's mind to an expectation of some future action by another person. California law defines an implied agreement as an agreement "the existence and terms of which are manifested by conduct" rather than by written or spoken words, and in most (but not all) states, implied agreements between unmarried partners of long standing can be fully enforced, *if proven.* Now, it is not just any old course of conduct that will establish an implied agreement; the claimant must be able to show that an "intent to promise" can be inferred, reasonably, from the party's conduct. And so, even when the actions are accurately remembered, one person's opinion of what's reasonable rarely matches precisely with another person's. Because of these potential discrepancies, there can be a great deal of confusion and conflict when you try to enforce an implied agreement in the context of a nasty dissolution.

Not that anyone should totally disparage implied agreements—we depend on them on a daily basis, especially in our personal relationships. There would be economic gridlock if there had to be a formal contract for every agreement. The problem arises when a similarly casual sort of approach is taken with regard to more serious commitments. Allow your lover to pay for the repairs on a house you alone own, whisper lovingly that you love "our house" now that she has repainted it, and your partner might reasonably conclude that she's become part owner of the house. Put your partner's name on the title to your car so you can more easily qualify for financing based on her better credit and allow her to pay for repairs and she might rightly conclude that the car is partly hers. Casually comment to your partner, "Don't worry, I earn enough for us to handle it" when he balks at buying a new computer and you may just have implicitly agreed to share a portion of your income with him.

Since "conduct" is so notoriously vague in expressing meaning, the "terms" of an implied contract are rarely what they appear to be. On the offering end, implied agreements frequently come with many hidden strings attached. The giver may view her generosity as valid only so long as (a) the love is running strong, (b) the funds are readily available, and (c) no pressing financial crisis demands a shift in expenditures.

In most situations, such a shift merely results in a crushing sense of disappointment, and if the relationship is still a loving one it's likely that the offers can be retracted and arrangements revised. But if the relationship has gone sour in the meantime or if, as so often occurs, the partner at the receiving end of the earlier assurance has genuinely relied on his perception of an assurance to his detriment, his feelings are not going to be so easily assuaged. Reliance on the unspoken assurances can be devastating to the partner who is financially dependent. Implied assurances can, in effect, become an economic house of cards, held aloft by loving energy that immediately deflates if the love evaporates.

In many instances the promises will be honored and the bounties of life will be shared, even after a dissolution. But more and more these days—and especially in an era of limited personal resources—such a response is quite unlikely. Memories of the earlier behavior will be recast according to the current needs of each person, and most likely there will be honest disputes as to how to interpret long-forgotten (or misremembered) events.

That is why the doctrine of implied agreements can create such problems in a gay divorce. Regardless of how many fragments of conduct can be reconstructed, the terms of the implied agreement probably will not be clear or easy to prove. In most states the legal standard for proving an implied agreement is very strict (and in some states implied agreements are rejected altogether), so most attorneys will discourage all but the most determined ex-lover from filing such a claim. Since the one needing to "prove the case" usually doesn't have much money, finding and paying an attorney to take on such a case will be very difficult.

In the end there is only one certain method of avoiding the uncertainties of implied agreements: get it in writing.

WHEN IS AN AGREEMENT NECESSARY?

Most relationships can be sorted into one of three camps when it comes to deciding if you need a formal agreement. If you aren't living together, aren't sharing your finances, and don't own anything together, you probably do not need a formal written agreement. Now, if either of you is supporting the other to any significant degree or if you are sharing the use of a particularly valuable item of property, you should compose a limited agreement covering just those particular matters. If it is just one or two things you are sharing, such as a motorcycle or a car, it should be easy to write up a one-page letter clarifying who owns what and who is paying what expenses. You may need to document some one-time-only mutual obligations (like paying for a joint vacation), and you will want to be alert to shifts in your arrangements. But a detailed written agreement probably can wait until later on in your relationship.

At the other end of the relationship spectrum are couples who definitely should have written agreements. If you co-own a house and your ownership share or payment obligations are anything other than a fifty-fifty allocation, or if one of you is supporting the other one financially for any length of time, you will want to put things in writing.

Those who reside in either extreme camp should readily know what they need or don't need. In between the two extremes, though, are relationships in which a formal written agreement is advisable but not necessary. This in-between group includes couples who own a house in equal shares, those who have worked out a reciprocal sharing of expenses that balances out by the end of the year, and those who run a small business owned by one partner in which the other partner works part-time and earns a fair salary. For these couples a written agreement may not be essential, but having an agreement still has a great deal of value as it will help you clarify some of the stickier kinds of uncertainties and confusions. In fact, for these in-between couples the process of reaching agreement is probably the most important element of the process; writing the agreement itself should be a fairly simple task, and implementing it should not be difficult at all.

GETTING YOUR AGREEMENT IN MOTION

Obstacles to Agreement

The two types of obstacles to making an agreement are educating yourselves about the law and about your finances and confronting the emotional barriers to reaching consensus.

The first step is to organize your financial and legal affairs, which may require a fair amount of education and commitment. This book and the resources listed at the end can be helpful, as can the advice of a professional accountant, financial planner, or attorney. You also may need to get advice on any property you own and make a candid assessment of your financial resources. If you are buying a house you will need to study the value of houses in your area, what you can afford individually and collectively, what the loan terms will be, and what your tax situation will be according to each particular strategy. If you are considering early retirement, for example, you will need to talk with your insurance and pension agents to know what your benefits are and what your expenses are likely to be. If one of you is saddled with child-support payments or an IRS lien, you will want to know exactly what is owed and under what term. Unless you have extremely elaborate financial and legal problems, one professional alone can usually advise both of you.

Part of your educational process also involves coming to terms with the realities of your financial needs. If you are liable for child support, review your divorce decree to be sure you know its precise terms. If you are a co-owner of a business facing future lease or equipment purchase obligations, get up to speed on what these will be. On the luckier side of the coin, if you anticipate inheriting some property or have accumulated sizable savings, take stock of what you own and where it is invested. You will need this information when you sit down to talk with your partner.

The second obstacle may be far more difficult to overcome. Whenever the subject of commitment is raised, long-simmering fears of dependency, abandonment, rejection, and entrapment come to the surface. No one wants to face the realities of losing a lover, quitting a job, breaking a promise, or being the victim of a loved one's rejection. The uncertainties about whether you are going to live as "I" or "we" will pervade your entire discussion.

Even after both of you are able to start talking about these difficult subjects, chances are you are not going to agree totally on *how* to handle them. These disagreements may inject a high dose of stress into your relationship. Discovering that your partner doesn't intend to share ownership of his house with you or acknowledging that you consider your earnings yours and yours alone can bring up deep-seated emotional issues and make for some very sensitive discussions.

But unless you are willing to talk about these matters and go on to make clear and realistic arrangements, you are stuck with two very unpleasant choices. You will either have to cower by yourself in your own private legal corner, sharing nothing and giving nothing to the person you love most of all, or, equally unappealing, share and give all without any binding assurances or legal protections.

The Need for an Agreement

The first task—and one that is often ignored—is to recognize the need for the agreement process. You may think your relationship is so blessed as to be beyond such banalities, but it may very well not be. You need to face the harsh limits of the legal protections for gay couples honestly and come to terms with what those limits really

Eric Marcus, a keen observer of gay relationships, believes that apart from the emotional resistance we face when we try to address these hard issues, the practical burdens of reaching agreements can create major obstacles for same-sex couples. We lack the training it takes to be able to talk about and handle these delicate topics, we lack any sense of how our lives together actually should be arranged, and we lack any social structure that establishes rules and procedures for dealing with these problems. Marcus goes so far as to suggest that in an ideal world we would all be sent to "relationship counselors" to help us straighten out these issues before we make commitments.

mean in the context of your own lives. Don't let your partner accuse you of not trusting him or her when you express these anxieties! It's essential to admit the transient human nature of any partnership; as perfect as it now seems there are bound to be some flaws, so there is always a potential for future dissolution.

Once you recognize the need for an agreement, you have to create a space to explore all the relevant issues. You will need emotional space in the form of patience, tolerance, and courage, and you will need physical space as well. Select a safe and comfortable place to talk out these matters. You may want to go away for a weekend to a rustic cabin or cozy hotel to get away from the kids, the phone, or the household chaos. And you are going to need time to discuss the issues as well as some time apart from each other to think about your discussions.

You should also implement a "holding pattern" while you sort out the long-term issues. You may want to keep assets separate until you decide what you want to merge, and you may want to rent rather than buy until you've worked out your financial arrangements. Waiting can be a problem if you face immediate practical pressures to buy a house, relocate your business, or make an investment decision, so if you need to take prompt action before you have the time to resolve the big issues, be cautious. Make sure you document what you are doing, minimize the irreversible actions, and try to keep your arrangements flexible.

Confronting Your Issues

You can then confront the particular issues that are most important in your relationship, organizing them in a manageable format for efficient discussion. Take stock of what personal matters *you* need to deal with. But remember, if an issue is perceived as important for either of you, it is something *both* of you need to deal with.

If your relationship is new, you likely are not going to be concerned about securing lifetime financial support, although if one of you is facing a terminal illness or a disability that prevents you from earning a living, this may be the very first item on your list. If having children is the top priority and your biological clock is running, this should be an early topic of discussion. There is a time and a place for every such discussion, and when to ask about each particular concern is something only you can decide. You may be tempted to conceal some of your less-attractive anxieties, but if you do so for too long, you're bound to face problems later on when your true emotions surface.

I encourage you to compile a detailed list of the topics that are most important to you and then make a second list of what you think is important to your partner. It is likely you will both include basics like the house, the car, and the kids. But make sure you also add other items like retirement plans, commuting problems, and taking care of your parents. Then, when you sit down to discuss your issues, compare your lists. You may be a bit distressed to see how many of your partner's items you never thought to include, but as a result of the process you will each have a much clearer sense of what topics need to be on the table.

I strongly recommend a full and complete disclosure of each party's financial assets and obligations. Not doing so undermines the construction of an honest foundation, one of the most fundamental requirements for an equitable and rational relationship. This is scary stuff and may be cause enough to postpone the agreement process—*and that is okay*. If you really don't feel you can trust your partner with such intimate information, then you should wait a while before you merge your economic lives.

Overcoming the Emotional Obstacles

The next phase may be the most difficult: getting past the emotional obstacles you've so carefully identified to reach a general sense of agreement on each major issue. No one is suggesting that until every little issue is fully resolved you are doomed to be alone in life. The optimum solution is to reach sufficient emotional clarity to be able to either (1) make the agreements necessary to live the kind of life you both want to live or (2) acknowledge that until certain specified emotional changes occur, a more cautious and less-intertwined life will be appropriate.

And how do you reach this goal of emotional clarity on central relationship issues? Two approaches are generally available. Some people prefer to talk in terms of principles, focusing on their underlying, gut-level emotions. These folks prefer to explore their childhood wounds, unpacking their baggage and examining their most intense sentiments. Once these people achieve clarity on the most fundamental level, it is usually a cinch to sort out the details and go forward to work out an agreement.

Others prefer to proceed right to the details and hammer out the specifics of their merging lives without lingering very long on the underlying emotions. These couples focus on questions such as whether to share the costs of life together and whether to rent or buy their first house. For them, tackling each particular decision directly, rather than talking about their feelings openly is the best way to sort out their feelings.

Either approach will work, and for most couples a combination of the two will work best. The situation becomes sticky when one of you wants to follow the "just-the-facts" approach while the other one wants to dig through every pocket of doubt and uncertainty—

or at least in more pockets than the practically minded one wants to. If this is your quandary, you are stepping into treacherous territory, so proceed with caution. Be conscious of this difference, be charitable to your partner's preferred manner of approaching these questions, and be prepared for a fair amount of gentle caring, open self-examination, and possibly some outside counseling. This is the meat and potatoes of relationship formation, so don't run away from it even if it is difficult at times.

REACH AN AGREEMENT, AS SPECIFIC AS IT NEEDS TO BE

The next-to-last step starts with scheduling the agreement-formation discussions. Don't make light of this task, as mishandling it can lead to disastrous results. If your partner is about to sit for her psychology board licensing exam, consider postponing the house-purchase discussion for a while. If one of you is thinking of changing jobs in the next few months, you may want to hold off moving in together and pooling your incomes. At a certain point, depending on how hectic your collective lives are, you may realize that there is no perfect time—but there may be one week that is better than all the rest!

If one of you is consistently canceling the meetings or changing the subject matter and the months continue to roll by without any resolution, you may need to force the issue a bit. Be sensible over what is a minor irritation and what is a major crisis, and don't precipitate a crisis prematurely. If you are doing fine renting and house prices aren't skyrocketing, putting off the decision for another year may not be so horrible. But if one of you is facing increasing pressure at work to leave and the other doesn't feel able to open a new business without a bit of economic security at home, you will need to face the music. For some couples counseling is the only way to push a partner into addressing things, but be careful: the reluctance to discuss these issues can itself be a message of impending rejection.

You should also give some serious thought as to where the discussions are going to take place. Some couples prefer to commune during dinner in a series of evenings. Others want to get away for the weekend, away from the demands of the house and the job, before plunging into these treacherous waters. The setting for the discussion can make all the difference. Our clever real estate broker knew my partner and I were undecided about buying our first house together, so he offered us the use of his cabin in the woods for the weekend. Maybe we would have decided to take on this venture in any setting, but sitting in front of a fireplace on a rainy California evening, far away from the rest of the world and free from any intrusive phone calls, certainly helped push us along.

One of the last preliminary steps of the agreement process is deciding whether you need any professional assistance in the discussions themselves. Most folks prefer to talk about these issues alone and bring in a professional attorney, therapist, or mediator only if things gets complicated or ugly. Others feel different and want a third party in the room from the start. If you are particularly lost in financial or legal discussions or if you are heading down particularly tender trails, inviting a skilled professional might help the process along.

Once you have made it through all of the preceding steps you are ready for the heart of the matter: making the agreement itself. This is where you sit down, tackle each of your particular concrete issues one at a time, and explore all of the different ways your concerns can be met, consistent with the relationship principles you've already agreed on. You proceed through the list of items that are not in dispute, taking notes of how you agree to handle them, and then go forward to try to resolve the matters that remain in dispute.

Keep a thorough list of all the items to be discussed, and whenever you reach consensus on a particular point take out a fresh sheet of paper, write out the basics of your agreement for that particular item, and check it off your list. You probably will want to break for a while after a few hours, so you will need to have a clear sense, in writing, of what has been accomplished and what is left to be resolved. Don't worry about the format or precise language of your notes, just be sure you both understand what you are agreeing to.

Disagreements are bound to surface during this critical stage of the agreement process, and relationship survival requires knowing how to overcome serious disagreements. The central ingredients of conflict resolution are (1) honoring the legitimacy of your partner's perspective, (2) remaining open to making compromises wherever possible, and (3) abiding by the agreements you've made, even when it requires serious shifts in your expectations.

Quite often a solution can be achieved that meets both partners' needs fully. But frequently some degree of compromise is necessary, and that's where reaching agreement gets dicey. There are times where you legitimately feel you must hold to your principles, but be open to some self-criticism here. If the relationship is working well for both of you and requires some compromise to survive, your collective betterment should outweigh following your own individual direction alone. Don't let your pride of independence undermine an otherwise satisfying relationship!

Another aspect of resolving conflicts is to be sure you are truly able to abide by the compromise you have just agreed to. Don't act with such resentment that you try to reclaim something sub rosa that you officially gave up in the compromise, and don't make agreements you know you can't follow. One of the most common causes of dissolutions occurs when one party feels forced into a solution he isn't really ready to make and then plays out his discontent by creating conflicts down the road.

Getting stuck can happen for many reasons, each of which is important in its own way. Sometimes the problems arise because of genuine practical conflicts over what to do. Other conflicts arise when there is an unrelated dispute and one or both of you fixate on areas of practical disagreement as a surrogate for deeper conflicts. In each instance, you may need to take some time off from the agreement-making process to deal directly with the problems that are really causing the conflict or hold back from making major decisions. Trying to reach agreement by steering around the conflict's sore point isn't going to work.

Sticky problems also can arise when there is a need for more information, some of which can be obtained and some of which just takes time to surface. If one of you faces an uncertain job situation or has a medical crisis, you may well need to wait this out before making any big decisions. Other information, such as tax consequences, real estate logistics, or legal advice, is available but takes time to obtain. In these situations a short break in the process will be required.

Another common stumbling block is the distraction of more pressing issues in your individual or collective lives. Families come to visit, jobs demand your total attention, kids and friends get sick. There are only so many hours in the day, and spending your precious Sunday afternoons talking about taxes and real estate is the last thing you may want to do. You need to be both realistic and practical. At some point you are going to have to have these conversations or you are going to be leaving things to chance—or, worse, to the presumptions imposed by the law. A few weeks or months of delay is okay, but beyond that you may just have to put some of those other tasks aside.

And then there is the hardest sticking point: resistance to making a commitment of any kind at all. As wonderful as falling in love is, it always packs with it a very fundamental problem: the potential loss of your self-sufficiency. Spend a few years with a dedicated partner sharing the burdens of life, and reclaiming your self-sufficiency in the event of a dissolution is not going to be easy. Fear of commitment also may be a rational response to the unknown. You don't know whether you'll be able to reach agreement with your partner, the law doesn't always protect same-sex couples, and one can't always count on lovers to be true to their word.

But unless you overcome your fears of commitment, you will never enjoy the wonderful benefits a long-term relationship can offer. The remedy is to move forward incrementally, reducing your fear of commitment while at the same time providing yourselves a deepening base line of assurances that addresses your rational concerns. As you strengthen yourself you can work to build a more secure relationship, one that addresses those concerns that you shouldn't try to eliminate. Get your name on the title to the house, sign an agreement that provides for merged savings accounts to cover yourselves in troubled times, and try to earn enough to purchase disability insurance, and you will feel safer.

As part of the agreement process you also need to have an open discussion about dissolution, disability, and death. Talking about the possibility of a breakup can actually be constructive if you make a commitment to treat each other decently, honestly, and gently should it happen. You will trust each other more and thus grow closer, and you will be less afraid of tackling problems if they do arise. Agreeing to participate in mediation and arbitration ahead of time will enable you to deal with the lesser conflicts, thus helping minimize the greater problems.

While you can't avoid some illnesses and death, you *can* avoid some of the painful economic consequences that can result from your demise. Dealing with the hard stuff ahead of time is one of the most loving things you can do for your partner. Depending on your health status you may be able to purchase life insurance, and, whatever your condition, you can certainly organize your practical and financial life to minimize the burden on your partner. Writing wills and signing powers of attorney are important parts of this process, but sorting out your relationship agreement is equally important. The decisions you make about property ownership and financial planning should be done with a clear sense of what would happen if one of you got sick or should die during your relationship.

It is equally important to talk about extended-family issues. Sometimes concerns arise about a family-owned business, sometimes it's a family farm. Since same-sex couples tend to be less connected to their nuclear and extended families, we sometimes fail to consider their role in agreement making. It is naive to think they don't matter when money and property is involved. Issues of family property or a business or pressures your partner is facing to help support an impoverished parent or sibling definitely are going to affect your partnership arrangement.

DOCUMENT YOUR AGREEMENT

When all these steps are completed you are ready to document your agreement. Simple agreements you can do yourself by writing up a letter or formal agreement, summarizing all of the key points and making all the financial arrangements as clear as possible. The resource books listed at the end of *Legal Affairs* contain sample agreements for you to use as models.

More complicated agreements may require an attorney to help you identify problems that need to be addressed, provide you with alternative solutions for your disputes, and then write up the agreement in enforceable and comprehensible language. One final reminder: you'll need to carry out the paperwork called for in your agreement. If you are adding a name to the title of your house or car, you'll have to obtain the necessary forms, fill them out, and turn them in to the proper authorities. If you are changing the name on a bank account, one or both of you is going to have to take time off from work to do that. The same goes for changing your insurance beneficiary, your pension documents, and your investment accounts.

Don't forget to identify which assets you plan to keep separate. You may not even need to list them if they are separately owned and were acquired before the relationship began. Such separate assets would include a privately owned business, the proceeds of a sale of a house years earlier, or gifts from a parent or a former lover. Don't be unreasonably greedy here and overreact to your partner's retention of personal assets—preserving a private realm of personal savings or keeping separate one's business debts is part of maintaining a healthy relationship.

There may also come a time when you need to change the terms of your agreement. This is something you can only do if both of you want to, as changing the terms of a contract without the other person's consent is a breach of the agreement, not a change. If you feel things are out of balance or inappropriate for your changing lives, don't hesitate to talk about making some revisions in your arrangements. Doing so will mean going back through all the steps and phases described in this chapter, but if that's what is needed, don't be afraid to discuss this with your partner. Make sure your new arrangements are written down, so you don't create too great a gap between what is on paper and the way you are living your lives. You may not have to see a lawyer or do anything formal, as it may simply be a matter of signing a one-page letter explaining how the debts are going to be handled or how you are shifting ownership of one of your cars. But take the time to make the change in writing.

4

The Basic Ingredients
of Every Agreement

Remember the old adage about how once you identify a problem you're well on the way toward solving it? The same applies for agreements. Knowing what to cover in your contract will greatly aid the agreement-formation process.

Every couple's discussions will focus on different priorities, with some points more prominently featured than others. When constructing your agreement start with the big items, then tackle what you need to and are able to. Pace yourself a bit if necessary. Rome wasn't built in a day and your legal affair won't be either!

This chapter surveys the major arenas that same-sex couples have to address. Most topics will warrant some discussion time at one phase or another of your relationship, but if any subject isn't pertinent to your particular situation or doesn't warrant any formal action at this time, turn the page and move on.

THE PLACE WHERE YOU LIVE

Renting Your Home
If you are nesting in a rented home or apartment, the top four subjects for you to tackle are: (1) who is legally responsible for the rent; (2) how you are going to divide the rental costs; (3) how

"management" decisions are going to be made; and (4) who gets to stay in the place if you break up.

Who Is the Tenant? Responsibility for paying the rent is primarily based on the written terms of the lease, as well as (in some cases) specific actions each of you takes. Rental arrangements can be oral or written; oral leases are usually month-to-month; if you are month-to-month tenants, whoever pays the rent or is acknowledged as the payer by the landlord (by receiving a payment from you or by sending you a notice) is usually considered the legal tenant. Therefore, if both of you want to be considered tenants, you should both meet with the landlord and sign the lease if there is one, and both pay the rent, either with two checks or a single check written on a joint account that has both your names on it.

As month-to-month tenants, either of you can be evicted and the rent can always be raised at any time, unless there are rent control protections in your town. So long as your landlord is decent and both of you are responsible and pay the rent, you should be treated with equal dignity. Unless there is a rent control ordinance, however, you can both be evicted if either one of you causes problems. If either you or your landlord prefers to use a term lease (which protects you from eviction or rent increases during the course of the lease but binds you to pay rent for the same period of time), then you will need to decide whose name is going to be on the written lease.

In most instances you can choose to list one or both names, and there are pros and cons of each option. If both names are listed, then the landlord can pursue either of you if the rent isn't paid or if you move out before the lease expires and the landlord cannot find a tenant to replace you at the same rent. If you break up, from the landlord's perspective anyone whose name is on the lease has the opportunity to stay put for the length of the lease. This prevents one of you from forcing the other one out as a trespasser or subtenant if conflicts arise, but it also means that neither of you has any legal primacy for the apartment.

If only one of you is named on the lease, however, then the landlord *probably* will only be able to come after that person for payment if you breach the lease. But at the same time, the unlisted partner may not have any legal rights if the listed tenant moves out or the lease is terminated. He or she also will definitely be in a worse position if both partners are trying to hold on to the place in a breakup situation. Don't be greedy here; you can't enjoy the leasehold benefits without taking on the payment obligations. Choose the option that makes most sense for both of you overall, given your long-term plans and each of your financial conditions.

Sometimes you don't have any choice in the matter. If one of you was there first and the landlord only wants to deal with one tenant (or the lease prohibits adding someone new), the decision has been made for you. Some landlords insist on having *every* occupant's name on the lease, and you may need to list both names to be able to show that you can afford the rent. In such cases, unless you are willing to keep your lover's presence a secret, both of you will have to sign the lease.

Homophobia can create special burdens for tenants, and in certain towns you may face serious discrimination if the prospective landlord suspects you are a gay couple. In these situations you will need to make a delicate personal and political decision. Some couples will insist on being open and accepted as a couple and thus take on the personal and legal challenges of contesting the actions of a biased landlord. Others may want to maintain a lower profile and only have one partner present himself to the landlord as a single person. If you select the path of discretion make sure you have a side agreement covering who has what rights to the apartment and what each person's obligations are.

Rental rights and liabilities based on conduct rather than on a lease can be dicey. Even if you aren't named on a lease, the law in most states declares that whoever pays all or a part of the rent under his own name (or with his own check) or is known or accepted by the landlord as an occupant is a legal tenant. If this is something you don't want to happen, be careful who sends in the rent checks, but if it is what you want, keep an account of who is paying the rent. If the lease prohibits having a roommate, contact your landlord and try to negotiate an amendment to your lease.

In those cities that are covered by rent control protections, deciding whose name goes on the lease will have special importance. In those venues, the law bestows on the "named" tenant significant protections against rent increases and a near guarantee that you won't be evicted except for specified reasons. In most such cities, however, the unofficial "occupant" (i.e., lover) is deprived of these benefits if the named tenant moves out or dies, which may leave one of you totally adrift. If you are renting an apartment that is covered by such protections, carefully read up on your local law. If an unlisted occupant isn't protected by the rent control laws, you should try diligently to get his or her name listed. If the stakes are really high and the rent control rules are at all confusing, consult an attorney or talk with your rent control board to learn how to handle the situation.

My general advice is that it is better to list both names on the lease unless doing so will alienate the landlord or create unnecessary tension in an otherwise good landlord-tenant relation. Listing both names is better because it gives each of you equal legal footing, thus preventing the landlord from evicting one of you just because the other one moves out. It also protects the "survivor" if you share an apartment in a co-op or in public housing that restricts who can rent there.

Who Pays the Bills? The second big item facing renters is allocating the monthly bills. As with any other household expense, it is up to the two of you to decide whether you want to split the costs equally or base your payments on how much each of you can afford—or on some other nonequal formula. In order to be sure that your arrangements are equitable, take the time to estimate *all* your likely costs, including utilities, food, and furnishings, and try to agree on a comprehensive budget. Make every effort to establish a consistent monthly plan if at all possible rather than making ad hoc budgetary decisions every month.

It is vital that you be direct with each other about what each of you can afford. Don't make a financial arrangement that is financially unrealistic, as this will only generate strife later on. Money conflicts can be the death of *any* relationship. If the only way you can afford that fancy apartment is if your partner covers two thirds of the rent, admit this from the beginning rather than borrowing the shortfall from her each month.

One of the benefits of being a same-sex couple is that you can choose between a range of cost-sharing alternatives. Some couples decide to split their housing costs along a socialist model ("from each according to his ability, to each according to his needs"), whereas others divide costs equally—even when that allows the higher-earning partner to accumulate some personal savings. If one of you has a lower income, has located a bargain apartment all by yourself, or is facing major nonhousing expenses such as college tuition or medical costs, consider these factors when you decide how much each is going to be paying each month. Figuring out what feels fair to both of you is part of the domestication process.

Once you have figured out how the costs are going to be shared, it should be easy to write a memorandum stating your arrangements. A one-page letter that explains who is going to pay how much each month will suffice. If both of you sign it, you've got a deal. If everything is going to be split equally and both names are on the lease, you may not even need anything in writing at all, but writing it down won't hurt. Just remember, this agreement affects only the two of you; if the rent doesn't get paid in full the landlord can evict *both* of you, even if you're the honorable one who has paid your full portion of the rent.

The Day-to-Day. Deciding how to handle the ongoing household chores is your third task, and it should be quite simple unless one of you is taking on special projects. Be realistic here. If the landlord is giving you a break on the rent, for painting the interior of your flat, for example, resolve who is expected to do this work. Most such arrangements don't have to be written down, but it is good to spend a few moments discussing them, and, if the situation *is* complicated, put it in writing.

Who Has to Move? Deciding who gets to keep the apartment or house if you part company is the fourth topic, and it is probably the biggest source of potential conflict for couples who rent. Even though you hope you will never have to face this decision, discuss it—if only to acknowledge its sensitivity and importance.

In some cities moving on is no big deal, as there may be dozens of apartments available for roughly the same rent. In other cities this will be a semibig deal, as other places are out there but hard to find and at higher rents than you've been paying. In cities like San Francisco, Boston, and New York City, losing your low-rent apartment can be financially devastating. When the options are scarce and you lose valuable rent control protections as long-term tenants, losing a prime-location, low-cost, or rent-controlled apartment can cost you thousands of dollars per year.

Since breaking up almost always means only one of you gets to stay in that dream rental and the other one has to hit the streets, deciding who has first right to hold on to the apartment may turn out to be the single biggest economic decision you have to confront. While in some situations it may be necessary to postpone the decision, try to reach a solution as soon as possible.

Here are a few suggestions on how to handle the issue of priority between renters if you break up:

- If only one of you can be the legal renter, arrange your finances accordingly. In some rent control jurisdictions only the original renter can benefit from the low rent and subsequent new roommates aren't protected, so nothing is gained by adding a second name to the lease. In these situations, you may want to take some of your collective rental savings and create a "relocation fund" to pay part of the excess rent of the unfortunate soul who may have to move out.
- If one of you occupied the apartment before the other one moved in, it is only fair that this person have first right to stay if things don't work out, so you may want to engineer a slightly unequal allocation of the rent obligation. Creating a relocation

fund for the vulnerable partner might be a good idea in this situation as well.

- If one of you has special needs and the apartment is just what you alone need, be it proximity to a workplace, special environmental concerns, or unique facilities (such as a darkroom or a potter's shed), it may make sense to give this partner the first right to stay if the relationship goes sour. The one getting special benefits from the place, however, should also consider paying slightly more rent each month, which would enable the partner without special needs the option of building up a small kitty to cover a potential relocation.

- If the rental unit is of equal benefit to both of you and you found it together, there may not be any objective basis on which either of you should be bestowed preferential rights in the event of a breakup. In this case the key is to recognize this fact from the outset, and agree ahead of time to go into mediation to resolve such disputes later on, if things get ugly. You might also consider creating a relocation allowance here as well, if you can afford it, to cover some of the costs one of you definitely will face if things go badly between you. This will greatly ease the mediation process, as there will be an established financial "reward" to help heal the wounds of whoever has to move out.

Owning Your Home

If you are fortunate enough to be buying a home or condominium, putting together your agreement is going to be more complex. This probably will be the largest single purchase you ever make—many of us have put our life savings into the down payment, and our monthly interest payments alone exceed what we previously paid in rent—on top of which we face insurance bills, repair costs, and property taxes. Second only to having children, buying property together is likely to be one of the biggest emotional events in your relationship as well.

In some instances you may already need to confer with an attorney as part of the property purchase. Your attorney should provide you with a detailed list of co-ownership issues to discuss and help you with your agreement. Use this opportunity to talk out the details, get the expert advice you need, and draw up an agreement. But remember, you can only have a comprehensive discussion if your attorney knows you are lovers and are buying the property together, so be sure to choose an attorney—gay or straight—with whom you feel comfortable.

For some couples the co-ownership aspects of your purchase may be very simple. You may be able to rely solely on the language of your deed or you can write up your own agreement, using a form obtained from one of the resource books listed at the end of this book or modifying a form used by a friend. But be careful here: unless you intend to own everything fifty-fifty and are holding title consistent with that arrangement, chances are you will need some kind of separate written agreement. If you are at all intimidated by the prospects of doing this, don't be afraid to turn to a lawyer; investing in a house is just too big a deal to treat lightly.

Here are the key points every real property co-ownership agreement should include.

1. The form of ownership (joint tenancy or tenancy-in-common), a recital of each party's initial contributions, and detailed provisions regarding loans from outsiders or from either owner

2. How ordinary payments (mortgage, taxes, insurance, utilities, urgent repairs) will be paid and how you are going to handle defaults by either of you

3. How decisions regarding optional expenditures (renovations, nonurgent repairs) are going to be made and how payments are going to be allocated

4. How records are to be maintained and how you are going to balance out overpayments and underpayments for the property

5. Whether or not labor contributions are going to be compensated

6. Whether there are any portions of the property that are under one person's sole control and management, i.e., a studio
7. Whether you will ever rent out any portion of the property
8. Who will get first rights to buy out the property if you break up and, if there's an internal buyout, how you will determine the property's value and the value of each person's partial interest in it
9. How you will handle the sale of the property to a third party
10. How the costs of a sale will be allocated
11. Whether you are going to use mediation and arbitration if the conflicts cannot otherwise be resolved

Home ownership debates are best understood by recognizing from the outset that every residence plays three central roles in our lives. Our house is (1) the physical place where we live, (2) a financial investment, and (3) a symbol of our relationship. These three roles are interwoven together, and, as a result, every decision we make about our house reverberates on all three levels.

Some of the potential difficulties of owning property can never be completely anticipated or avoided. Market values drop, roofs leak, and foundations crumble. But many of the more common co-ownership problems *can* be avoided, and those that cannot can, at least, be mitigated. Your goal as a new co-owner, therefore, is to create an agreement that serves both of you as a practical yet flexible structure that will endure throughout your relationship. Doing so is just as important as preventing dry rot in your walls or repairing fire hazards such as outdated electrical systems!

Buying In. The first and most important topics for home owners to address deal with the interrelated matters of the form of title, the relative amount of each person's investment, and the allocation of your respective ownership interests. This is the arena where couples are most likely to make their biggest mistakes, and, not surprisingly, it also can be the source of the ugliest real estate wars in the event of a separation.

Property ownership by unmarrieds in nearly every state of this country comes in one of two packages: joint tenancy or tenancy-in-common. Joint tenancy means you own the property in fifty-fifty shares *and* if one of you dies while you co-own the property, the other one automatically gets the decedent's half interest—regardless of whether the decedent had a will or what the will says. The transfer to the co-owner is instantaneous upon the death of a joint tenant.

Tenancy-in-common, by contrast, allows you to own the property in any percentage split you want, not just fifty-fifty and if one owner dies, that person's share goes to whoever is named in the will as beneficiary. If the co-owner dies without a will, his or her share goes to whoever the state law says should get it, usually a parent, child, or sibling.

In order to select the form of ownership that is right for you, you first need to make two big decisions: what percentage each of you owns and who is to get your share if you die while co-owning the place. The two factors are interrelated and the decision is never easy, but there are a few simple rules that will help you sort things out, though if you can't come to a solid decision on the question after reading this section, you may need to spend an hour or so with an attorney who is familiar with your particular issues.

There are three main components of these intertwined decisions. Visualize the decision-making task as a series of forks in the road:

1. Your first decision involves the percentage of ownership each of you will acquire, based on what each of you has contributed and how you want to organize your financial lives. Regardless of how much you contributed to the purchase, if you have decided to own the property in unequal shares you *have* to choose tenancy-in-common; if it's a fifty-fifty split, you can choose either form of ownership.

2. If you want your portion to go to someone *other than* your co-owner upon your death, you also have to go with tenancy-

in-common. But, remember, if you don't write a will, your parents or siblings will end up owning the property. If your partner is your preferred heir, however, you can take title either way; if you select joint tenancy, your heirs can avoid the costs and delay of probate, but, depending on your particular economic situation, your heirs may face extra tax burdens down the road.

3. Depending on how much your property is worth and what you have decided to do with it upon your death, the estate expenses and tax consequences of each option may favor one over the other. If you expect to have more than $600,000 in assets by the time you die or if the property has a lot of equity, you should consult with an accountant or estate planner before making your decision and build your structure around his or her advice.

Depending on your allocation of ownership percentages and your estate planning choices, your title options may be limited to only one choice. Once you come to terms with the estate tax implications, there's a decent chance that one form of title will probably emerge as your best choice.

If you are putting in equal amounts of down-payment money and plan to contribute equally to the monthly costs and the maintenance expenses, the title decision should be easy: you should be equal owners. If you plan to name each other as heirs, joint tenancy may be just right for you. Don't forget that if both your names are on the deed, under either form of ownership, with no *un*equal percentage allocation stated, a fifty-fifty split is what the law will presume.

If one of you is contributing more than the other for the down payment, renovation expenses, or ongoing monthly costs, you will have to decide whether the person paying more is going to own a greater share of the property, or, alternatively, whether the richer one is making a gift or loan of the extra contribution. If unequal ownership is the route you are following, tenancy-in-common is the form for you. Remember, under both title options the law is going to presume that having both names on the title means equal ownership, so if this is contrary to what one or both of you have in mind, you will need to sign a side agreement confirming the specific terms of your unequal ownership.

There are three basic methods of accommodating unequal contributions to the acquisition of your residence:

a. The richer partner can opt to be generous and make a gift to her or his partner of any extra contribution, or you both can agree to exchange that extra payment for a significant contribution of another variety that the other one is making to the relationship. There is nothing wrong with being generous, and it can be one of the noblest expressions of deep and abiding love. But watch out here, as in some relationships generosity can become manipulative or even oppressive, and for some people giving or receiving gifts can become a terrible emotional burden. I encourage generosity, but I recommend that if one of you is going to be generous in the purchase of the house, make sure it is done openly and discussed thoroughly.

Making unequal contributions of any significant size to co-owned property is one of those situation in which it is *essential* that you have a written agreement to document the generosity so the donor isn't tempted to rewrite history and try to characterize the gift as a loan. And if the gift is worth more than $10,000 per year, you also should check with your accountant on how best to handle the long-range tax consequences that will arise from such a large gift.

b. The richer partner can make a loan to the poorer one, to be repaid either during the course of the co-ownership or later on, either when the property is sold or if the parties break up. Be careful here, though, as the interest on the loan could saddle the poorer partner with a huge debt, and if there's a drop in property values the debtor could be left without any proceeds from which to repay the debt. Some folks agree ahead of time that if such an unfortunate event occurs, the loan will be forgiven in whole or in part.

There also can be tax ramifications to such a loan arrangement as the interest is income, and you'll need to decide how much interest, if any, is going to be charged and when the loan is going to be repaid. Don't be afraid to tackle the deeper emotional issues that inevitably will arise when you start exploring long-term loans to one another.

By the way, loans of this kind can always be forgiven. There wouldn't be a nicer anniversary present than to forgive part or all of that down-payment loan!

c. Finally, if you feel uncomfortable with either the gift or the loan approach you always have a third option: you can agree from the start that the richer partner will own a larger proportion of the residence. If you follow this model you'll have to decide the size of that larger portion, agree on whether the monthly costs are going to be split by the same percentage or equally, and resolve how to accommodate this inequality if the co-ownership terminates. Allocating monthly costs pro rata sometimes feels awkward since it's likely you are using the house equally. But if the relationship lasts as long as you hope it will and you split all the monthly payments equally, the initial imbalance in the down payment eventually will be nearly equalized by the equal monthly burdens.

In such a situation it usually makes sense to choose the equal payments option and make an annual adjustment to your allocation percentages as the poorer one catches up or, alternatively, agree on a compromise allocation from the start. For example, you might agree that even though one of you paid two thirds of the up-front costs, so long as you each pay an equal share of the monthly costs for up to ten years you will own the property on a forty-sixty percentage and, then, on a fifty-fifty basis if the relationship lasts ten years or longer. If you are having trouble deciding what is the fair thing to do in such a case, get out a calculator and figure out how the different scenarios will play out over time. Use different appreciation assumption because if property values go up the one who owns a larger percentage of the property may end up a whole lot richer, whereas if property values stay flat the richer partner will simply have spent more and gotten little extra in return. In addition, bear in mind that an agreement to share property pro rata means you share the losses by the same percentage, which can become a real burden if the market drops precipitously.

To a great extent, picking the best solution for house co-ownership depends on how you structure the underlying finances of your relationship. If you have decided to share your resources and merge your economic lives, your property arrangement should be a reflection of that sharing. Conversely, if you are keeping your financial lives separate in part or completely, you'll need to establish what your financial principles are and then integrate your sense of what is fair with your realistic estimate of what each of you can afford to contribute. You can then translate that equation into the specifics of the co-ownership agreement.

What's the best solution when there is an unequal contribution to the purchase? If the excess contribution is a onetime event, most couples find it easiest to use the loan model, agreeing not to charge any interest if the loan is going to be repaid or forgiven fairly soon and forgiven altogether if values plummet. Put a fixed value on each person's contribution, whether it is for the down payment or for a particular renovation project, and reach an agreement on how to repay these capital investments if the property is sold. It will then be easy to divide up any remaining proceeds of sale (the profit) according to how you are handling your monthly payments, which will probably be closer to an equal allocation. But before making any final decision, give due consideration to both the pro rata ownership and the gift model, as each is a viable option for the same-sex couple.

Whatever you decide, don't ignore the implications of unequal contributions. Unresolved issues in this area probably constitute the lion's share of same-sex dissolution litigation. A typical case is that of Brian and Joe. Joe inherited a lot of money in the third year of their relationship, and when they bought a house Joe put $90,000 into the purchase, although Brian only had $10,000 to contribute. They took the house as joint tenants (for inheritance purposes) and never really discussed how to treat Joe's extra contribution. When they broke up ten years later, Brian expected to get half the proceeds of the sale, whereas Joe thought he should get 90 percent of the proceeds. It cost them more than $20,000 in attorneys' fees and a year of aggravation to resolve this dispute, and eventually the arbitrator split the proceeds on a 60 percent–40 percent allocation, a compromise that left Joe feeling quite aggrieved. Brian, however, felt that even though the division wasn't fifty-fifty, he got close to what he was entitled to, though the process was way too expensive and very draining.

The next item for discussion is how you are going to handle *unforeseen* costs like improvements and major repairs. On top of the unwelcome repairs you will inevitably face, one or both of you may well want to do some improvements. If you are equal owners it makes most sense to share these costs equally, but if you own the property in unequal portions you will need to choose between splitting the costs by the same percentage as you own the property (pro rata, that is) or equally.

You will need to reach a consensus on how much each of you can afford to contribute to the improvement as well as on how you are going to handle responsibility for the costs long-term. If ready cash is a problem for one of you, be open to having one partner come up with the money straightaway and plan to have the other reimburse her or him over time. Most couples feel that the costs of long-lasting improvement, which by definition are optional, can be budgeted ahead of time and should raise the value of the property—should be shared pro rata based on the percentage of ownership, and this is usually the fairest way to go. By contrast, the ongoing maintenance, which keeps the value constant and is more related to the day-to-day use of the property, is less predictable. These costs, therefore, usually are shared equally.

Don't forget: this is *your* relationship and *your* agreement, so you can always revise it so long as you *both* agree on the revisions. At the outset you should try to settle on terms that make sense for both of you given your immediate situation, but stay open to the possibility that the arrangement may need to be adjusted if financial positions shift or the relationship deepens.

Taking Charge. The next set of co-ownership questions involves your decision-making procedures. Home ownership *must* be a consensus activity, regardless of who owns what percentage of the house. While it is just fine for one person to take the lead, no one should be allowed to redo the kitchen or refinance the mortgage without the other's consent. If this puts obstacles in the path of efficient property management or prevents one of you from doing what you desperately believe needs to be done, then so be it. The arduous process of reaching consensus will force you to overcome those conflicts, which is precisely what should take place.

Agreeing that you'll act only by consensus in making major decisions allows you to postpone working out the details of such decisions until you really need to face them. Trying to decide about renovation projects in the abstract, years before you actually are going to do the work, is a near impossible task. If you agree in a written document that you will each play an equal role in the decision making when the day actually comes, you will feel far better protected and thus it will be easier to make the initial leap into co-ownership.

The same goes for deciding if either of you is going to be compensated for any excess labor contributions. I recommend that neither partner be given an automatic right to compensation for her labor. But if down the road one partner is considering taking the summer off to paint the house, it only makes sense to consider reducing her mortgage obligations until she goes back to work full-time. But again, this is a decision that is better made at that time, not while you are busy with the purchase decisions and don't really know what kind of construction activities will be needed.

By the way, the key to surviving a renovation is to recognize that you are undertaking a very big project, something that may be optional. Don't minimize the scale of the challenge or deny the inevitable emotional reverberations of almost every aspect of the situation, and take it slow, be considerate, remain flexible, and keep a good sense of perspective. Acknowledge that there will be disagreements on how to deal with your contractor, and approach potential spats with love and compassion, not with a judgmental air. Be patient enough for consensus, and don't expect to get your own way every time.

Following these rules won't eliminate the possible crises, but they should at least help you keep them manageable!

Splitting Up. You can avoid many of the nasty battles of a potential breakup by making a few rational decisions ahead of time. If you can reach agreement about contributions and procedures during the loving times, a breakup will be far less tortuous and expensive for you.

The goal of this phase of the discussion is to construct the rules and procedures for handling your real estate divorce, should one occur. Some aspects of the task, like calculating the percentages of ownership, will flow directly from the ownership decisions you already should have made. But since you can't know ahead of time exactly what conflicts will arise, it also helps to commit to following certain procedures for resolving any variety of conflicts early on, while you are still friends. Working these methods out ahead of time, such as agreeing that you will attend a few mediation sessions, will also reduce your fear of a separation, something that actually can be a key ingredient to sticking together.

If you have already figured out who owns what share of the property, you should agree to honor that allocation in the event of a dissolution, thereby handling the single biggest source of conflict. You can then proceed to spell out how you are going to apply the ownership allocation. Based on the methods of compensation for any extra contribution you agreed on, this may mean buying each other out, paying back a down payment loan, or dividing up the proceeds of a sale in unequal portions.

Your ownership agreement also should include how you are going to value extra contributions to improvements each of you may make. You'll need to decide when something is going to be construed as a gift and, if it isn't, how you can most reasonably agree on a value of the contribution. Some couples agree on a dollar-for-dollar reimbursement, and others choose to get an appraisal of the improvement. You may want to agree ahead of time to accept a neutral appraiser or the average of two brokers' opinions of the market value. Remember, in most states neither party gets *any* compensation for extra contributions or renovations unless there is a prior agreement between the parties, so don't fail to make such an agreement if that's your intention.

Another separation issue to confront is how you are going to handle conflict. It is impossible to know precisely what the fights will be about, so you need to design a system that can accommodate conflicts without destroying your lives. In a buyout setting you may have a disagreement about the value of the property, so you may want to agree to use an appraisal process. You also may want to slow down the process to give each other some breathing time to make those all-important decisions. If this is your preference, you should agree on who is going to live in the house and at what cost while you are deciding the larger issues.

You may also want to agree, ahead of time, to help each other out financially in the event of a breakup, especially if one of you is going to face major relocation expenses. You will certainly want to include mediation and arbitration as part of the conflict resolution process, as this one provision alone can save you years of litigation and thousands of dollars in legal fees should you face a major conflict down the road. The details of these procedures are covered in the breakup discussions in chapter 7. Make sure you understand the consequences of these procedures before you agree to abide by them.

A comprehensive co-ownership agreement also should address whether one of you will have a first right to buy out the other if staying together doesn't work out and, if so, what procedures you will use to effectuate such a buyout right. If you don't want to establish an automatic "first dibs" on the property, you should agree to use mediation or arbitration to decide who will get that first opportunity and on what financial terms. It usually makes sense to agree from the start that if neither of you buys the other one out within a few months you will sell the property and distribute the proceeds according to your ownership ratio. Your agreement should also cover whether special considerations are going to be given if one of you is disabled or facing a serious illness.

Finally, your agreement should spell out what is going to happen if one of you dies while you are co-owners. To avoid any legal inconsistencies, make sure these details are coordinated with the writing of your will. Property agreements usually aren't legally sufficient as will substitutes, so unless you hold your property as joint tenants and have nothing else to leave to your partner, make sure you have a will. It's something every lesbian or gay man needs!

Writing It Down. There are several different ways you can formalize in writing the terms of your co-ownership agreement. If your lives are fairly simple and you feel able to tackle these topics by yourselves, study the sample agreements in the resource books and read the chapters in this book on separation matters, and then you should be able to put together your own basic agreement. In fact, whether or not you plan to see a lawyer to help you through this exercise, you should write down a summary of your agreement in your own words. Then, even if you never get around to writing up anything more formal, at least you will have some concrete evidence of your intentions.

For those whose lives are a bit more complicated or who are feeling uncertain about how to handle these arrangements, gather up your homemade agreement and spend an hour or two with an attorney, who will refine it and add any points you may have missed. This should cost you only a few hundred dollars.

It makes sense for those of you who are either blessed with a valuable piece of property or dealing with especially complicated arrangements to hire an attorney from the outset to draft an agreement. You should both use the same attorney, and if you select someone who is familiar with these sorts of agreements, you should not need to pay more than $500 to meet and have an agreement drafted.

While you can combine the elements of a property agreement with other financial matters, most attorneys recommend that you make separate agreements for different topics. This helps you keep your life better organized and enables you to conclude one set of discussions before you deal with other matters. It also preserves your privacy in the event you ever have to reveal one document to an arbitrator or professional consultant.

A Most Honored Guest. You need to pay special attention if one of you is living in a house owned solely by the other person. The most common scenario occurs when one of you already owns a house and the other one moves in as the affair develops into a relationship. You may have long-term fantasies about renting or buying a place together, but depending on how comfortable the place is and how your financial situations evolve, what starts out as an interim solution may end up being a permanent way of life.

The key to making sense of this awkward situation is to be clear about who is an owner and who is not. This clarification may sometimes be painful and can cause some pretty sour feelings, but continuing confusion in this realm can have even more devastating consequences. The basic guideline is that the one who is not a legal owner should be kept free of many of the major cost burdens and should have a lesser vote in making the major property decisions but should contribute something for the rental value.

You should openly acknowledge and make accommodations for the inequality of such a situation. Put aside your rules on political correctness about egalitarian relationships here: inequality in the home need not always be inequitable so long as there is adequate compensation for the one with lesser status. As a nonowning co-occupant it is only fair that you contribute *something* to the ongoing property costs, but it probably should be something less than half. If the mortgage is really low it may make sense for the nonowner just to pay for utilities and minor repairs, but if the mortgage is high it may make sense for the nonowner to pay an amount roughly equal to half the rental value. Remember, nonowners cannot take a tax deduction for any mortgage interest payments unless they can deduct the rent as a business expense. In most instances, the nonowner, given his role as a lover as well as co-occupant, should be consulted when major decisions need to be made, but it is inevitable and only fair, however, that the owner's vote count for more if there are conflicts.

If the "guest" is making significant contributions to the property greater than half of what the market rent would ordinarily be, it is essential that there be a written agreement clarifying whether and when she is going to be compensated for these contributions. In addition, you should both consider contributing to a special savings account for the nonowner's future property purchase, either of a new place together or the buy-in of a portion of her partner's place. Nothing makes a relationship deteriorate more rapidly than having one person pay for repairs or improvements on a house she does not own without an agreement that will address this situation when the time comes. This can create a terrible sense of insecurity and injustice, which can be fatal to an otherwise happy relationship.

And if the guest is contributing equally to the ongoing costs and wants to be part of the decision making, it is only fair that sooner or later she be converted into an owner. Chances are there will be a transition time when the guest begins to function more like an owner than she legally is before any official change. Sooner or later, when one or both of you begins to realize that this in-between status will no longer work, you will either have to take the leap together and move into a jointly owned home or engineer a buy-in by the long-term guest.

This is not only a financial but an emotional transition as well. Both partners' perceptions of self and home definitely will shift in ways that may surprise both of you. The emotional logistics of buying into your partner's property include the obvious shift in control over the home and a greater sense of equality in the relationship.

Being a sole owner can be scary, but at the same time it offers an emphatic sense of security and control as you can always boot out your guest and yours is the vote that counts in the end.

Since neither of you is in an "arm's length" buyer-seller relationship, it usually isn't fair to charge full price for a home the buyer already has been occupying and probably contributing to as well. At the same time, there has to be recognition that the owning partner has been keeping up the place long before the guest arrived and has probably put up a hefty amount of money up front. Thus, some kind of compromise price, midway between a price so low that it's an outright gift and the full retail price, should be established. Keep in mind that once you decide on a fair price, the seller can always offer the buyer an even greater "discount" in the form of a partial gift. Whatever you decide, be sure to put the terms in writing so that neither party is tempted to renegotiate the deal later on.

Once you've figured out the financial terms, you need to deal with the legal and practical issues of the buy-in. Every state has a different mechanism for adding a co-owner to the title, and you should talk with a real estate broker, title company officer, or local attorney to learn what forms and procedures are required. For some couples there can be significant tax consequences of a buy-in, most likely in the guise of a gift tax. And in some places your property taxes can go up dramatically. You also may need a written agreement to support your claim for a tax deduction on the mortgage interest if your name isn't listed as a borrower on the loan. Some cities also charge a transfer tax even on the sale of a *portion* of property, although you should examine whether you can be exempted from this tax as domestic partners.

The Silent Owner. When only one person's name is on the title, the one who isn't named is not technically an owner. She may have an "equitable" interest in the property, which means she is entitled to some portion of the equity because of contributions of money or labor, but *legally* she may still be a renter or a guest. Allowing such a situation to remain for a long time without a written agreement can have terrible consequences. In the most painful scenario, the record owner (the one on the title) can evict the nonowner upon a breakup, and it may be very difficult for the nonowner to recover any compensation for his or her payments or renovation work.

Despite these risks, some people put up with this situation, as owning real estate can disqualify those on welfare or the medically indigent from receiving certain payments and can create problems if you get sued or are evading an aggressive creditor. One of the perks of being unmarried is that your partner's wealth is not available to your creditors and will not disqualify you from public benefits, and, therefore, shifting (otherwise known as hiding) your assets and placing them in your partner's name may be a tempting strategy. Some people elect to keep their name off the title to avoid the costs of a transfer or to maintain their privacy, especially if they are worried about the very real consequences of openly co-owning property in a homophobic world. But however legitimate the reason may be, there are serious downsides of entering into such an arrangement.

The first such problem is that there's a good chance that what you are doing is illegal. It's called defrauding creditors, and if you get caught, the penalties can be severe. The same goes for helping your lover hide his or her assets to get on welfare. Facing a criminal charge or a civil lawsuit for hiding assets from a creditor or the government will not help you in any way, now or later.

The second downside, and one that is actually more likely to occur, is that if you are the one keeping your name off the title and a dispute subsequently arises with your partner, you may never be able to recoup your investment. If the one whose name is on the title gets into trouble and her or his creditors come after the house, you may not be able to shield your hidden partial ownership of the property. Even more likely, if you get into a spat with your partner you may be prevented legally from making a claim for your partial interest in the property, and if the owner dies without making you his or her heir you can end up homeless and broke.

The law in most states says that if you have kept your name off the title in order to do something illegal—like defraud a creditor—

you cannot rewrite your story later on just to benefit yourself. The courts will label you as having "unclean hands" and deny whatever claim you may assert, however genuine it may be. Now, of course, if your partner is honest there is nothing to prevent her or him from reimbursing you on an informal basis. But if your partner doesn't feel quite so generous or claims not to have the funds to pay you, you will have a very hard time winning a court battle. The best way to avoid these problems is to shun this kind of arrangement altogether or to spend some time with an attorney beforehand learning about the likely consequences of your particular scheme.

If no illegalities are involved, you can have your attorney draw up an agreement establishing that one of you is holding the property "in trust" for the two of you. By signing this binding agreement between yourselves, you will have established a record of the investment, making it clear who has what rights to the property should a conflict arise.

ASSETS AND OBJECTS AND DEBTS, OH MY!

Once you have worked through your real estate issues and written up a cotenancy agreement, dealing with everything else should be fairly simple. The basic legal concepts that apply to all other property, whether it is a vacation house, artwork, or the furniture, are the same. You need to decide who owns what portion of what, who gets to control what, and how to handle the distribution of any jointly owned property if things don't work out.

The easiest way to cope with these matters is to agree on a "default" provision, that is, an agreement on how possessions and debts are going to be handled in the absence of an agreement to the contrary. Getting clear on this foundational level will establish your basic system and therefore eliminate many of the potential areas of conflict, greatly reducing the need for a lengthy written agreement. Your default system probably should look something like this:

a. Anything that either person owned or owed prior to moving in together or that was acquired solely with the personal funds of one person remains the property or the debt of that person

b. Anything that is bought with joint assets and any debt incurred jointly will be a joint asset or debt, and if there's a breakup it will be divided equally between the two parties

c. Anything either person receives as a gift from the other or from someone else will remain the recipient's property

d. If either partner wishes to establish ownership of property contrary to these provisions, there must be an agreement written up and signed by both parties.

With this sort of system in place only two issues are left to resolve. The first is keeping track of what objects fall into which category. Identifying what you had before you moved in together shouldn't be hard, so the only real challenge is to clarify who owns the things you acquired after you joined households. If you aren't planning to live together for a while—or ever—you'll want to establish a set date for the commencement of your relationship. As part of these procedures, you'll also need to establish what was a gift and what wasn't.

If you have merged *all* your finances, these questions are readily answered since *everything* will be jointly owned. If you are keeping some of your property separate, though, you will need to maintain a list of what is separate and what is jointly owned. You can keep a list of many small items in your heads, but for really big items, like appliances, artworks, or major pieces of furniture, a written list is strongly advisable.

Then, once you set up this system there should be only one last cumbersome problem to deal with: how to apportion and value the jointly owned property. My recommendation is that you opt for one of the following two easy-to-remember systems. You can either (a) agree that everything that is jointly owned is going to be owned fifty-fifty regardless of who pays for what or (b) agree that if there's a dissolution the jointly-owned objects will be distributed pro rata, based on what each of you has paid, in total, for the personal property purchases.

It naturally follows that if you opt for the pro rata system rather than the fifty-fifty division, you will need to agree on a means of keeping track of payments or contributions to the joint account. For the first few years many couples keep a ledger book listing all payments for joint purchases. After a while this may become too tedious, and then you can either agree on a fixed formula or keep your check registers and credit card receipts, to be reviewed only if you break up.

The *principle* here is what counts: be clear as to what is a gift and what is a joint investment, and don't allow your grandiose sense of generosity to get ahead of your true feelings. If you want to hold on to ownership of things you have bought or brought with you, remember that you have that choice, and the decision to merge your possessions should be a conscious and careful one.

For unmarried couples the law presumes that items bought with joint funds (i.e., from a joint bank account) are jointly owned fifty-fifty and items bought with personal funds are owned exclusively by the purchaser unless there's an agreement to the contrary. Accordingly, you should organize your financial lives along the same principle and try to avoid creating ambiguity about shared possessions. Be conscious of what is going into the joint account, if you have one, and if you ever want to recharacterize an item or make a gift, talk about it openly and keep track of what you are doing. So long as your practical arrangements are in sync with your emotional needs, organizing your personal property should not be difficult.

Sharing your lives can be a wonderful adventure, and pooling your resources and your possessions can be a vital component of that merging process. But don't bring something home pretending it's a gift when in fact you expect to take it with you or get reimbursed for it later on, and don't allow your partner to saddle you with half the cost of purchases that you aren't prepared to absorb.

Money and Debts

Handling your financial affairs demands that you first make some fundamental decisions as to how you wish to live as a couple and then establish practical methods of abiding by those decisions. The primary decision, of course, is whether you are going to function as independent (the Atomic Model), partially integrated (the Fusion Model) or wholly merged financial units (the Nuclear Model). Each approach has its pros and cons, and, rest assured, two people can be emotionally linked even if they remain financially independent.

Don't minimize the deep emotional overtones of these discussions. At least once every few months I meet with clients who state, emphatically, that they are keeping their finances separate but fall into terrible conflicts when I recommend they put this in writing. Suddenly, the poorer one's unspoken fears of rejection and resulting poverty surface, and if these are not handled well they can lead to the relationship's demise.

Resolving these foundational issues about money is critical to the survival of your relationship, and there is no right or wrong choice here—so long as the two of you can agree. My standard advice is to avoid the extremes: don't let yourselves stay totally isolated economically, but at the same time, be willing to allow arenas of separation if either of you need to. I strongly advise my clients to take their time here: don't wait until you are 100 percent certain of your relationship to start sharing finances or you will never do it, but do hold back for the first year or two until you really know each other. Try to keep your financial decisions focused on your practical priorities, and don't be tempted to let your decisions here become a proxy for the emotional commitment you are both looking for.

Once you have made your fundamental decisions and chosen one of the three basic options (Atomic, Fusion, or Nuclear), there are a few special protocols you should know. First, be aware of two central rules: (1) unless there is an agreement to the contrary, each of you owns your own assets and debts, and (2) if the asset or debt is in both your names, the law will presume it's a joint fifty-fifty item, again unless there's an agreement to the contrary.

These rules are simple to master; what gets complicated is dealing with the hurt feelings they can cause and applying the rules to your real-world decisions. As for the financial assets, think very carefully before putting an account in two names or adding your partner's name to an existing account. Whether it's a stock account, a checking account, or a credit line, adding your lover's name means you are giving her ownership of half of its contents. If this isn't what you want to do, write up a side agreement or change your financial plans.

Most accounts allow you to add someone's name as a "death beneficiary," which means that person is entitled to receive the money on your death but not until then. You also can sign a power of attorney that gives your partner decision-making authority over the account but not ownership of the funds. Decision-making authority usually means the right to spend all the money without your prior express consent, so be very careful here!

Careful couples usually open separate accounts as well as a joint account, so they can shift their assets between accounts as they make specific agreements about merging finances. Not having separate accounts can cause problems regardless of your basic arrangement, as even a wholly merged couple will, from time to time, need separate accounts for gifts, sole business ventures, or special personal obligations. Having separate accounts also helps you avoid parking money in a joint account "for convenience," even when you don't view the funds as joint assets.

Joint accounts can work in one of two ways: some require both signatures, either each time or just for checks above a specified amount, and others allow either party to write a check for any amount. A joint checking account is one of the most monumental acts of trust, and since it can often be inconvenient for both parties to sign every check, the trust must not be betrayed.

Debts, for the most part, follow the same rules. If the credit card account is in both names you will each be fully liable for the debt, regardless of who makes the purchase. If this isn't what you want, don't get a joint card. As with checking accounts, it may be smart for each of you to have personal cards as well as a "house card" so you can separate your personal expenses from the joint ones. Debts incurred directly in connection with a jointly owned residence, such as mortgages, taxes, and major home repairs, are also going to be considered joint debts.

Be extra careful if one of you has past due debts or judgments. If you open a joint account or buy property together, you could inadvertently expose the "good" partner's assets to the "bad" partner's debts. Since one of the best benefits of being unmarried is that you are not automatically liable for each other's debts, don't jeopardize that benefit by combining your assets without knowing what all of your partner's liabilities are.

Earnings and Support, Now and Forevermore

One of the central tenets of a traditional marriage is that each partner pledges to support the other one, not just during marriage but "until death do us part." This doctrine of mutual support is one of the integral elements of the status of marriage, and it forms the legal basis for many of the financial components of marital law. It's what makes each partner liable for her spouse's debts, and it is what gives each partner the right to demand alimony upon divorce. Unmarried couples do not have any of these rights or obligations unless they agree to take them on contractually. Nonetheless, don't be afraid to talk about these matters. They are very important, both of you know they're important, and keeping silent about them is in no one's best interest.

The best approach is to reach agreement on the general economic structure of your relationship first, using the Atomic, Fusion, or Nuclear models. You can then translate the basic format of your relationship into a specific agreement that deals directly with both present earnings and future support.

The major questions here are to a large degree quite philosophical: if one of you has greater earnings, more savings, or an inheritance, are any of these funds going to be used to support the two of you together? Or are you going to hold down your collective spending to a level you can both afford and allow the more flush partner the option of accumulating separate savings and, from time to time, make specific gifts to the partnership at her whim only? And, under either option, if there is a breakup, is the richer one agreeing ahead of time to help out the poorer one?

There is no right or wrong answer here; what counts is that the decision must be a conscious one that is truly acceptable to both of you. Dealing with money is hard for almost everyone, straight or gay, and it is rare that anyone goes through life without facing serious financial struggles at one time or another. Indeed, even when there is enough money to cover the basics, for most folks serious emotional issues and justifiable insecurities about money abound. Moreover, money can reflect the success of our parents, as well as our own priorities, abilities, and good luck. Face it, money can dramatically change how we live and our sense of who we are.

Without any traditional model to tell us how to live our lives, our actions reflect our feelings and therefore can convey a heavy message at times. In addition, lesbians and gay men often face particular conflicts about money arising out of our understandable sense of isolation from family and the precariousness of our sense of independence. Those who cannot turn to their parents or children for assistance or who have suffered in the employment realm as a result of discrimination are particularly vulnerable. The best way to resolve these problems—in most instances, the only way—is to acknowledge them openly and tackle them head-on.

Once you have settled on a set of operating financial principles that works for both of you, here are your options for handling the practical aspects:

1. If you don't wish to pool your finances and plan to keep all your earnings in separate accounts, no written agreement is needed unless you are living in one of the very few locales that honors spousal rights for same-sex couples as a matter of

course. Without an agreement to the contrary, generally neither of you will accrue any rights to the other person's accounts since there will be no evidence of a contract and no commingling of separate funds.

2. If you are combining certain funds, say, for housing expenses or future vacations, but keeping everything else separate, chances are you won't ever accumulate much in joint financial assets as you'll be spending the joint money almost as fast as you deposit it into the joint account. Neither of you will ever accrue any rights to the separately held funds, and you should agree in writing to share ownership of the things purchased from the joint account and the joint assets. So long as you stick to this arrangement and the legal titles on the accounts are consistent with the way you want them, you probably don't need a written agreement about finances.

3. If one of you is supporting the other to any significant degree, either by pooling your resources or having one person pay all the bills from her or his own account, you should formalize this arrangement in a binding written agreement. Some couples want to make it clear to each other that this arrangement is a form of voluntary generosity that can be cut off at any time, whereas others are willing to provide legally binding future protection to the dependent one. In order to avoid confusion down the road over which category you are in—especially if major decisions are being made about the expectation of support—it is *strongly* advisable that you put things in writing. The written agreement can easily be changed if you both agree on the proposed changes, but you can create terrible problems if you allow a pattern of temporary support to create a precedent of permanent support without any written document to establish your agreement.

4. Apart from any agreements you reach about pooling resources or providing support while you are together, it is critical that you also talk about whether or not either of you is

willing to provide ongoing support to the other one if the relationship ends. Unmarried couples have no automatic rights to alimony or spousal support, and generally speaking the law is only going to honor such claims if there is proof of an actual contract. Even though oral and implied contracts in some states are enforceable in this arena, it is highly unlikely that a court will award such support without a written agreement, as proving an oral or implied deal is just too daunting and it is unlikely that a judge or jury will accept one person's word about it.

If you are both able to agree that one of you will have the right to long-term financial support even after the relationship ends, it is *essential* to put this arrangement in writing. But, if there has been a protracted pattern of support and you don't want to have this construed as postseparation support, you should put that in writing as well.

Here are a few words of caution about long-term financial issues:

- Don't pool your separate money in a joint account unless you intend to convert the funds to joint ownership and have a clearly written side agreement on how to handle the funds.
- Don't "lend" money to each other without having a written IOU, as it is just too easy for memories to fade over time and loans to be perceived by the borrower as gifts.
- Don't continue supporting your partner for a long period of time unless you make the limits of your intentions clear to him in writing.
- Don't assume that your idiosyncratic ideas about what is fair and reasonable are the same as your partner's. Everyone has her own opinions about how money is to be shared and spent in a relationship, and these opinions arise from childhood patterns, the immediate economic situation, and moral and polit-

ical values. Working out a mutually acceptable arrangement requires that each person enter the discussion with equal respect for her partner's opinions.

Joint Investments in a Joint Future

All this being said, it is crucial that every long-term same-sex couple devote serious attention to the challenge of making joint investments for their joint future. One of the most unfortunate features of many long-standing gay relationships is the apparent lack of faith in the relationship's longevity. This lack of faith manifests itself in many ways but most vividly in a reluctance to take on long-term risks and to make long-term investments of both money and energy for the sake of a better collective future. Moving beyond this rugged individualism begins with a candid exploration of what is truly possible despite the legal handicaps. "Investment" can take many forms, but there are three basic types.

Career Advancement. The most common investment is one in which one partner supports the other while she or he pursues an academic degree or certification program. The economic basis of this deal is obvious: both parties live on less for a few years in return for one person's obtaining a degree or license that will eventually increase their collective earning capacity. The exchange is a fair one so long as the couple stays together, as both will benefit from the career advancement of the temporarily dependent one. Building a career or a new business takes a long time, and especially for those who do not have the help of supportive parents, the assistance of a partner may be the *only* way to accomplish these goals.

Family law for married couples recognizes the value of such an exchange, and in most states the economic value of a professional practice or business is an asset the couple will share should there be a divorce. This provision protects the supporting partner, as she will be assured a financial interest in the business or professional practice she helped finance, assuming that the newly educated one goes on to make a better living. The law, however, generally doesn't grant any such protections to same-sex couples unless they sign a contract between themselves, so to create such arrangements, ask your partner to join you in creating a plan. Here's what to do:

1. Give some serious thought as to how you want to change your life. For many folks it may be as simple as finishing your high school or college education. For others it may mean writing a book, setting up a small retail business, or taking some night classes. More ambitious folks may want to go to law or medical school.

2. Figure out what it is going to take to accomplish your goal financially, practically, and emotionally. Conjure up a clear sense of whether this is going to mean moving to a new city, resigning from a job, or just cutting back to part-time. Calculate what it is actually going to cost and how long it will take, factoring in your lost income as well as the educational or business investment expenses.

3. Sit down with your partner, discuss whether this is a plan both of you can endorse, and decide what is a fair arrangement for both parties. Be realistic as to what is feasible, financially and practically, and try to make a realistic assessment of the long-term benefit of the proposed investment. Law school definitely is worth more than film school financially speaking, but measured by emotional fulfillment the film venture may well win out. Be clear about what each person's limits are, financially and timewise.

4. Create a legally binding "safety net" that protects both parties. Talk through how you want to handle things if the relationship doesn't survive the process or if the investment doesn't pay off financially. If a breakup occurs fairly soon after the schooling is finished, it's only fair that the assisted one repay, to some degree, the support that made it all possible. If your relationship survives, the reimbursement should come in a sharing of the increased income. Alternatively, if you are keeping your finances separate, repayment could be based on the out-of-pocket cost of the investment (i.e., the

tuition or the start-up costs of the business), on the total amount of assistance provided by the supporting one, or on some portion of the increased income or value resulting from the investment. Indentured servitude for the rest of someone's life is *not* the optimum model; rather, a sense of reciprocity and fairness is what you are looking for. If the two of you stay together a fair number of years and share in the benefits of the new career but things go sour later on, each of you should be willing to move on without any reimbursement obligations.

Working Together. The second kind of joint investment occurs when you work together as a couple on a single long-term project that will benefit both of you, assuming you stay together for awhile. This can be a business venture in which one of you devotes full time and the other one keeps a day job during the venture's initial year, or it may be something less complicated, like renovating your kitchen or building a deck off your living room. Each of you will be contributing something to a project that is of unique value— perhaps one partner has the skills and the other the funds, or maybe one has the credit for a loan and the other valuable business contacts.

Working together on a joint adventure can be both thrilling and magical, but if mishandled it can be devastating to a relationship. Since there are no automatic legal protections for either of you in case of a dissolution, you'll need to come to an agreement about handling each issue. You should base your agreement on what each person is going to invest in the project, what you expect it to be worth, and how you can allocate its benefits between yourselves if things don't work out as planned.

Relationship as Teamwork. The third and most subtle form of joint investment involves contributions of neither money nor labor but, rather, gifts of the spirit and emotional support. Building a partnership demands a major shift in the way one thinks about oneself and the other person. It compels each of you to shift your self-image from an individual to a family, where your personal needs may, at times, come second to those of the partnership. If we *don't* find a way to make these sacrifices and put our individual needs aside from time to time, it's unlikely our relationship is going to flourish. One of the truly special features of a same-sex relationship is that no one will ever complain that the burdens are being assigned according to gender. Feeling free of the anxieties of being forced to play the "wife" or "husband" role, either partner should be willing and able to demand or offer help without feeling he or she is the life-long domestic spouse or the eternal breadwinner.

Refocusing your view from that of two individuals to being a family happens magically as the trust and affection deepens, but not without some conscious effort. Heterosexual couples can rely on their upbringing and the wedding to jump-start this process, and for any couple, straight or gay, raising children is bound to cement these ties. But those who live in a world without weddings and, so often, without kids around to inspire such connections, effort may be needed to move consciously toward collective thinking. Since uncertainty about the long-term legal obligations can hinder these already fragile bonds, a vital part of the unification process is, necessarily, the clarification of each partner's legal rights and obligations.

So add to your list of topics deserving discussion the issue of making long-term investments of personal emotional and financial energy in your relationship. Doing so will open the door to a depth of commitment that will only strengthen and expand your budding relationship.

THE ESSENTIAL LEGAL DOCUMENTS

In stitching this legal tapestry together, it is preferable to create a series of separate documents rather than try to squeeze all your concerns into one single agreement. Each document will then have its own purpose and its own structure.

1. *Real Property Agreement:* If you own property together and your arrangement is other than fifty-fifty ownership of a single-family residence with both of your names on the deed, you need a written contract setting forth the terms of your co-ownership agreement. In most states this is called a co-tenancy agreement.

2. *Cohabitation Agreement:* If either partner is supporting the other one, if there is a significant amount of financial commingling, if promises are being made about separately or jointly owned businesses, or if assurances are being made about long-term and/or postdissolution support, a cohabitation agreement is needed. A cohabitation agreement generally includes a disclosure of assets, a list of separate and joint property, statements regarding the allocation of property subsequently acquired, agreements regarding present and future support obligations, and an agreement to resolve future conflicts by mediation and arbitration.

3. *Powers of Attorney:* As an unmarried couple you lack the automatic right to make decisions about each other's finances or health care. If you want to give these powers to your partner, you need to sign general (for business affairs) and health care (for medical affairs) powers of attorney. In some states these documents only last for a set number of years, so be sure to keep your papers current and valid. Durable powers of attorney remain effective even when the principal has lost consciousness, so be careful if that is what you are signing—and be certain that your bank accounts are integrated with your financial sharing arrangements.

4. *Wills and/or Trusts:* Since none of these agreements survives either of your deaths, you should also sign wills or trust documents. A will and a trust achieve the same goal: establishing who gets your possessions upon your death. Married couples don't need to worry about such documents unless they want to disinherit their spouses (which they can't do 100 percent

in some states!), but those of us who are unmarried need to make our own arrangements. If we don't take care of this before we die, the law will transfer our assets to our "next of kin," that is, our parents or siblings. If this is not what you have in mind, it is essential that you compose and sign a legally valid will or trust document.

5

The Children of Lesbian
and Gay Families

*In the old days only straight folks had kids, and coming out meant
never being able to raise children. In one of the most dramatic
social shifts of the century, lesbian and gay families now include
children. It's a marvelous development, though not without its
complications.*

THE EVOLUTION OF LESBIAN AND GAY FAMILIES

In the past, the only homosexuals who gave birth to or raised children were women who married, had children, and were awarded
custody if the marriage broke up and the father didn't take advantage of his wife's homosexuality to assert full custody. In this way
the lesbian mother was created. On rare occasions a divorcing dad
who was awarded custody went on to discover his gayness, and
some of these divorced men subsequently formed liaisons. But
parenting among same-sex couples was usually the unintended result of a prior heterosexual union.

As a result, up until the mid-1970s the only legal issue gay parents regularly faced was that of child custody in a divorce. This was
a time when almost every court in the land presumed that homosexuals were unfit parents. If a lesbian wanted to retain custody of
her child, staying in the closet or quietly working out a settlement
with her spouse were the only ways she had of retaining a connec-

tion with her children. Thousands of lesbians and gay men were forced to give up their children as a result of such prejudice.

Thanks to a valiant effort in the past two decades by hundreds of lesbian mothers, who were joined by gay fathers, supportive therapists, attorneys, and political activists, the walls of negative stereotyping finally began to tumble. The reasons for this change are many and varied: homophobia in general has declined, psychological studies have proven that being raised in a gay family is not detrimental to children, and increasing numbers of individuals have found the strength and the legal resources needed to challenge unfair custody decisions.

Fortunately, many straight parents have come to realize that an ex-spouse's homosexuality need not be viewed as a social disaster. Lawyers and psychologists have worked to educate judges, and hostile trial court decisions have been reversed. Increasing numbers of appellate courts have ruled that homosexuality per se is not grounds for denying a parent custody of her or his child. Thus the prospects for lesbian and gay parents seeking to retain custody of their children are better today than ever before, although the battle is far from over and egregious decisions still emerge.

The real innovative development of the past twenty years is that lesbians and gay men can create their own families with children, intentionally and without a past heterosexual relationship. This trend was slow in emerging; in the early years of the gay liberation movement, families were often viewed as something to escape from and making babies was something only straight people did. Staying home to take care of kids was seen by feminists as a sign of oppression, and bringing a toddler to the playground was the last thing a politically correct gay man would do.

But in a remarkable convergence of political transformation, social liberation, and genuine individual change in the decades after Stonewall, what began as isolated acts of lesbians choosing children has burgeoned into a major trend. Starting in the mid-1970s an increasing number of lesbians who had never been married began having children of their own. While every birth has its own story, there has been an unquestionable shift in feminist politics, a changing attitude toward children and families among lesbians in particular, and a growing institutionalization of lesbian family culture overall, all of which have contributed to this dramatic societal shift.

Artificial insemination has become widespread, and many cities have sperm banks that accept lesbian clients. A sperm bank open to serving the lesbian community was opened in Northern California in the early 1980s, and within a few years a budding lesbian baby boom began to appear. Current estimates of children born to or raised by lesbians range in the millions; some studies assert that between six and fourteen million children live with lesbian or gay parents. Homosexual parents have created their own magazines, their own social support networks, and an infrastructure of attorneys, schools, counselors, and political groups, all working to protect the rights of lesbian and gay parents and their families.

For the first decade of the lesbian baby boom most moms took it for granted that only the biological mother would be the legal parent. Legal status was not a top priority, and being a single mother was an acceptable option. The notion of a child having *two* legal mothers seemed beyond comprehension.

Then, in the mid-1980s, a group of adventurous lesbians began to challenge the single-mother model for same-sex couples. Nonbiological mothers began to question why they should remain legal outsiders forever, and the prospect of losing one's children in the event of a dissolution—or the death of the biological parent—loomed ever larger. Activists and lawyers soon realized that straight stepparents had been adopting their partners' children for decades and asked: Why shouldn't lesbian partners be able to do the same?

The first known second-parent adoption occurred in 1985 in Oregon, and within the next five years a network of lawyers across the country began making similar applications to local courts. Many early efforts were rebuffed, but over time judges in many states began to get the point. Soon thereafter joint two-parent adoptions of a child were allowed when the legal ties to its birth mother were terminated, although most of the early adoptions were second-parent adoptions by the birth mother's lesbian partner, situations in which the birth mom remained a legal parent.

Predictably, there was a wide array of responses by state legislatures and courts. In many states it was discovered that nothing in the statutes expressly barred such adoptions, making it possible to obtain legal victories on a one-by-one basis. Some states passed favorable legislation, while others did the opposite. In several states lower courts denied the applications but were reversed by appellate courts, and in some parts of the country adoptions by unmarried couples were banned regardless of sexual orientation. At least fifteen states currently allow gay second-parent adoptions officially and others do so on an occasional basis, and the list is growing longer every year. Since the law in this area is changing so quickly, it is crucial that you consult an attorney to see what laws currently apply in your state.

In the past few years same-sex parenting has finally broken the gender barrier. Woman have raised children without men for centuries, but men daring to be parents on their own is something quite new. Think back on the first time you saw a gay male couple holding a child with not a mother anywhere in sight and you will realize how revolutionary this really is. I still remember the first time I watched two men hover over their month-old daughter, checking her diaper and passing a bottle between them—this was social change of a momentous magnitude!

A SURVEY OF THE LAW

Parenting decisions must begin with an honest and thorough understanding of how the laws are written. Your choices about children for the most part will be irrevocable, and this arena is constrained by the law more than any other aspect of our domestic lives. Even though the rules are notoriously local in this realm and specific legal advice is essential, a basic knowledge of the rules will get you started.

Laws Affecting Children Are Local

The first legal principle you should know is that statutes affecting parents and children are overwhelmingly local and, at the moment, quite volatile. What's allowed in one state may not be allowed across state lines, and what happened yesterday is no guarantee of what will happen tomorrow. Compounding the law's changeability is the fact that the actual day-to-day practices of the way laws regarding kids are enforced can vary enormously from town to town and from judge to judge. As a result, your educational effort must be extremely fine-tuned. Examine your state laws and the most recent court decisions in your state so you can begin your inquiry with a solid grasp of where the law currently stands in your particular locale.

The two most important questions you need to have answered are (1) whether second-parent adoptions or joint adoptions by same-sex couples are allowed and (2) whether, in the event of a dispute between the two of you, the nonlegal parent has any rights or responsibilities for a jointly raised child. More than any other doctrines, these will shape your new family arrangements. You will also want to learn how the adoption process works, what it will cost, whether lesbian and gay parents are discriminated against in the process, and what other rules (i.e., insurance for dependents or welfare eligibility) might affect your child-rearing decisions.

In some states, for example, second-parent adoptions may be possible but aren't authorized by statute, and thus the outcome will depend on the judge who hears your application. Some judges defer to hostile social services agencies who may appear in court and assert that you are unfit parents. In other states you may need to customize your strategies based on which county you live in, and you may even want to consider moving to a more enlightened area. Don't be caught unprepared, as this is one area of the law in which you *must* seek guidance of a seasoned *local* attorney.

The Basic Legal Doctrines

Here are a few general principles to observe as a foundation for structuring your same-sex family:

1. The birth mother and the birth father (the one who provides the sperm, either through sex or artificial insemination, unless there is a *doctor-handled* insemination) are presumed to be the legal parents, even if they aren't married to each other. If a sperm donor is anonymous the birth mother will be the sole parent. In order for anyone else to be declared a legal parent, formal action by a court is absolutely necessary. No private arrangement or contract between the parents alone, no matter how long-standing and sincere their relationship, can substitute for a judgment issued by a court.

2. Historically, adoption involved the termination of the birth parents' rights and obligations and the creation of a new parenting relationship, with the adoptive parents taking on all rights and responsibilities and the birth mother severing all ties to the child. The notion of an adoptive mother being a coparent with a birth mother is contrary to this model. A nonprofit agency handled most adoptions, and neither the birth parents nor the adoptive parents knew much, if anything, about each other. This original model of adoption still shapes many laws. In a limited number of states same-sex couples are allowed to adopt the child of an unrelated mother jointly, just like straight parents, but in many other states they cannot. In some states gay people can only adopt as single people and an adopting parent's partner will have to sit on the side, hoping to become a legal coparent later on if second-parent adoptions are allowed.

3. In some states, in certain narrow categories, partners of a legal parent can become adoptive parents without terminating the birth parents' rights. Traditionally, such second-parent adoptions were allowed only for heterosexual stepparents, i.e., when the new husband or wife of the custo-

dial birth parent wanted to become a coprimary parent with his or her new legal spouse following either a divorce or the death of the other birth parent. In about fifteen states so far a second-parent adoption is also allowed if the lesbian or gay partner of a birth parent wants to become a legal coparent— in effect, a homosexual stepparent adoption. But despite the enormous progress in this area of law and favorable rulings from some of the most influential courts of the land, in many states gay second-parent adoptions are still banned. In other states neither the courts nor the legislatures have issued decisive rulings on the subject, leaving it up to the local judge to decide what to do.

4. Sperm donors in most states have no rights or obligations as fathers if the insemination is handled through a doctor. But if the donor delivers his sperm directly to the birth mother or does a direct donation through a sperm bank and no doctor is involved, or if he goes on to develop a parentlike relationship with the child, in many states he may acquire legal rights and obligations as a father. Surrogate birth mothers, who carry a child so that another parent or parents can adopt it, remain legal parents until a court-approved adoption is granted, and then they have no further rights or obligations.

5. In the event of a same-sex dissolution, if the nonbiological partner has been declared a legal parent through a second-parent adoption the custody and visitation disputes *should* be resolved just as if the couple were straight. It is rare, however, for a *non*legal parent to obtain custody or visitation rights if the legal parent objects. Only in a few states can nonlegal parents seek limited visitation of their ex-lover's child, either by demonstrating they fall within the state's laws protecting a "de facto parent" or "psychological parent" (the person the child considers her parent) or by making use of certain states' expanded child-visitation laws for nonparents. But these laws were designed to provide grandparents or foster parents rights to visit children they were involved with

over a long period of time and were not designed for homosexual partners. As a result, it has been very difficult (but not impossible) to persuade local courts to apply these doctrines to same-sex parents.

6. Private contractual agreements between adults regarding the lives of children are generally *not* enforceable if they contradict the "official" legal rules, on the grounds that they violate the doctrine that two people cannot enter into a contract regarding the rights of a third person. Such agreements, however, can be reviewed as evidence of what the parties intended to do, and as such they can influence the outcome of a dispute.

Answers to Frequently Asked Questions About Children

1. *Can a same-sex couple jointly adopt a child when the birth mother is giving up all rights and obligations as a parent?* This depends on whether the couple is arranging an adoption through a public agency, a private nonprofit agency, privately through an attorney, or directly with the birth mother. Many private agencies help same-sex couples, but most public agencies won't. If the birth mother and the agency both say yes, approval will be much easier—but not guaranteed. Bear in mind that every adoption must be approved by the local judge, and some won't approve a gay adoption even when the birth mother says yes.

2. *Can a single applicant adopt a child if it becomes known he or she is gay?* Officially speaking, most states do not prohibit lesbians and gay men from adopting, but this is not always true, and even where it is allowed, discrimination runs rampant. This is a hot political topic, and in some states the religious right is fighting to prohibit any unmarried person, gay or straight, from adopting. Be realistic: sometimes it is better to keep your sexual orientation quiet during the adoption process, as torturous as this will be to anyone who has been out for a long time. Foreign adoptions can be particularly

tricky, as gay applicants can encounter discrimination in many foreign countries.

3. *What is the role of the birth father in an adoption?* Under every state's rules a known birth father has specified rights that cannot be terminated without notice and an opportunity to be heard in court. This can be tricky, as often the birth mother doesn't want to tell the birth father about the adoption, especially when a same-sex couple is adopting the child. Some couples take the risk of claiming that the father is unknown so no one needs to be notified, but this is very risky. If the birth father later emerges and tries to invalidate the adoption, you can risk losing custody of your child.

4. *Under what conditions will second-parent adoptions be allowed for same-sex couples?* In many states you will have to pursue an appellate battle to win this right, but even in the fifteen or so states where second-parent adoptions are allowed, finessing your application is tricky. Court approval is required, and you may face resistance from the social workers who evaluate your application, and certain judges may not be willing to grant your application regardless of what the law says. Be prepared for an exhausting examination of your relationship and your home life, and don't try to do this on your own! Make sure you retain the services of a qualified local adoption attorney who has handled such cases.

5. *What are the options for insemination through sperm donors?* If you are considering using a sperm donor you have several choices: known or anonymous private donors, sperm banks, or a private doctor's services. It is imperative that you educate yourself about your state and local laws to be sure you understand the rights and duties of the donor. You also need to be very careful if you initiate a close relationship with a known donor after the birth, as you may create an implied parental relationship that is contrary to your prior legal arrangements. If the donor is legally recognized as a father, he will gain the right to make decisions about the child and

could seek custody or visitation rights—and he also could be subject to financial obligations of child support. By the way, similar issues arise for gay male couples who do an open adoption (where the birth mom is known to the men) and go on to develop a close relationship with the birth mother.

6. *How will the courts handle a custody dispute if a same-sex couple with children breaks up?* If both partners are legal parents the courts are supposed to apply the same rules they apply to straight divorces: the decisions are based on what the judge perceives is "in the best interests of the child," and joint or shared custody is the common outcome. But few courts are familiar with lesbian custody disputes and many judges are uncomfortable with this situation, so it is very hard to predict the outcomes. For this reason, make every possible effort to work out your arrangements by yourselves, through mediation if necessary, and then request that the court affirm your agreement. But if one of you has not been able to become a legal parent, winning a legal right to legal or physical custody or even occasional visitation is going to be very difficult. You definitely will need legal counsel here.

CONCEIVING THE POSSIBLE ARRANGEMENTS

Same-sex couples can bring children into their families in a wide variety of ways, and, not surprisingly, each method engenders its own particular practical and legal questions. Here is a summary of the most typical means by which lesbian and gay couples bring children into their lives and a brief review of the legal issues that arise in each situation and some suggested topics for further discussion.

Kids from a Prior, Heterosexual Relationship

Many lesbians and gay men have children the old-fashioned way, in a sexual relationship with someone of the opposite gender. For many years this was the only way homosexuals became parents. If you and your spouse are getting a divorce, watch out for the following conflicts:

- The parent's homosexuality may become an issue in the custody battles with the ex-spouse; many straight parents are totally accepting of their gay ex-spouses, but some of them aren't. If you are facing a custody battle, you need to evaluate this situation *very* carefully and decide whether you are willing and able to fight this battle openly. If your partner is pressuring you back into the closet to avoid a custody fight, try not to let your political values blind you. Try to look carefully at the big picture in making your decisions.
- If the ex-spouse is alive and legally competent, it is almost impossible to terminate his or her rights, so it is unlikely that the new lover will ever become a legal parent. In some states a nonlegal parent can ask for visitation rights in the event of a breakup of a same-sex relationship, but this request is not frequently granted. Both of you must, therefore, recognize the legal imbalance and accommodate yourselves, emotionally, to this reality. This shouldn't prevent you from having a wonderfully loving relationship with your partner's child; it's just that everyone has to recognize the legal limits of your bond.

Single Parent, New Relationship
If either of you is the sole legal parent of a child and beginning a new relationship, at some point you will need to decide what your formal arrangements with the nonlegal parent will be.

First, ascertain whether second-parent adoptions are allowed in your state, and if they aren't, find out if a nonlegal parent has any rights if the two of you break up. Then, armed with this information, discuss with your partner whether you want the nonbirth parent to become a legal parent. This is going to be a very difficult decision; while the law will set the parameters on what is possible, ultimately your decision should rest primarily on emotional and practical considerations rather than legal factors.

If you can't both be legal parents but you want to function as equal coparents, you have only two choices: change the law through the courts or the legislature or orchestrate an informal arrangement between yourselves and stick by your agreements, since it is unlikely any court will enforce them if you don't.

Joint Conceptions

If you are considering having or raising children together and both of you plan to be involved from the start, you have several options. Men and women can either adopt as single people or try for a joint adoption, working either directly with the birth mother or by going through a private or public agency. Lesbians, of course, have the added option of natural childbirth through insemination from a known or unknown donor or through intercourse with a friend.

Have a candid and thorough discussion about whether this is something you both want to do to help you decide whether you should both try to be the legal parents. Be open about your long-range intentions legally and practically, and try to sort out your expectations for parenting. Remember, it's okay for one partner to say from the start that she is going to be the secondary parent. Don't feel compelled to mirror the heterosexual marriage model, in which both parents are supposed to be 100 percent involved in every child-rearing activity.

Make sure you ascertain whether two-parent adoptions are allowed for same-sex couples in your state, and, if they are, learn precisely what is involved in the process. Adoption is always traumatic regardless of your sexual orientation, and facing discrimination will only add to the difficulties. If you are both committed to being legal parents, make sure you have a realistic sense of what's involved. If second-parent adoptions aren't allowed in your state, be honest about how you are going to handle the emotional tensions that will result from the imbalance.

If you plan to use a sperm donor, you will need to deal with the donor's rights and obligations and the nonbirth mother's role. If you are using a known donor or are eager to know the donor and have him involved in your lives, be clear from the start what that means legally and try to formalize the agreement with the donor. Even though it's not certain it will be enforceable, reaching an agreement is a valuable method of resolving issues and the contract can become evidence in any future dispute. If you don't want the donor to be a member of your extended family, give serious consideration to using an anonymous donor—or at least limit contact with the donor until after the child is grown. Even though you can't finalize a second-parent adoption until the child is born, in many states you can initiate the process and sign an informal agreement between the two of you early on that assures the nonbirth parent that her rights will be protected. When married couples use a donor, both spouses have to sign the consent documents, and this is also a good model for same-sex couples to follow.

Factors and Reasons
Even after you've scoped out the laws and sorted out your respective emotions, you may still find it hard to decide which route to

Berkeley's Sperm Bank of California offers three options: it provides sperm from anonymous donors whose identity is never known, sperm from donors who allow themselves to be contacted by the offspring when they reach adulthood, and medical testing of known donors. According to founding director Barbara Raboy, the Sperm Bank is unique in its emphasis on providing detailed data about the donors to the women and allowing the women to choose their donors. Raboy offers some important words of caution: be sure the donor's sperm is healthy and the donor's family medical history is a safe one, deal openly with the legal issues affecting the rights of the donor and the birth mother's partner, and be conscious of your personal fertility issues.

take. Here are some additional suggestions to help you resolve your dilemmas:

- If your relationship is a new one or if one of you has serious doubts about having children, give the issue some time to incubate. Just as it was wrong to be told that we couldn't have kids, so too we should not now flip sides and assert that everyone *must* have kids. Deprived of the ritual assumptions of marriage and given our socialization, this is not going to be an easy decision for anyone.
- Be candid about how much uncertainty and stress each of you can absorb. If raising a child who isn't legally yours is not emotionally bearable, you shouldn't start down this path unless you're sure you can both be the legal parents. If being out of the closet is not acceptable, a legal fight for a same-sex adoption is not going to be tolerable for you.
- Ascertain the likely costs of each option, and compare options as part of your discussion of who is to be the legal parent. One of you may have better health insurance and family leave benefits, and this is important. A private adoption can cost as much as $20,000 and an agency adoption can easily exceed $5,000, while a sperm bank or private insemination usually costs less then $500.
- Pay attention to how your relationship as a couple fits into your extended-family environment. There's nothing like a new baby to bring parents and siblings back into your lives, though chances are your sexuality will remain controversial. Reflect on how you and your child are going to be received in your families and at your workplace, and incorporate these issues into your decision-making process.
- If you are not the legal parent of the child you may face serious legal obstacles if your partner dies or is seriously incapacitated. You can minimize the potential problems by having the legal parent sign a document nominating you as the child's

guardian, but only if you discuss the situation openly with your partner.

- Seek out a lesbian/gay parenting group in your community; most major cities have active support and information groups that can provide emotional counseling and practical information about doctors, agencies, and costs. These groups offer a marvelous source for friends who share your interest in parenting, opening you up to new possibilities and relieving some of your isolation.

Elizabeth Hendrickson, former director of the National Center for Lesbian Rights and now an attorney in Oakland, California, offers a useful method for dealing with some of the imbalances inherent in same-sex parenting. She recommends that each couple evaluate which partner is likely to feel the most vulnerable by not being designated the legal parent. Vulnerability takes two forms, she says. Some folks are much thinner-skinned about legal uncertainties, and for them the prospect of having to rely solely on the goodwill of their partner can be excruciating. Others may feel they will be disfavored by the larger world if they are not the legal parent, either because they are poorer, of an ethnic or racial minority, or more isolated from their extended family. Try to acknowledge this imbalance, Hendrickson recommends, and then try to correct the imbalance by designating the more vulnerable partner as the birth parent or, in the case of an adoption, the primary legal parent if both can't adopt jointly.

FORMALIZING YOUR COPARENTING ARRANGEMENT

There are four methods of formalizing your family arrangements: (1) by your conversations and expressions of feelings, (2) by your own written contracts and documents, (3) by your deeds and actions, and (4) by binding legal action. Each has its benefits and burdens, and you should give particular consideration as to how you want to commemorate these momentous decisions.

Express Yourself Clearly

The first method—and it's an essential foundation for crystallizing parenting plans—is thinking out the issues and talking out your wants and needs clearly and directly. Don't be vague or indirect here: if you want to raise your children in the countryside, say so; if you want only one child and insist on residing in an urban area, speak up. You can always negotiate a compromise, but compromising begins with a clear declaration of where each party stands.

The key questions to discuss include, at a minimum, the following:

- For lesbian couples, is one of you going to get pregnant, and, if so, which one?
- If pregnancy isn't an option, which approaches to adoption will you try?
- Is it essential that both of you be legal parents, and, if so, is that legally possible where you live?
- Who is going to pay the costs of the birth or adoption?
- Are both of you willing to be open about your sexuality?
- Are you both willing and able to support the child for the long term? Raising kids involves obligations as well as rights, and it is essential that both of you directly confront this aspect of the equation.
- Are there any particular decision-making issues that are especially important to either of you?
- What are your values, priorities, and goals for your family?
- What is your vision of what would happen if you separated? Is this vision consistent with what the law says about your relationship with the child?

A mutual plan will empower you to proceed with your intentions. If the discussions precipitate disagreements or conflicts, it is *essential* that you deal with them thoroughly. See a counselor if you think this will help, and consider attending a local gay-parenting discussion group. Don't let yourself be rushed into a decision here.

Children are precious, autonomous creatures who will be with you for the rest of your life.

One of the marvels of same-sex parenting is that it *never* happens by accident, so your family is truly intentional and your child will know he or she is wanted. You should embrace the difficult challenge of creating your family as a wonderful opportunity, so be deliberate in your actions. Even if you don't want to execute a written contract or take binding legal steps, you can always send your partner letters stating your loving feelings and intentions. This will help cement your bonds and serve as a touchstone you can reflect back on when you want to recall what led to your decision.

The Benefits of Contracts

Every attorney will tell you—and you should definitely consult one if you are adding children to your family—that a contract between two adults regarding the fate of a third party generally is not legally binding. Your child, unlike your house or your car, is an autonomous legal being, and as such she or he has rights neither of you can sign away.

The consequences of this doctrine are far-reaching. It means that agreements between you and your partner (and also your donor or birth mother, if one exists in your case) most likely won't be enforced by a court should you fall into disagreement in later years. An agreement to relinquish custody in case of a breakup or an agreement not to seek child support from a partner can be set aside by a judge—and readily is. The legal standard in every state in the country for resolving legal issues about kids is "the best interests of the child," and if the agreement conflicts with that standard, the court can nullify it.

This does not mean that agreements between parents about their children are without any significance. In fact, most attorneys who counsel same-sex couples recommend that such agreements be drafted and signed. A coparenting agreement will typically contain provisions covering whether one of you will be the biological mom or dad, whether you will both seek to become legal parents, how the financial burdens will be shared, and how you intend to handle custody matters should a separation occur.

Such contracts are recommended for the following powerful reasons:

- Drafting an agreement will force you to visit an attorney, who will explain the law to you and make sure that both of you understand the risks and complications of creating a family together.
- Drafting an agreement will force you to discuss the important parenting issues openly and clearly, which will flush out possible areas of disagreement between you. As with so many contracts, you may discover that it is the agreement-formation process that is important, not the resulting written product.
- If you run into conflicts early on, you will be forced to find practical solutions, and chances are you will be able to use these solutions if problems arise.
- The agreement will serve as a written reminder of how you felt at the outset, and this information will be useful in guiding future conflict resolutions. If one of you steadfastly states in writing that you would help support your lover's child even if you broke up later on, you will probably be more likely to do so than if you just give a vague assurance that you won't remember clearly.
- Even if an agreement isn't legally enforceable, most folks keep their promises and will abide by the terms of the contract. Putting your agreement in writing gives more weight to your promises, as it lends them moral and persuasive value if there is a subsequent conflict.
- Many judges rely on such agreements as evidence when making a decision, even though they aren't legally binding. It is surprising how often judges refer to such agreements when making decisions, even though the official grounds for the decision will be "the best interests of the child." The judge will likely pay attention to the agreement in forming her or his "in-

tuitive" sense about the conflict. If an agreement says the donor is not going to have any parental involvement or that the nonlegal parent understands she has no rights upon a separation, this acknowledgment will definitely shape the dispute's outcome.

- Eventually, some judges will enforce the terms of an agreement between parents regarding a child despite all the general legal doctrine to the contrary. Yours may be the test case, and this alone may motivate you to abide by your agreement.
- In addition, you can sign a series of related documents that *are* legally enforceable. You can each name your partner as the preferred guardian in the event one of you becomes incapacitated or dies, you can provide medical authorization rights to each other, and you can notify your child's school or doctor that your partner has authority to be consulted on major decisions. Each of these agreements can have an impact in a future dispute—especially a nomination of guardianship upon incapacity or death—and they will reinforce the emotional and personal commitments underlying them.

Practice What You Preach

The third way of manifesting your intentions is to act consistently with your agreement. This may seem odd to mention, but, in fact, people frequently act contrary to their stated intentions. If this happens you either need to change your agreement or change your actions. Allowing inconsistencies to remain unchallenged for years can create enormous confusion in a subsequent dispute.

For example, if you agree that you are going to apply for a second-parent adoption, do so. If years go by without either of you pushing for the application, acknowledge this in writing, setting forth your reasons for not doing so. If your sperm donor agrees not to get involved as a close parent to your child but in later years actually does get involved, recognize this change and rewrite your agreement. The worst possible situation occurs when actions reflect one set of intentions and documents state the contrary, as this creates a dissonance that can give rise to inconsistent expectations with chaotic legal results.

This is serious business, and it warrants seeing an attorney whenever there is a major change in the way your family structure operates. But even if you can't get to the lawyer right away, make written notes of the changes and exchange detailed letters. This will prevent either of you from denying that you were aware of the changes, which should reduce the level of surprise if a conflict later arises.

Legal Action

The best way to concretize your family arrangements is to construct a legal structure that meshes with your intentions and expectations. In most instances this means obtaining a second-parent adoption or adopting the child jointly and formalizing the legal relationship with the donor if one is involved.

This is not a process to be taken lightly. Unlike a marriage, an adoption in most instances cannot be undone since invalidating an adoption requires proving fraud or deception. Adopting a child means supporting your child for eighteen years—even longer if the child is disabled—and for a lifetime interaction with the child's other parent, even if the relationship ends. This is how your child will view things and how the court will as well—and it is how it should be.

And this is one area where same-sex couples will be treated just like married couples. Once you establish that both of you are parents, you are both legally bound to support the child financially and each of you has an equal right to custody and visitation, regardless of how nasty your personal relationship may become. The family law court will hear your petition and can prevent one parent from leaving the state with the child without the court's prior permission, and the district attorney can pursue you for unpaid child support if you fail to live up to your legal obligations.

The precise procedure for a joint adoption or a second-parent adoption will differ from state to state. Because of the complexity of the process and the chances of judicial discrimination, you will need an attorney, and the fees often will be in excess of $1,500. In some counties where second-parent adoptions are routinely granted, some attorneys provide the service for a fixed fee, often as low as $1,000. There may be nonprofit resources in your local community to help you for even less, so check around. Make sure you use the services of an attorney who knows what he or she is doing, especially if you live in a homophobic environment.

Kate Kendell, current executive director of the National Center for Lesbian Rights, offers several helpful suggestions for couples choosing children. First, lesbians choosing children need to spend a lot of time discussing their intentions to make sure they are aware of each other's expectations before acting. Second, using a known donor is risky unless you intend to include the father in your life—don't tug at the donor's heartstrings by inviting him into your life only partway unless that is what he truly wants. Third, recognize the limits of the law in most states, and if a second-parent adoption isn't possible, sign a private agreement and abide by it as the morally right thing to do, even if it is not legally required. Fourth, honor the emotional reality of coparenting if you break up with your partner, and agree to share custody or allow visitation even if she or he isn't a legal parent.

AND IF THERE'S A SEPARATION

Divorce can be brutal on kids everywhere, and same-sex dissolutions are no exception. Indeed, because of the inhospitable social milieu facing many children of same-sex couples and the frequent lack of extended family support, a breakup may even be harder for children of lesbian and gay couples.

Custody and visitation disputes arise for same-sex couples in one of three scenarios: (1) when both partners are legal parents, (2) when only one partner is a legal parent but the law grants nonlegal parents some rights, and (3) when the law denies nonlegal parents all rights. Here are some guidelines for each situation.

Both Parents Are Legal

If both of you are legal parents, chances are your custody and visitation disputes will be handled just like those of married heterosexual couples. Both parents have the right to legal custody (which means that the child is legally yours to care for), and the details of physical custody (where the child actually lives) will need to be worked out between the parents on a practical and reasonable basis. If the parents cannot agree on the details of the physical custody arrangements, the local family-law judge will hear both sides' arguments and make a decision. Custody decisions usually remain open for future reevaluation, however.

It is extremely rare for either partner to be granted sole legal or physical custody. Most courts order shared custody with some alternating arrangements. The sharing is usually as balanced as possible; one parent does not get sole custody and the other one only weekend visits. You will need an attorney who can tell you how decisions are generally made in your particular local court if you are facing a custody battle.

If you both are legal parents the court can order you to pay child support if the child is living primarily with the other parent. The court can also order either of you to come up with your fair share of insurance and tuition costs or any other special expenses related to the child's upbringing. All of this works just as it does with straight couples, but most judges are not familiar with homosexual dissolutions and often feel some discomfort with your situation. Moreover, in most states your other financial affairs are generally not handled by the family law court, as you are still an unmarried couple.

This distinction can create some awkward and tortuous legal proceedings since from your angle the financial and child-rearing issues are clearly connected. Paying child support and having physical custody of your child are obviously related to who gets the house and how the financial assets are distributed, even though the law usually doesn't see it this way. For this reason, in some counties you can ask to combine the financial and child-custody conflicts into one courtroom proceeding, even if technically they are different lawsuits.

The most consistently proclaimed message to everyone in a custody dispute is *mediate*. Do it soon, do it often, and do it with the intention of resolving all your issues this way. Pushing the dispute into litigation will only cost everyone an enormous amount of money and strain everyone's emotions.

If the Nonlegal Parent Has Parental Rights

In some states nonlegal parents can seek access to the child as a de facto or psychological parent. If you are in a jurisdiction that allows nonlegal parents to seek custody or visitation privileges, it is critical that both of you accept two features of this legal reality: you will both have the opportunity to go into court and argue for custody or visitation, and it is likely that neither of you will automatically be granted sole custody. In legal terms, the nonlegal parent will have *standing*, a doctrine that determines what category of persons have an arguable legal claim the court must consider, to argue for partial custody or regular visitation, and thus the doors of the courthouse will be open to hear his or her claim. This does not, however, establish what the court will do when it listens to the claim—that decision will be based on the "best interests of the child" standard.

If you are the birth parent in such a jurisdiction, don't challenge your partner's right to make her or his requests. Be assured that courts almost never award sole custody to a nonlegal parent if the legal parent contests the request, but they often grant extensive visitation rights and in some states they may grant shared custody. It is imperative that you check with an attorney to learn what is customarily done in your county. If you aren't able to reach an agreement through mediation, be prepared to abide by the court's decisions.

If you find yourself in a jurisdiction that has traditionally allowed heterosexual stepparents or foster parents to make requests for custody and visitation, logically speaking, a same-sex partner should have the very same rights. Unfortunately, not all courts agree, and it may take an appeal to a higher court to open up the stepparent door to same-sex couples.

The law in this area is especially fluid these days, and more and more courts are looking beyond the legal technicalities to evaluate who actually functions as a loving and caring parent. This trend is happening with foster parents, grandparents, and nonmarital straight couples, and in many courts it is slowly happening with same-sex couples. Many judges recognize the unfairness of denying gay couples the right to adopt jointly, and, when faced with a custody dispute, they are often inclined to protect the concerns of the nonlegal parent.

A court in Pennsylvania recently acknowledged the importance of the nonlegal parent and allowed her the right to seek partial custody of the couple's young child. The judge concluded that since the nonbiological mom had lived with the child and her birth mother in a family setting and had developed a close relationship with the child with the participation and acquiescence of the birth mom, it would be unfair to cut the nonlegal parent out entirely. The judge took note of the fact that both moms had participated to some degree in the insemination decision, and observed that the child had taken both mothers' names and was covered by related legal documents. The judge also based his decision on his observation that the nonbiological mom had shown a "constant, sincere interest in the child and that the child had recognized [her] as a significant person in her life."

Out in the Cold

Unfortunately, in many other states nonlegal parents have absolutely no rights to seek custody or even visitation. The standing doctrine labels them "strangers to the court," and they are not even allowed to submit requests for custody or visitation. In states where nonlegal parents lack standing, they aren't even able to enter the courtroom to argue that shared custody would be in the child's best interest.

Almost everyone involved in the same-sex parenting debate agrees that keeping nonbiological parents out of court altogether is horrible, and most attorneys and authors hope the law will change to allow courts to decide each family's dispute on a case-by-case basis. Some creative attorneys are trying to use other legal approaches, such as the guardianship process to gain visitation, and most observers believe that eventually the courtroom doors will be opened. But in many states (even in California, which probably is home to the largest number of same-sex families with children), as of now the door remains closed to nonlegal parents.

If this is your situation and you have developed a close personal bond with "your" child—even though you knew from the outset that you were not a legal parent—you are facing some very daunting hurdles. Don't give up in total despair as most of these situations eventually resolve themselves amicably. If your bond with your partner's child is a strong one, a bit of emotional distance from your ex should reduce the strife and allow a friendly solution to emerge. If things don't work out to your satisfaction, try to initiate formal mediation with a paid mediator.

Your goal in counseling should be to establish a practical and fair arrangement that allows you a minimum amount of time with the child you have been living with and loving for so many years. The strongest argument in your arsenal is that this is best for the child, so try to rely on this approach rather than arguing about who is right or wrong legally. Having a parent disappear can have horrendous emotional consequences for a child, and every mother and father knows this. If you can't persuade your ex-lover of this reality, try invoking the wisdom of therapists, extended family members, and friends.

You can also raise moral and political arguments in support of your continued involvement. Unless there was a clear agreement from the outset that the child was going to be your ex-lover's alone, it is just plain wrong for one homosexual to take advantage of the legal barriers to deny her or his partner access to a jointly raised child. If the only reason you aren't married is because of discriminatory laws, it isn't fair for one homosexual to use those laws to harm her or his ex-lover.

On the other hand, if the requests are being rejected for legitimate reasons, and especially if the legal parent believes her or his partner is harmful emotionally or physically to the child, listen carefully to these accusations. You will probably need to work with a counselor whom you both trust, and if the grounds for denying you access to the child are legitimate, a counseling process should bear this out and help you work out a jointly acceptable solution.

If mediation fails and neither party is ready to give up, the nonlegal partner can file a legal action for custody or visitation, hoping to change the law through a series of appeals. This is a very difficult process, as you probably will lose the first round in court, and it will take years and cost thousands of dollars in attorneys fees—with no certain results. If you are considering taking this approach, make sure you speak with an attorney experienced in this area, and give it a lot of thought before you decide to launch such an effort.

The same rules of thumb apply when there is a known sperm donor or birth mother and you have actively encouraged or allowed this biological parent to grow emotionally attached to your child. While the donor or birth mother may not have legal rights in your case, the moral obligations need to be considered. If you don't want to raise someone's expectations of involvement with your child, don't include him in your family events or treat him as a parent. However noble your intentions may be, doing so will only cause pain later on.

One special note for single lesbian or gay parents: don't ever underestimate the intense bond that can be created between your child and someone you are dating. There is an enormous reservoir of unvoiced parental cravings in the lesbian and gay community, and a few joyous weekends with the child of a new love can tap these feelings very deeply. If the new relationship suddenly ends, both the partner and the child may feel devastated, so be careful how you respond to the child. If at all possible, allow the relationship to continue on a friendship basis so the interaction with the child can survive, even if it is only on an occasional basis.

THE DEATH OF A HOMOSEXUAL PARENT

The consequences of a death or the disability of a lesbian or gay parent can create serious legal problems. If there has been a second-parent or joint adoption, the surviving coparent will remain a legal parent with full rights and obligations as such, but without a joint adoption the nonlegal parent may have no rights at all. If there is another legal parent out there (such as an ex-husband or biological parent), that person will likely have the first right to seek custody of the orphaned child. In order for the partner of the deceased parent to stop this, she or he would have to prove that the legal parent is totally unfit—a very difficult task.

Fortunately, in most states a parent can sign a nomination of guardianship, which informs the court that you have a preference as to who should have custody of your child should you die. You can name your partner as the preferred guardian, and in many states the court will honor that preference, though it may not be binding on the court. A guardianship nomination usually can be included in a will, and every homosexual parent should do this. If there is no nominated guardian and no second legal parent out there, or if the legal parent does not actively seek custody of the child, a local judge will make the custody and guardianship decisions.

Therefore, if you have children it is essential that you meet with an attorney and sign the guardianship nomination. If you anticipate a problem or if one of you is facing a life-threatening illness, have a frank talk with anyone you think might object to your lover being named guardian of your child, and tell her or him directly what you want to happen. There is nothing like a deathbed statement to restrain a parent or sibling from filing an objection to your lover's becoming your child's guardian. Without such a direct discussion, in fact, your parents or siblings might even feel they are doing the right thing in seeking to be your child's guardians. This is bound to be one of the most difficult conversations you will have, but it is something that you must do for the sake of your partner as well as your child.

6

Public Affairs
in the Happy Times

Even the most reclusive same-sex couples live in a larger public world. As we become more mainstream and interact more intimately with our friends and families, and as we seek greater recognition from governments and other institutions, our relationships will inevitably be affected by the outside world.

We may fantasize that we are insular and self-sufficient when we are single, but when we enter into a long-term relationship it is certain that we exist in the context of a larger social universe. Our friends and family quickly notice and comment on our courtship, and as we debate whether to live together our conversations are inevitably shaped by other people's expectations and even regulations on how we should run our lives. There's no escaping the fact that many of our internal legal and financial arrangements are powerfully affected by the strictures of the larger public realm.

THE SOCIAL REALM

Conceiving the Impossible
The first and one of the deepest ways in which the larger public sphere impacts your domestic life is in the shaping of your desires and dreams. We may delude ourselves into believing we are autonomous independent creatures, forging our own bold paths

through the thickets of life's challenges, but it isn't so. As children and then throughout our adolescence, we are constantly assaulted by images and recommendations that continuously tell us how life is meant to be lived.

As lesbians and gay men we endure an especially complicated bombardment. We are, of course, inundated by the universal societal expectations of what love, marriage, and family are meant to be, as they are shaped by the particular framework of our own families. It is axiomatic that each of us is offered a two-layer set of family-life messages: an overlay of overt doctrines and moralities as to how families are *supposed* to function and then, just as significant, the more vivid reality of the actual relationships that exist within our own immediate family.

At the same time we are also victims of a less conscious and more diffused assault: the story of what it is to be a homosexual. Long before many of us identified ourselves as gay, we heard the messages of what being gay means, and then, when we each in our own way realized that it was us they were talking about, for a time those distorted impressions and prejudiced images took hold. And, with few exceptions—especially for those who grew up before Stonewall—the messages we received weren't pretty. For so many years being gay meant being unhappy, ostracized, lonely, deprived, and isolated.

Let's not deceive ourselves into thinking that the public signals sent our way cease after we come out. Despite all our protestations to the contrary, we all remain vulnerable to the society-wide messages of how we should live our lives. Indeed, in time our own lesbian and gay communities can be equally influential in pronouncing how life is to be lived. For decades it was standard operating procedure that all lesbians had to be coupled in a butch-femme marriage, and many gay men in the 1970s felt obligated to seek their highest goals solely as sexual predators, the Don Juans of the gay underworld.

Egalitarian coupling and nesting are the current rage, so much so that being a single gay man or a childless lesbian couple may soon be just as denigrated in our community as being homosexual used to be in the straight world. Norms and expectations exist in every society, and it is naive to think that one can plan a life oblivious to such models and images.

The remedy to this dilemma is to listen closely to what your surroundings tell you, and, then, listen even more closely to what is really important for *you*. Don't buy into the notion that homosexuals aren't able to partner for life, but at the same time don't feel compelled to couple up if that's not what you want—and not if the current prospect doesn't meet your innermost needs. Don't feel obligated to be monogamous if you have a need to explore more freely, but don't be afraid to cling to that picket fence if you know that's where you want to be. Be aware of the dialectic between the self and society and don't pretend to be oblivious to the outside world, but don't let its external pressures overpower you.

Please Ask—I'll Tell!

It's easy to broadcast to all your closest friends that you are in love, or at least auditioning a potential Mr. or Ms. Right. What is more delicate is announcing that things are getting serious, for two reasons: not being out and not having an established vocabulary for our relationships. These issues can be very problematic for some couples, and, surprisingly, they are directly tied to many of the legal predicaments same-sex partners face in the courtship phase.

The outness issue can be the most tender of problems, excruciatingly so when you are in love. It can be sheer torture if you can't share the most joyous experience of your life with those you live and work with. Imagine sitting silently in the lunchroom as your office mates hover around a colleague who glowingly tells the story of her recent engagement. Remember how it felt when your mother beamed with excitement over your brother's upcoming wedding plans and how angry you were when your boss took an extra week of paid vacation for his honeymoon last year. Being a single homosexual in the closet can be pure hell, but staying hidden when a new romance is blossoming can feel even worse.

Staying closeted will also make it nearly impossible for you to resolve many of the legal and financial matters you will face. Conversations with real estate brokers, bankers, lawyers, and tax accountants can grow totally unwieldy if you keep the nature of your relationship hidden. You'll find it impossible to ask the right questions, professionals won't be able to give you the right advice, and you'll be afraid to address the important issues out of fear that the true nature of your relationship will be discovered. There is only one way out of this trap: come out. Do it slowly and carefully if that is your style, as there is no single right path that fits everyone, but find a way to tell the people who are important in your life that you are gay.

The second quandary is vocabulary. What do you call your relationship, and how do you label your loved one? This is a problem that has plagued our community for decades, and as much as we try to avoid it, the labels we use shape the way we think. "Lover" can be awkward in straight company, and while some men have elected to seize the dominant language in an ironic way, referring to their boyfriend as "husband," referring to a girlfriend as "wife" hasn't caught on so well. The term "spouse" or "significant other" works for some, and "partner" or "life partner" makes sense so long as no one confuses your new affair with a business venture. If you are really stuck on the labeling question, you can always say "the woman/man I live with." It's a mouthful, but it says what it needs to say.

My preference is "partner," but, whatever the term, the moral is that labels send a powerful signal to others and to you. They express the way you conceive your relationship and in turn shape the way others treat you. In some circles calling your partner boyfriend, for example, may trivialize your connection, whereas a label like spouse or partner is bound to sound far more permanent and serious. If you can come up with a new set of terms that is just right for us, you will be famous, though when legal marriage is eventually allowed for same-sex couples, a whole new set of terms will emerge!

Formal Announcements

The heterosexual rituals of engagement and marriage are elegant and well defined, and as our community grows bolder and, in a sense, more assimilated, many same-sex couples may opt for formal announcements of their joyous events. Most gay couples only send an announcement when they are holding a commitment ceremony, but limiting the opportunity this way really isn't necessary. Straight couples have been announcing their engagement and/or marriage for centuries, and moving in together is a big-enough event in itself to justify notification to all concerned. More and more, we are all rediscovering the benefits of traditional social rituals, and there is no reason lesbians and gay men shouldn't reap these benefits.

Most couples send announcements only to those in their social circle. If you are ready to spread the news boldly, however, in a few towns you can announce your commitment in the newspaper right alongside the traditional heterosexual engagement or wedding announcements. This is a brave endeavor and remains a rare phenomenon. Unfortunately, in most cities you may be denied the opportunity to do this unless you take legal action, and in the few states where the question has been litigated newspapers have generally been given the right to deny gay couples equal treatment. If you get turned down, don't expect much protection from the courts; instead, try to organize your community and apply public pressure from advertisers to open up the announcements page.

If you are gutsy enough to try this route and your notice gets published, you will be providing a very valuable service to the entire gay community. There's nothing like an engagement or wedding announcement in the society page to warm the heart of every other budding same-sex romantic and calm the nerves of young, frightened homosexuals. It may even pull at the heartstrings of one or more recalcitrant homophobes.

Let's Have a Party!

To some folks, formal weddings are a dreaded burden to be avoided—whether as participant or guest. For the participants they can mean enormous expense, public exposure, and dozens of details to fret about. For gays and lesbians who have been around for a while, weddings may feel like the antithesis of sexual liberation; for guests, they can mean yet another stuffy event to attend and another present to buy.

Others view the burgeoning gay marriage industry with absolute delight. To an increasing number of younger couples it is an opportunity to share the joy, celebrate the romance, and flaunt conventional taboos by appropriating an event that for centuries was denied same-sex couples. Weddings have long been an opportunity for showing off, reaching out for community support for your relationship, and formalizing your commitment, and there's no reason you should let anyone deprive you of this experience. Of course, whether to hold a public celebration of your relationship is an entirely personal decision. And, other than signing contracts with caterers and musicians, it has little binding legal consequence. But legal issues are not wholly irrelevant, in two respects.

First, a public ceremony really does establish your relationship as a solid social bond in the eyes of your friends and family and, most likely, in your own eyes as well. Ask anyone who has participated in such an event and she will tell you that her relationship has been forever changed.

A wedding transforms your private affair into a public partnership in a way few other experiences can do. Chances are that you will now immediately think of yourselves and begin to organize your lives as a couple. If this is what you want, then call the caterers! But if this image and this symbol are at odds with your innermost feelings, feel free to postpone the ceremony. The private aspects of commemorating your love are what really matter, so don't ever let the outward expression overstep the reality!

Second, while courts have consistently ruled that private or religious vows of emotional commitment are not legally binding contracts, the ritualized promises of a formal ceremony can play a role in any future legal dramas, though until legal marriage is opened up to us, perhaps a minor role. Since most legal rules for unmarried couples are notoriously *unclear*, discussions over implied agreements unavoidably expand into discussions about each party's intentions.

For this reason a ceremony with promises of mutual aid and comfort uttered in front of several hundred close friends may be mentioned in a subsequent legal battle—and it should. Even if the courts of law don't dip into such treacherous waters as a touchstone for resolving dissolution conflicts, it just isn't right to stand up and pledge your love and lifelong commitment only to abandon your partner and renounce all your financial obligations a few years later. You should take these vows seriously, and so should your partner. And, who knows, yours may be the very case in which a judge decides to redraw the legal line and enforce your promises.

So if the ceremonial promises you are planning to make aren't in sync with your innermost intentions, don't schedule a formal event just yet. Have a housewarming party instead. For now, delight in the love of your informal affair, and, when you are ready to move forward, go back to the drawing board of the relationship discus-

Jewish tradition offers a unique kind of marriage contract called a *ketuba*, which is a detailed agreement based on language and provisions that date back centuries written up in a flowery and elegant script and often illustrated and displayed proudly in the newlyweds' home. Traditional ketubas talk of commitments to honor and respect each other, and, in recent years, many lesbians and gay men have commissioned a ketuba using their own special terms. Once the contract was enforceable under traditional Jewish law, but nowadays it serves only as a symbolic statement of emotional commitment.

sion and work out the emotional issues. Whatever you do, *don't make vows you don't intend to keep.*

With This Ring I Thee Wed

Exchanging rings has little direct legal consequence, but it can have an enormous psychological impact on how you see yourselves as a couple and on how those around you relate to the two of you. Wearing a ring says to the world, "I am no longer just an individual; I also am half of a committed couple." Like the other rituals of partnering, wearing a ring reinforces the importance of your link to your partner in a powerfully public way. It tells potential suitors to stay away, and it signals potential creditors to ask some pointed questions about who is paying the bills. And if your sexual orientation is not yet public your ring will precipitate recurring coming-out discussions as you explain to the questioner who your special partner really is.

Wearing matching rings also provides you with a marvelous opportunity to ask your partner "Will you?" and gives her or him a chance to say "I do." It also offers both of you an opportunity for a private ritual that can be incredibly tender. Treat the question with the importance it deserves!

The Law of the In-laws

Once upon a time marriage was primarily a merger of two families and only incidentally a union of two individuals. Decisions about a prospective marriage were made by the heads of the households, and the choice of partners had as much to do with family fortunes and business opportunities as any romantic concerns. Marriage in traditional culture also served a variety of interfamilial and multi-generational social functions: the wife produced children and the husband provided economic stability—often to his wife's family as well as his own. In some cultures extended families provided a network of household labor, emotional support, and kinship connections. As a result, keeping a marriage alive meant responding to the demands of one's in-laws as much as meeting the needs of one's spouse.

While the economics of the family have been radically transformed in recent centuries and a romantic basis of marriage has evolved as the universal norm, many of the emotional dynamics of earlier years live on. Talk to anyone in a traditional marriage and he will regale you with stories of in-law problems: what your spouse thinks of your parents, how your parents treat your spouse, who shows up at what family events, and how everyone behaves when he gets there. One of the rare "privileges of oppression" for gay couples is that, for the most part, we have been exempt from these pressures.

Think about it. How many of you are expected to host your in-laws for two weeks each year or regularly deal with a torrent of invasive criticisms and "helpful" suggestions about how you should run your household? Have any of you considered taking your beau to meet your parents before deciding whether to live together? And how important is it to you that your aunts and uncles approve of the way your lover earns her or his living? Homophobic ostracism has carried with it a modicum of privacy and distance that, depending on your particular family situation, you may soon think back on with a fair degree of fondness.

The closer we come to full social acceptance and the more vocally we seek family approval of our relationships, the more we expose ourselves to pressures that have been so oppressive in many straight marriages. Yes, along the way there should be a bounty of extended-family love, joyous social events, and practical support, as these are the benefits we are fighting for. But don't deceive yourself into thinking that these benefits come without any strings attached!

In-law pressures include the burdens of socializing as well as the scrutiny of others' judgments, and in many relationships in-law problems can play a major role in the legal and financial dynamics of your relationship. If either of you is part of a family business or facing financial pressures from your extended family (say, for example, to support an ailing parent or help with the tuition for an orphaned nephew), your partner's actions will certainly become a hot topic of discussion—most of which will take place behind your back—among your extended family.

The pressures from your extended family can also affect your own legal and financial decisions in ways that are hard to spot at first. If your partner suddenly evinces fear of sharing a house she has long owned or insists that the car stay in her name alone, it's possible that parental objections are lurking somewhere in the deeper recesses of her consciousness. If your parents balk at lending the two of you money for a down payment even though they've done the same for every other child (all of whom happen to be heterosexual) and you find yourself reluctant to confront them with their hypocrisy, this pressure will color your house-buying experience and could create problems in your partnership. Start organizing your estate planning or setting up a jointly owned business and your parents' financial influence will surely come to the surface.

The key here is to acknowledge that these relatives are out there and that an integral part of their accepting you is paying attention to you. As a result, they will start forming opinions about how you should organize your life, and you will soon begin to care about what they think as well. This is a price of acceptance you cannot avoid paying, so take a cue from your straight friends and attend to these issues seriously. Doing so will guarantee that you will be attentive to the problems and, let's hope, find mutually satisfying ways of addressing them.

My Name Is Your Name

The social rules about surnames for married couples go deep in our cultural history and differ widely across different ethnic and national groups. Consider the voluminous criticism that arose about Hillary Rodham Clinton's name-change oscillations and you'll readily concede that the surname debate remains a fervent one in the heterosexual community. This should not be a surprise since the wife's taking of the husband's name was for centuries *the* universal symbol of being a married woman.

While there is a definite trend among heterosexual married women to keep their "own" surnames (which, of course, are the names of their fathers), especially among professional classes, this remains a minority trend. A wife's retaining her own name still carries with it the stamp of feminism—intentionally so for many women. Using hyphenated names is still rare in this country, and husbands rarely take them on. Wives and children usually still take the husband's name.

Doing so is no longer required legally, and in most states anyone can change her or his name so long as there is no fraud. Names can be changed in two ways: either by use or by court order. If you act consistently by telling everyone about the change and don't defraud any creditors, in most states you can take on a partner's name or hyphenate your names as you like. While your name may legally remain as it previously was, by custom you can use your new last name as an alternate name—which is what traditional married couples have usually done.

For lesbians and gay men, though, changing your name by court order is the preferred way to go as it avoids confusion with government officials, banks, and employers. In most states there is great latitude about what name you choose, so there is nothing per se that prohibits a same-sex couple from electing to use the same last name. But, not surprisingly, in many states you may face judicial opposition if you attempt to take your partner's name. You know that the real basis of the opposition is homophobia, but the judge is unlikely to admit this and he will couch his concerns in terms of fear of fraud against creditors or employers. If you think you are going to face these sorts of arguments, consult an attorney in your city who is familiar with the local rules and can help steer you through the process.

If the two of you are going to be coparenting a child, the surname issue becomes a bit more complicated. You'll need to choose a surname for your child, and if the name is other than the surname of the birth mother a court order is usually required. You have three choices here: choose one partner's name, use a hyphenated name, or choose an entirely new name for your family. The hyphenated name is the most logical option as it reinforces the family as a unit without the confusion that will result from giving everyone a new name. The situation is the same as it is when you want to change your own name: be prepared for resistance from the court if either of you is not the child's legal parent.

The surname issue will also arise in the course of an adoption, and, if you are adopting as a single parent, it may be difficult to select a hyphenated name. Remember that the decisions you make will shape the public's perception of the two of you and of your child, so try hard to integrate the naming decision with your underlying philosophy and household agreements about your child.

I Now Pronounce You a Couple
You may believe that the real purpose of a ceremonial vow is to cement your relationship between yourselves, but, in fact, its primary purpose is to announce to the rest of the world that henceforth the two of you should be treated as a couple, not as two individuals. This is a far-reaching change in perception that has endless and often unpredictable consequences. Your partner offends a guest at dinner, for example, and you are expected to face the resulting criticism and smooth the social waters, you land a new job and your partner's economic status is suddenly elevated, or you take a controversial stand in your community and your partner finds herself ostracized. You are a team, for better or for worse.

There is nothing wrong with this change so long as you are prepared for it and welcome it. But be realistic here; well before you begin to notice and respond to the legal impacts of the changes in your relationship, you will feel the interpersonal effects of the public perceptions strongly. To some folks, who you choose as your partner is in itself a reflection of who you are. This was true in the days of nineteenth-century novelist Jane Austen, and it remains so to this day. The more public you are about your choice, the greater the resulting impression will be on your friends and family— positive or negative.

THE LEGAL/FINANCIAL REALM

Credit Cards and Debts

The law for unmarrieds is that everyone "owns" his or her own debts, regardless of who benefits from the proceeds of a loan. However, if you cosign a credit card or loan application or if the loan is secured by a house you jointly own, each of you will usually be liable for the entire debt. Whatever arrangement you make between yourselves is your business alone, but legally the bank can come after either of you if any portion of the bill isn't paid. If you co-own a house, a car, or anything else of value, your partner's creditors can legally seize his or her portion of the jointly owned property to satisfy an unpaid debt. In most states this can only happen after a lawsuit has been filed and the creditor has won his case, and either of you can usually go to court to segregate your portion of the property to isolate it from any collection activity. If a creditor suspects you are hiding the debtor's assets under your own name, your personal assets can definitely be in jeopardy. Be scrupulous in keeping your finances as separate as you can, and don't engage in any major transfer of assets without consulting an attorney.

Likewise, a person who files bankruptcy needn't automatically drag her partner into a quagmire, but you may need to do some careful planning if this is a likely prospect. If you co-own real estate and bankruptcy is a possibility, you definitely should speak to a bankruptcy attorney at the earliest possible time since certain financial transactions can be undone against your will when a bankruptcy petition is filed. Again, you need to be extremely careful in separating out any joint assets prior to a bankruptcy filing to avoid any impression of hiding your assets.

Insurance for Everyone

You are likely to face two types of special insurance problems as a same-sex couple: determining what is reasonably necessary coverage and responding to the widespread discrimination against gay couples. There is very little guidance here and even less legal protection. In fact, unmarried couples, whether they are gay or straight, can encounter horrible obstacles in the insurance realm.

Life Insurance. This is designed to provide economic relief to a dependent spouse upon the death of a financially supporting family member, most commonly a husband and/or father. Most policies are purchased by the insured, who designates the beneficiary, usually his or her spouse. In some instances it is possible for one person to purchase a policy on another person's life, with the purchaser designating her or himself as the beneficiary. This option assures you that, as the policy owner, you are in control of designating the beneficiary and paying the premiums rather than leaving this up to the insured.

Insurance policies are either term or whole life, which is sometimes called universal. A term policy costs less annually in premiums, but if you ever stop paying your premiums you receive nothing at all. On the other hand, whole life policies incorporate a savings plan in which you pay somewhat more each year in premiums and accrue some savings, which you can either borrow against or rely on to cover future premiums. Be sure to ask if the premiums are guaranteed to stay low or whether they can increase later on, and *insist on a renewable policy* so the insurance company can't suddenly dump you.

Same-sex couples face discrimination in the sale of life insurance in several respects. First, insurance companies are bound to raise the HIV issue with male couples, and sellers of life insurance generally have the legal right to require an HIV test. Some companies have even been known to deny coverage to an HIV-negative man who lives with someone who is HIV-positive. It's unclear whether the courts will allow this kind of discrimination, but if either of you is HIV-positive you can expect serious obstacles to purchasing life insurance. Since some companies just don't like gay people, you may receive a lousy reception even if you are both HIV-negative.

Second, unless you own a home together, it can be very difficult to buy insurance coverage for each other's benefit, whether you are buying your own policy or buying a policy on your partner's life. If you own a home together, you can usually buy a policy on your partner's life (listing yourselves as "co-owners" rather than lovers), or you can sign up for mortgage insurance, a widely available type of life insurance that is designed to cover your partner's share of the mortgage obligations if she or he should die.

Obviously, even before you hit these obstacles you need to ask yourselves if you need or can afford life insurance. If you are both financially independent and are likely to stay this way for a while, life insurance may not be necessary. But if either of you is dependent on the other one to pay your basic living expenses, give it serious consideration.

Disability Insurance. If you are self-employed or work for a company that doesn't provide disability insurance, you should consider buying a disability policy. Disability insurance provides you with income if you can no longer work for health reasons, and it will supplement your Social Security benefits. Disability insurance is especially important if you are buying a house together or have little savings because if one of you gets sick it may be impossible for you to afford to keep your house. How much disability insurance you need depends directly on your savings, your monthly costs of living, the degree to which you can carry each other during difficult times, and how much you can afford to pay in premiums. A policy that provides $20,000 a year upon disability can easily cost you more than $1,500 a year in premiums.

Disability insurance is something everyone buys as an individual and not as a couple. HIV-based discrimination is rampant in the insurance industry, even if you are willing to do an HIV test and it comes out negative, since some insurers just can't accept safe sex as a reality. Locate an insurance agent in your community who serves other gay clients to get candid advice on where to apply.

Property/Renters' Insurance. If you own a home and have a mortgage, you will be required to carry homeowners' insurance, as a major theft or a fire can be devastating. In contrast, renters' insurance is optional and can be expensive in some towns, but if you have a fair number of valuable possessions, you should seriously consider purchasing it.

Same-sex couples often face discrimination in this insurance market. If only one of you owns the home, then only the homeowner's personal property is covered by homeowners' insurance— the nonowner's personal belongings are *not* insured. If you are not an owner and you have a significant number of personal goods, obtain a separate renter's policy or ask to be added to the homeowners' policy as an additional insured. Second, as renters you may be forced to buy separate policies rather than get a single policy as a family, and this can cost you several hundred extra dollars per year.

Umbrella Coverage. Those of you with substantial assets should consider purchasing an umbrella policy, otherwise known as a personal excess policy. This is a high-limit insurance policy (often for $1 million or more) that is triggered only when you face a significant claim (most likely from a major car accident) that exceeds the limits of coverage provided by your ordinary auto or homeowners' insurance policy.

The cost of an umbrella policy is not all that high (usually less than $300 a year) since it's rarely needed. However, to qualify you generally have to purchase the maximum amount of auto insurance, which can add several hundred dollars per year to your premiums. Same-sex couples often face discrimination here as well, as most companies require that each of you buy your own policy, whereas married couples get to share the cost of a single policy. If the costs are significant, you should consider filing a discrimination claim here.

Automobile Insurance. Depending on which state you live in you may be legally required to purchase automobile insurance, but it's something no one should be without anyway. Remember, your own policy will provide you with coverage if you get into an accident caused by someone who is uninsured or underinsured. Some companies have been known to discriminate against same-sex couples by only allowing one partner to be the insured, labeling the other partner as a codriver, and many companies don't offer multicar discounts to unmarried couples. *Don't let a company do this to you!* It is blatant discrimination, as the codriver usually has far less protection (such as no coverage when you rent a car).

Health Insurance. As an unmarried couple you will be forced to buy individual policies if you aren't covered by your employer, which may add significantly to the cost of your premiums, and if one of you has health problems, it may prevent you from obtaining private insurance altogether. This may constitute discrimination, and it is one area where domestic partnership legislation and changes in corporate policy can be of vital importance.

If you are coparenting a child, you will need to be especially careful in purchasing health insurance. Be sure the legal parent is signing up for the coverage and that your child is fully covered. If getting health insurance is going to be difficult for one of you, it makes sense to take this into account when you decide who is going to be the child's legal parent—if both of you together cannot be legal parents.

Tax Consequences. There is at least one tax advantage for same-sex couples. Tax authorities consider transfers of assets or money between same-sex couples as arm's length transactions. In other words, the price you set for property conveyed between yourselves is presumed to be fair, and a transfer of property between the two of you is presumed to be a legitimate and valid transaction. This can come in handy, say, for real estate sales, as you can meet statutory deadlines for selling property and can shift ownership of property between yourselves to comply with various tax rules. You may even be able to contract with each other to perform domestic services and thus shift some income to the one paying a lower rate of taxes, something married couples can't do. Same-sex couples formerly had the benefit of doubling the tax-free profits earned on the sale of a residence after age fifty-five, but the 1997 tax laws changed all that. Single folks can earn up to $250,000 tax free, and married as well as unmarried couples now can take up to $500,000 in profits tax-free whenever they sell their residence, as often as every two years, so long as they've lived there two out of the past five years.

The list of negative consequences for same-sex couples is, unfortunately, quite a bit longer. Here they are:

- You can't file a joint income tax return, even in situations where that might result in lower overall taxes for the two of you.
- If you buy or sell a partial interest in your partner's home and you don't qualify for the standard residential exemption, either when you are moving in together or if you break up, this is considered a taxable event. As a consequence, the seller of the partial interest in the house may owe the government taxes on any profits he or she made on the sale.
- If you give an asset to your lover or make an interest-free loan, you may be liable for gift taxes on the amount of the gift. In most instances you don't actually have to pay the tax at the time of the gift, but this will reduce the total amount of property you can bequeath tax-free upon your death. If you have accumulated an estate of more than the federal legal limit (currently $600,000, but soon to rise to $1 million) your heirs may have to pay a heftier tax on any inheritance. Gifts to charities, given either while you are alive or upon your death, are generally tax-exempt.
- Unlike married couples, upon your death you cannot bequeath your entire estate to your partner tax-free. Instead, you are limited to a set amount (unless you give your property to charity, of course). The current amount for federal tax exemption is $600,000 (which will go up to $1,000,000 by the year 2000); state exemptions vary considerably.
- If you are pooling your assets, in theory the richer partner could be considered to be making a gift to the poorer one or the poorer one could be viewed as receiving income for services rendered. If either of you ever gets audited, it is *conceiv-*

able that the IRS could hold the richer one liable for a gift tax or could make the poorer one pay income tax. While it's highly unlikely you'll ever face this kind of audit it's not impossible, so you should speak with a tax specialist if you are doing a fair amount of income sharing or asset pooling. If one of you merely pays more each month for expenses in a shared home, however, that isn't considered a gift or income to the other one—unless the amounts are extremely large.

- If you are coparenting a child or two you will need to decide who will get the dependent exemption and who is considered the "head of the household." You'll want to be legally consistent here, so don't present one arrangement to the IRS and another one to your local court.

- If you own a home in joint tenancy and one of you dies, the IRS can base the decedent's estate tax on the value of the entire property unless the surviving partner can demonstrate that she or he contributed to the purchase and upkeep of the place. In effect, the tax authorities are trying to recapture, tax-wise, the effects of any gift of joint-tenancy property between the two of you. Therefore, if you are lucky enough to own a residence that has a fair amount of equity or if it looks as if you are accumulating a fairly large estate, do your partner a favor: schedule an appointment with a skilled estate-planning attorney or tax accountant who has experience helping same-sex couples, as you may be able to minimize your tax exposure. Remember, if you die without a will your assets will pass to your parents or siblings, which may not be where you want them to go.

Government and Private Benefits

As an unmarried couple either of you can qualify for public benefits regardless of your partner's wealth and income. If one of you is disabled or has AIDS, being unmarried actually can be beneficial. You can obtain Social Security disability and, in most states, free

Chris Kollaja, a San Francisco accountant in the office of A. L. Nella & Company, a well-established firm serving a predominantly lesbian and gay clientele, offers several valuable tips. He encourages couples to keep their finances separate for at least the first three years to minimize tax problems and reduce the risk of conflicts. For relationships that survive this initial period, you can begin to think of yourselves as "we" rather then "me." Taking your time will greatly ease the difficulties of sorting out the tax and legal matters and also enable you to make better decisions and share the burdens equitably. Chris also recommends that every gay person initiate a savings program immediately, regardless of whether he or she has children. This will protect you in later years, and at the end of your life it will enable you to "leave a legacy" to the charity of your choice.

medical coverage without forcing your partner to deplete all of her assets.

Being unmarried may also enable you to qualify for a variety of private and other public benefits as well. Most often you can apply for a student loan without having to disclose your partner's income, and you can qualify for low-income housing based on your assets alone. Since your partner's credit rating won't be haunting you, this should make it easier to qualify for certain private benefits or government programs.

On the other hand, there are a slew of public and private benefits you won't be entitled to as an unmarried couple. On the public side, you won't qualify for retirement benefits based on your partner's earnings when your partner retires or dies. You won't be able to receive unemployment benefits if you are forced to quit your job to follow your lover to a new city, and most likely you won't receive any workers' compensation benefits if your partner is killed on the job. If one of you is a citizen of a foreign country, you probably won't be eligible for citizenship based on your long-term relationship, although in a few instances gay immigrants have been able to remain in the country on the grounds that it would be an unfair hardship to force them to leave their long-term (same-sex) domestic partner.

The list of unavailable public benefits is a long one, and it differs from state to state. This is one area where unmarried couples—straight or gay—suffer tremendously. And until the laws are changed or same-sex couples can marry, there is nothing the two of you can do about it by private agreement. Furthermore, unless you work for an employer with an enlightened domestic-partnership policy, it is unlikely you will qualify for health insurance under your partner's employee coverage nor will you benefit from your partner's job-based life-insurance policy.

Some employees receive a host of tangible benefits from their employer or employee association that they generally share with their spouse. Spouses of certain university employees receive free tuition, corporations give discounts to employees and their wives, and military spouses are entitled to a plethora of private benefits. But unless the employer or association has a domestic partnership program in place, you're left out in the cold. While there's little the two of you can do about this all by yourselves, there are effective strategies for addressing these problems. Here are some useful approaches:

- Try to establish a domestic partnership program with your employer, employee union, or local government. This is one area where the state and federal government has little power, so you can organize your effort on a local basis.
- Publicize discrimination in the local papers, use the issue as an organizing tool for your local lesbian and gay political organizations, and tell your nongay political organizations to make this issue a top priority. Denial of benefits for long-term

couples is one of the most pressing political issues for our community.

- Share your story with family and friends. It is often difficult for straight friends and family to comprehend the practical effects of discrimination. Straight unmarried couples always have the option of getting married, but not us—unless the current prohibitions are lifted. Being denied health insurance or free tuition is something everyone can understand in monetary terms.

- If you are really angry and are ready to fight the good fight, contact your local gay legal organization and consider filing a legal challenge. These are uphill battles, and you will need the support of a talented attorney to have a prayer of a chance of succeeding, but don't give up hope. Every movement has its own Rosa Parks, and you could be ours!

PART II

The Hard Times

7

Breaking Up Is Hard to Do:
The Procedural Options

Given the stresses we live under, it is amazing any relationship survives. Love doesn't always last, and when it doesn't life can be hell. One of the reasons our breakups can be so arduous is the lack of a readily available custom-fitted legal-dissolution process. Learning how to manage your dissolution within the existing legal structure can greatly reduce the pain.

Discord never develops overnight. For some a sense of imminent dissolution hovers for months or years, peppered by wrenching counseling sessions, late-night arguments, disclosures of affairs, and temporary separations before lovers go their separate ways. Others opt for a different style of disintegration, keeping conflicts under wraps until a nasty incident or budding romance thrusts the dissension into the open. Whether or not you are the initiator of the dissolution, it is always difficult to broach the subject, which is why this path is inevitably strewn with mixed messages and ambivalence.

Dealing effectively with the demise of love requires an endless reservoir of rationality. Divorce can make even the most sane person crazy, the most tender one brutal, and the most generous one selfish. When you are in the depths of a breakup, you may feel that nothing could assuage the pain, but, in fact, this is not true. Eventually, you will realize that the separation probably is in both your interests, an insight that will help enormously but will not come easily. Getting a grasp on the most likely outcomes will help minimize the pain, as this knowledge can foster a degree of patience and flexibility that will be of enormous personal benefit.

Every dissolution goes through three stages: the pre-breakup phase, the breakup itself, and the eventual resolution of the resulting disputes. Each phase has its own set of problems and challenges, and each requires its own component skills.

THE UNCERTAIN FUTURE

Being able to hear the rumblings of an oncoming crisis is a valuable skill that requires a balanced and rational attentiveness and a hefty dose of patience. If your partner never calls when he's out of town and the two of you quarrel over every little expenditure, be alert. Pay close attention when important discussions about the future get postponed or romantic weekends away consistently get canceled. The lack of sex can surely be a sign of a troubled affair.

Regardless of how you choose to handle the troubles emotionally, you should follow this particular piece of practical advice: *avoid making major commitments during times of brooding emotional conflict.* If a storm is approaching and the sky is dark with clouds, torrential rains are on the horizon, so don't plan a home renovation, don't buy a house if you are renters, don't bail out your partner's business with your last $5,000 in savings, and don't agree to move across the country to follow your lover to a new job.

Unfortunately, most people do just the opposite. They think that a home-improvement project or a new business venture will pull them out of a funk. Most of the time this just isn't true. Having kids rarely rescues a failing heterosexual marriage, and remodeling a kitchen will be just as unsuccessful for homosexuals. The potential for failure is especially true for same-sex couples since it is unrealistic to expect a troubled couple to weather the difficult legally mandated agreement-formation process. Since contractual discussions are onerous in the best of times, it is unrealistic to expect legal certainty when things are not going well. As a result, taking precipitous action when the relationship is on the rocks can create even worse predicaments.

As tensions mount and irritations surface, try to be conscious of what's a temporary conflict and what's the beginning of a separation and when a separation is becoming a dissolution. This is not a simple assignment, and the oscillation between conflict, resolution, disagreement, and dissolution can last for months. You are more likely to stay sane if you can find a way to live more independently while the conflicts are emerging. Minimize your social and professional obligations, avoid major financial risks, and secure for yourself a "safety net" of savings and emotional support. Find ways that allow both of you to coexist in the midst of uncertainty. Reduce expenses, separate business obligations, and avoid new projects.

In the early stages of conflict you should focus on what is essential to protect yourself without abruptly heightening the tension. Try to keep your funds separate, and reduce the funds in a joint account. Try to cancel joint credit cards, or at least put a limit on them. Make sure you have access to critical documents, and take the time to learn how the household assets are arranged if you don't know already. If you have children or a serious medical condition, think seriously about how you are going to handle them in the event of a separation. Consider changing your will, which you can do without telling your partner. Spend a few hours with an attorney, privately, to learn where you will stand if things disintegrate.

At the same time, avoid taking steps that accelerate the problems or kill any chances to resolve the conflicts. It's okay to withdraw your half of common funds or block the draining of a joint bank account, but don't embezzle the entire account. It's fine to put a valuable piece of art in storage, but don't destroy or hide anything that isn't yours. Don't create additional problems for yourself by calling the police on your lover without justification, and don't harass your partner at work.

If the situation advances to the point where a dissolution seems imminent, the conflicts probably will emerge into the open and your range of options—as well as your need to protect yourself—will increase dramatically. This is the time to take control of your finances by separating joint assets wherever possible and preventing your partner from draining the accounts. If you can't reach a mutual agreement on your funds, consider placing them in an escrow company's or a lawyer's trust account, which requires joint approval of any withdrawals. Ascertain which bills must be paid, and set up a system for getting them paid. If there are tools or a car essential for your work, make sure you have access to and control of what you need.

You will definitely need to take some action to protect yourself, just as you did in the times of early tension. Some actions have consequences but should still be considered, while others are dangerous to everyone involved. Try to ensure that your basic needs are going to be met, and protect yourself from being the victim of theft, bodily violence, or any illness or stress that would prevent you from working. If it appears that the only way to accomplish these goals is to act aggressively, learn the consequences of what you are planning to do by speaking with an attorney beforehand. It really won't help you, long-term, to steal furniture you don't need, deprive your lover of the use of her car so she loses her job, or file a fictitious assault accusation against your lover.

Here are some specific ideas for dealing with each type of asset you may wish to protect:

Financial Assets and Debts

Your earnings are yours unless you place them in a joint account, and your savings are also yours alone unless you place them in a joint account. Debts are also yours alone unless you both signed the loan agreement at the outset. If you have been keeping things separate, then keep them this way, and if you have combined assets or debts, try to reduce your exposure and risk. Hold off depositing your bonus check into the joint account, and keep your salaries separate for a while. Call the bank and make sure both signatures are required for withdrawing money from a joint account, and, if necessary, send the bank written instructions.

Credit Cards and Contractual Liabilities

Wherever possible avoid exposure to debt arising out of your partner's actions. Call the credit card company and see if a lower credit limit can be imposed on any joint card, read the fine print on that credit card contract you got long ago, and take out a card in your own name to use if the seas really get rough. If you can't limit the credit line on a joint card, consider canceling it altogether. Monitor any contracts with repair companies or salespeople, and stay on top of the way your real estate is being managed. If you can't reduce your liability without raising a red flag in front of your partner, you'll have to decide whether waiting a while is worth the risk.

Housing

Comfortable housing is an essential requirement for sane living, so make sure you are not exposing yourself to having to live without it. If you are renting a place together, think about who is going to live where and who will be liable for the lease payments. If you are joint owners of a property, try to make sure there is enough money in the joint savings account to handle the mortgage and consider setting up an automatic payment system to ensure against default. If you are not the legal renter or owner, start looking around for a place to move to if things get worse.

Personal Property

Find out what is really critical for your life and livelihood, and evaluate what things have real financial value. Give serious thought to taking those things into your own domain, either by relocating them or by figuring out a way to gain control of them. You may need to act carefully to avoid raising your partner's suspicion, but if you are concerned about impulsive destruction of your car, your family heirlooms, or the tools of your trade, do what is necessary to protect yourself.

Business Assets and Activities

If you co-own a business or rental property, you need to avoid having your assets taken from you. Verify in what form authority has been given to employees or managers, and if necessary send them a letter with instructions to await joint approval before taking any action. Get up to speed on how the joint business is run and where the records are being kept so your partner can't take total control of your economic fate.

Kids and Pets

When married couples break up, the courts usually take immediate control over the children, whereas pets are usually left for the parties to fight over. While child kidnapping does occur, the law can be fairly effective in avoiding it. For lesbian and gay couples, however, legal custody is often not so clear, and it's rare that courts get involved quickly. If you fear that your partner will act destructively or selfishly, try to arrange temporary housing or be prepared to seek immediate legal protections for your family.

The Body and the Self

Finally, give serious thought as to how you can best protect your physical body and your reputation. Angry lovers can inflict serious harm on each other through domestic violence and, especially for lesbian and gay couples, through the ruination of each other's reputations. Please make every effort to avoid such disasters. Don't "out" your lover out of spite, and don't jeopardize his or her job by excessive harassment or annoyance. If, on the other hand, you anticipate being the subject of such abuse, consider speaking to a sympathetic coworker or boss to try to minimize the potential damage before it happens.

Keep in mind that the dissolution will unfold far differently if either of you is in a new relationship. If you are the lucky one, it is incumbent on you to be doubly sensitive, as you will be better insulated with a companion to comfort you—and perhaps a new place to call home. You should be as considerate as possible, willing to make compromises and financial accommodations and to provide encouragement for your ex. But if you are the one being left behind, you will need to recognize that emotional support is something you probably won't find at home, and so you should hustle for comfort very quickly. Search out friends and family members, and make a strong effort to establish a support network.

Even if you had an open relationship, hurt feelings are bound to exist when a breakup results because of a new affair. Lying to your ex about your new romance will only work for a while, and at some point you must be honest about what is happening. Treat your ex as a person deserving respect, not as an obstacle lying in the path to your future. If you have the misfortune of being the one left behind, make every effort to accept the reality as a reflection of underlying problems in the relationship, not the cause of the breakup. Punishing your ex-lover for leaving you will only make your own life more miserable.

Having an agreement that covers your financial affairs should help a great deal, and, if one exists, it is incumbent on you to review it and abide by its terms. Your obligations may be more extensive than you realized, and you may need to schedule mediation sessions straightaway. Some of the issues you are facing may not be covered by your agreement, even if it's a detailed one, so you may need to be thinking, immediately, of equitable ways to address them. Don't precipitate a climate of adversarial aggression just because you fear your partner may do so. Try to be the giving one, even when you feel otherwise.

A final component of your preseparation preparation is getting answers to crucial legal questions. Talk with an attorney or review one of the resource books to get a good grasp on how the law applies to your situation. If you share a house and don't have a written agreement, for example, learn how its division is likely to be handled, and if you're sharing custody and care of a child but haven't done a second-parent adoption, learn what that means for each of you. You may not want to orchestrate your separation precisely along legal lines, but you should be as informed as possible.

THE MOMENT OF TRUTH

At some point you come to the end of the road. Your boyfriend may propose that he live with a friend for a few weeks while he sorts out his feelings; you may tell your lover you've had it with his self-destructive chemical addictions; or you may burst into tears during a therapy session and both say, in unison, that the relationship is over. Most counselors recommend that you follow a few simple rules of decency to reduce the agony of separation and maximize the possibility of staying friends. When talking about the reasons for the breakup, focus your statements on your own perspective and try not to blame your partner. Remind her or him of how difficult things have gotten for both of you. Try not to make any unilateral decisions, and be willing to talk things out and try counseling for a limited period of time.

Once you emerge from the shock of the bad news, your most immediate concerns will involve children, housing, and money, all of which are unavoidably interrelated. Resolving these matters requires balancing the conflicting demands of (1) finding a place to live for each of you, (2) paying the bills and sorting out the immediate financial arrangements, and (3) figuring out where the children will live and who will pay for their care.

If you have a written agreement, review it, then make an appointment with an attorney to go over it if you need interpretation or advice. If you don't have an agreement or yours doesn't completely address your concerns, you and your ex will need to develop solutions both of you can live with. Keep in mind that your first arrangement is bound to be temporary, and don't feel pressured to make a permanent decision immediately. Try to be flexible and patient whenever possible, as this is a time to be accommodating, not overly assertive.

Your goal is to create a stable situation for both of you, one in which you can maintain your sanity, stay healthy, keep your job, help your kids, and allow yourself to discover that life is not over, even though the relationship is. You need to create a "safety zone" to get through the resolution process, to give you a balance that's vital for surviving the challenges that lie ahead. If you push for every little victory at the early stages of dissolution, you will wear each other out long before you've faced the more important long-term issues.

Avoid harassing your ex at work, especially if he or she isn't open about being gay. Make use of E-mail or voice mail whenever possible, and stick with specific appointments after work to deal with the pressing issues. If you are the victim of harassment, consider obtaining a restraining order against the harasser, even if that means coming out at work and in the courthouse.

Here's a crucial warning for the particularly volatile relationship: domestic violence in same-sex relationships is one of the dirty little secrets in our community, and it's essential that you be realistic about this possibility during a breakup. If you find yourself being

Greg Merrill of San Francisco's Community United Against Violence, a social service organization that helps eliminate violence against gays as well as within same-sex relationships, offers the following advice. First, have the courage to acknowledge that violence is occurring and that it is not okay. Always make a police report to help you document your problems at a later date, and tell the police you are in a domestic relationship with the batterer, as this will help them help you. Find a safe place to move to, and build up a support system to help you through the hard times. You *may* want to speak with a friend or family member of the batterer, but be realistic: most likely such a person will not take your side. And finally, even though the court systems are supposed to help you, in most counties they rarely do. Use a community social service agency and find immediate practical solutions, relying on civil or criminal prosecution only as a last resort.

battered, shoved, or grabbed or if your partner is destroying your property, stealing your things, or forcing sex on you, face it: you are a victim of domestic violence, and you need to act quickly to minimize the harm to you.

Here's a list of ten essential tasks to handle in the immediate breakup phase:

1. Find temporary housing for the departing partner at an affordable price. Make a fair deal for sharing the added housing costs, with a firm time limit on temporary arrangements.

2. Make practical arrangements for your children so their suffering is minimized. If both of you are legal parents (and in some states even when only one is), you can utilize the court system for custody and support orders. Consider mediation from the outset.

3. Separate your finances immediately. Stop using joint credit cards, and if one of you needs to borrow from the other, keep track of the loans and agree to balance up the finances later on. Don't steal from each other.

4. Minimize the battles over personal possessions. Emotions are too hot for you to focus on these details, so make interim arrangements to meet your needs, agree to disagree, and resolve things later.

5. Reduce the collective economic drain. Dissolution is expensive, and this is not the time to squander your resources.

6. Keep your interactions brief, sane, and calm, even if it means hiding your true feelings or having a third person in the room. There are practical details to sort out, and that's where you should focus your attention.

7. If you are ready and willing to deal with the emotions straight on, consider meeting with a couples counselor to make the dialogue more productive.

8. Compile a list of what lies ahead for you in the separation process and identify your highest priorities to serve as a guide through the resolution stage. This will make the future

feel more bearable, and it will help you select the best method for resolving your conflicts.

9. If the two of you are able to communicate, find as many possible areas of agreement as you can, and as soon as you reach an agreement, implement it. The fewer items remaining in dispute the easier it will be to resolve them.

10. Don't express your feelings by grabbing for more of the "goods" or creating artificial obstacles to the separation. You'll only cause yourself more pain, and you probably won't achieve any of the desired emotional results.

In her excellent book *Between Love & Hate: A Guide to Civilized Divorce*, social worker Lois Gold offers the following seven keys to a constructive divorce—and her advice applies equally to same-sex couples.

1. Take responsibility for regulating your own behavior, regardless of what your ex does.

2. Separate your emotions from the practical decision-making tasks.

3. Separate your job as a parent (or homeowner or employee) from the relationship conflicts.

4. Accept that you have contributed to the dissolution.

5. Try to understand your ex's viewpoint.

6. Be willing to negotiate and compromise.

7. Commit to using an equitable and nonadversarial settlement process.

RESOLVING THE REMAINING CONFLICTS

Once the farewells have been said and each of you has landed in a zone of safety, you will be ready to tackle the rest of the mess. Each dissolution presents its own problems that demand resolution; while certain issues like the house, the money, and the car will show up on nearly everyone's list, each couple will face unique disputes. Remember: *any* topic on *anyone's* list needs to be addressed. You may reject your partner's demands, but that doesn't mean they don't warrant discussion. Don't argue about what issues should be fought over, as this will only slow down the process.

From a legal perspective there are seven different methods to choose from to resolve your conflicts: direct conversation, formal mediation, represented mediation, represented negotiation, binding arbitration, nonbinding arbitration, and litigation. What follows is a brief description of what each method entails to help you select the right approach. Some of these options can work serially and some concurrently, and using one does not always preclude trying another. If you are confused, be open to meeting with an attorney at the outset just to evaluate your procedural options.

Direct Negotiation

If you are communicating directly with your former partner in an effort to find a mutually acceptable solution, direct negotiation is what you are involved in. This process is closer to mediation when you work toward a mutually acceptable solution without trying to convince the other person that you are right, sharing feelings and goals but not trying to win the other person over to your perspective. You posit solutions and see if any of them will work.

Negotiation more aptly describes a process in which you exchange offers, provide justifications for your position, and steer toward an acceptable middle course; here there is less sharing of feelings and more of a bargaining atmosphere. The line between mediation and negotiation is a fine one; the key feature of both is that you are talking to each other with no one else in the room. Some use the term collaborative mediation to describe a process of jointly crafting a resolution that meets their needs; commercial-style negotiation, by contrast, involves reaching a settlement somewhere in between the two positions, based primarily on the relative legal strength of each person's case.

Direct negotiation is just a more focused way of doing what former lovers always do: argue. But rather than being argumentative, you are trying to reach a solution. The two of you get to decide what the topics are going to be, financial or emotional, and you tackle them according to your own ground rules. You each present your goals and justifications, and you explore different solutions to see whether an acceptable compromise can be achieved.

The ground rules for effective conflict resolution when talking directly with each other are as follows:

1. Acknowledge that this is an important task, and carve out a special time and place for it. Don't engage in impulsive arguments over the phone; schedule your discussions ahead of time, pick a neutral location, and stick to the topic.

2. Select a method of communicating that is safe and practical for both of you. Some couples prefer to meet face-to-face, while others would rather use the phone. Letter writing can be effective, as it slows down the pace and allows you to think carefully before responding. E-mail can work beautifully, combining the speed of a phone call with the deliberateness of a letter. You proclaim your position and she responds when she's ready, nobody can interrupt because only one person writes at a time, and there's a record of what was said. If you are using the telephone a lot, don't call your ex at work unless it is absolutely necessary, and keep any calls short and unemotional.

3. Acknowledge when you aren't making progress and choose another mode of communication. Don't allow yourselves to be tirelessly stuck in repetitive arguments or ineffective diatribe. Step back, shift gears, and try another approach.

4. Don't expect to convince your partner of the absolute truth of your position; if you had been able to do this earlier, you probably wouldn't have broken up. If she or he is able to hear your side of the story and accept that it is your reality, proceed with your discussion of possible solutions.

5. Focus on solutions rather than principles. I often tell clients who are fighting over property to limit their discussions to

numbers, not words. Act as if you are at an auction, make offers and counteroffers, and see if there's a dollar amount you can live with. This approach has a much better chance of succeeding than spending the day arguing over whose legal theory or whose memory of an oral agreement is correct.

6. Focus on getting the process over with rather than viewing it as a chance to work through your anger or to stay connected to your ex. You can earn more money on your job, and you'll probably find more satisfaction looking for a new partner, rather than spending all your spare time arguing. Moreover, you are far more likely to reach an emotional resolution (with or without your ex) and forge a friendship with your ex *after* you have divided up the goods!

Formal Mediation

At some point one or both of you may conclude that the direct talks are not working. You may feel too intimidated by your partner, especially if there's been a pattern of domination and competition in your relationship. The revelation of a secret affair or the suspicion of prior deceit can block rational discourse, and if there is a serious prospect of violence, volatility, or chronic noncooperation, direct discussions between just the two of you may be impossible.

If you both prefer to mediate, then using a neutral mediator can work beautifully. Formal mediation takes place when a third party sits with both parties to help find a compromise that neither party would have otherwise considered. Mediators do *not* decide who is right and who is wrong, nor do they have the power to force either person to do anything. Instead, they are empowered to work with you as equals and to encourage you to settle your differences. They sit as your mutual counselor rather than as your judge. It is truly amazing—and everyone will tell you this—how often an intractable conflict resolves itself through mediation. The success rate is so high that most experts will tell you to give it a try, at least for a few sessions, even when the chasms of disagreement seem absolutely unbridgeable.

Mediation can be very effective for at least four reasons:

1. Mediators often provide substantive insight that changes people's minds. For example, if one soul believes he was harmed more than the other one and the mediator can demonstrate he wasn't, or if one person feels she is legally entitled to something when she is not, a mediator can quickly clear the air.

2. Mediators are able to unscramble communication problems since the anger in a breakup can be so intense that exes can't even hear an apology or explanation. If there's a third party in the room who actively improves the communication, it is amazing how clear the discussions can become.

3. Mediation is a performative or dramatic process. Ex-lovers want to express their feelings and have someone listen, and they want (quite justifiably) someone to affirm their pain. Many people need to explain themselves in a setting that includes professionals and yet is a safe setting, and those who feel wronged may want a public apology and a written record of the resolution. Mediation ensures that each side is fully heard, which can open up all sorts of solutions. Sitting in front of a mediator may expose the ugliest of emotions, but it's a controlled setting that often inspires exes to move beyond their feelings.

4. Mediation serves in two ways as a harbinger of what can happen if you *don't* resolve your conflicts. First, it involves going semipublic with your problems by locating and hiring a mediator, paying more money to a third party, and taking time away from work or play to deal with the dispute. This alone can create enormous agony, and when couples realize how unpleasant the process can be, a compromise may look more palatable. And, second, most mediators are very effective at telling the parties point-blank precisely how expensive, time-consuming, and unpleasant arbitration or litigation can be, and these warnings can serve as excellent prods to a settlement.

Formal mediation, therefore, is something nearly every couple should try at least for a few sessions. Mediators explore solutions, encourage brainstorming, and foster an atmosphere of mutual benefit that can help both parties crawl out of their pits of anger. Even when the effort doesn't solve all the problems, it usually resolves some of them and can thus focus attention on the remaining conflicts and pave the way for a more civilized way of resolving them. Since the cost of the mediator should be shared by both parties, a few sessions should not cost you more than $500.

According to Martina Reaves, an experienced attorney-mediator based in Emeryville, California, mediation can be especially beneficial for same-sex couples. The legal system is highly inappropriate for our conflicts, and with mediation the parties can control the process and fashion concrete solutions that are uniquely right for their lives. Mediation also offers the best chance for healing the relationship in a private and confidential setting. Reaves points out that it isn't always necessary to use a lesbian or gay mediator—working with someone of high quality and sensitivity is what matters, not his or her sexual orientation. You should also be sure to understand what your legal rights are before you finalize any agreement in order to know if you are waiving rights out of ignorance rather than by choice.

The preliminary tasks of mediation are selecting a mediator and scheduling the sessions. Begin by (1) locating prospective mediators and checking out their credentials, (2) speaking briefly with the proposed mediator to see if she or he is acceptable, and (3) working out the financial and practical details and arranging the schedules.

You will want someone who has worked with same-sex couples, regardless of his or her own sexual orientation. Talking to your friends or a personal counselor is often the best source of referrals. Make sure you get a reference from at least one person who has worked with the mediator, as any mediator can have flaws, and you want to find at least one person who can vouch for your selection. Typically, the mediator will talk only briefly with each of you separately and wait until you are together to hear the substance of the dispute. But don't minimize the value of this first contact, as it should help give you an intuitive sense of whether this mediator is the right one for you.

You also need to find someone who is affordable, conveniently located, and willing to see you at a time of day that is convenient for both of you. If there are particular items in dispute such as a house or a business, be certain that the mediator is familiar and skilled in these areas. Mediators are usually trained either as therapists or attorneys, so give serious thought as to which training is more appropriate for your problems.

If your conflicts are primarily emotional and you don't have a lot of practical issues to resolve, a therapist-mediator is probably right for you. If you are not primarily dealing with emotional conflicts but are arguing over money, property, or anything concrete, an attorney-mediator is probably the better choice. If the problems are a combination of the two, as is quite likely, you will then have to decide jointly which approach is more acceptable to you. For especially complex situations, you might consider having a team made up of an attorney and a therapist, though this approach can quickly become expensive.

My preference is for attorney-mediators, since I find sorting out property conflicts a lousy way of addressing emotional problems and generally it's more efficient to dive right into the practical tasks. While therapist-mediators can bring warring parties together, the agreements you come to with them may lack the precision needed to make them binding, or, worse, they may be based on incorrect assumptions about legal matters. If you are using a therapist-mediator I recommend you meet with an attorney first to ascertain what your rights are. Then have your attorney review your agreement before signing it just to be sure you haven't inadvertently given away more than you intended.

A *Guide to Divorce Mediation* is a book written by one of the nation's top mediators, Gary Friedman. It summarizes the mediation process and includes many good ideas that apply to same-sex couples. He says that for mediation to work both parties must have a motivation to mediate, enough self-responsibility to speak out and make decisions, a willingness to disagree and be assertive when necessary, and the courage to agree to a mutually beneficial resolution. In addition, the parties must agree to stop all litigation and to disclose relevant documents to each other, and they must agree not to use the mediation disclosures in court if the mediation fails. He also recommends that an attorney explain to both sides what would most likely happen if they did go to court so that the settlement is based on informed choices.

Represented Mediation

Some of you may want to avoid submitting your fate to an arbitrator or judge but feel you aren't able to get your point across all by yourself in mediation. If so, you may want to explore the option of represented mediation, in which the two of you explore settlement with or without the assistance of a mediator but with a personal advocate for each of you at the table. The advocate is most frequently an attorney but could also be a friend, financial adviser, or colleague.

The purpose of having an advocate is to help you handle the emotional strain, to tell your story as effectively as possible, and to respond to the overwhelming accusations that may surface. An advocate can serve as your private counselor during the mediation to review proposed solutions and talk out proffered settlements. Sitting through a three-hour mediation session can be a mighty lonely chore, and some people find it difficult to make major decisions alone under pressure. Having an advocate means there is someone at your side helping you decide what to say and what to do.

There are two possible downfalls of inviting an advocate along. First, if you are using attorneys as your advocates *and* paying for a mediator, the process can get quite expensive. You're each paying your attorney as well as half the mediator's fee, so a series of sessions will be costly. Second, having an advocate can make the process antagonistic if each advocate tries to argue her case rather than work toward a compromise. An experienced mediator should be able to control this tendency, but try to choose an advocate who is committed to the mediation process and doesn't see it as just an opportunity to argue the validity of your position.

Represented Negotiation

Represented negotiation is just a fancy term for what lawyers do all the time: argue on the phone and write letters advocating their client's position, trying to find a solution acceptable to both sides. To begin, you retain an advocate who will help you develop a position that takes into account the law as it applies to your particular situation. Your advocate will also address your personal goals, how much you want to and can afford to fight, and what you think your ex is likely to want and do. Your advocate then carries this message to your ex (or his or her advocate), either by phone call, letter, or personal meeting.

These presentations will combine argument, threat, manipulation, and intimidation, depending on the facts of the case and the style of the advocate. You can set the tone of the process to a great degree by letting your advocate know your priorities. If you are prepared to go to the mat and don't want to settle for anything less than 100 percent victory, you need an advocate who is comfortable with this approach and will carry that message. If compromise is your highest priority and reaching an amicable resolution is more important than maximizing your financial gain, a very different sort of message needs to be sent.

After a response is obtained from your ex, you and your advocate will confer and decide what the next step should be. Your goal is to exchange a series of financial offers and counteroffers, working toward a compromise, even though at the outset you may only exchange argumentative diatribes. In some instances the fight will focus on what the proper method of solving the problem is, and, in complicated breakups, there may well be a preliminary fight over exactly what is at stake.

After a series of inquiries, responses, and caucuses you will either reach a settlement or you will conclude that an alternative approach is needed. How long the negotiation process lasts depends on how much time and money each of you is willing to devote to the effort and how likely a settlement appears. If both parties start out by making exaggerated demands, it's going to take even longer to reach a middle ground. If the hired guns can't achieve a resolution you can always pull back from the precipice a bit, reconsider talking directly to each other, and try a less formal and less expensive process.

Represented negotiation has two attractive benefits and two confounding downsides. The best aspect is that you are free from having to deal with your ex-lover directly. You only have to talk to your advocate, who is on your side, and she or he does all the dirty work and explains issues to you in terms you can understand. You get to control when and how you deal with the conflict. The other positive feature is that a settlement is often achieved. Dedicated lawyers who are focused on the task at hand and open to finding solutions can work wonders.

The downsides are that the process can be expensive and slow. If you are paying your attorney by the hour, the sheer length and number of discussions can add up very quickly. Each round requires three sets of talks or letters: you talk with your attorney about what you want, your attorney writes a letter or talks with the other attorney, and then your attorney reports back to you and you jointly process the response.

The negotiation process also can take a long time. Between your schedule, your attorney's other obligations, and your ex's schedule, weeks can go by between offers and counteroffers. One person goes on vacation and the entire process grinds to a halt; an attorney has to handle a trial and suddenly two weeks are gone. It's not unusual to spend two months and incur $2,000 in fees negotiating the terms of a complex settlement—and if in the end the parties can't agree on all the terms, you can be right back where you started.

For these reasons, if you are going to use this negotiation process it is essential that you establish a time limit and a budget for it. If money is tight tell your attorney at the outset so the strategy can be tailored to your budget. A few face-to-face meetings or short telephone calls might work more quickly than a series of lengthy letters. If more than a month or two elapses and there's no clear sign of progress toward a workable solution, I usually advise my clients to cut the cord and move on to another method of conflict resolution.

Deciding whether to accept a particular offer can be a difficult decision. If the offer is within 80 percent of what you think you'd be awarded at a trial, I say take it, as the risks of losing and the costs of fighting just aren't worth the extra 20 percent. Unless there's a contract between the parties, the winning party in a same-sex dissolution can't force the other party to pay his or her fees, so continuing to fight just costs you more money. If, on the other hand, the offer is way too low, you should settle only if you're too emotionally drained or cannot afford to fight on. When the offer is low but not horribly so, make the decision based on your feelings and not on financial needs.

Binding Arbitration

Arbitration is a special forum for having a trial. Rather than going to the county courthouse and submitting the case to a judge appointed by the governor and paid by taxpayers, the parties hire a private individual—either a retired judge or an experienced attorney—to serve as their arbitrator. The parties agree by written contract to use simpler procedures and evidentiary rules, hold

According to Stewart Levine, an experienced San Francisco Bay Area attorney who lectures nationwide on methods of resolving conflicts, the key to settling your disputes by negotiation is mostly an internal emotional process of acceptance and letting go: accept the part you have played in the creation of the problem, accept that you are dealing with someone you voluntarily brought into your life, accept that the legal system is inadequate to deal with your situation, acknowledge that an adversarial approach will have terrible emotional and financial consequences for both parties, be open about your fears, and, most critically, let go of any fantasy of "winning" or getting even.

informal hearings on a faster schedule than would occur in a government-sponsored courtroom, and abide by the arbitrator's decision.

The preliminary tasks of arbitration involve getting your partner to agree to this process (unless it's already been agreed to in a prior written agreement), choosing an arbitrator, paying the arbitrator's fee in advance, and identifying the issues to be resolved. Presenting your case to the arbitrator, the next step, is often an informal process. Since you are not in court you do not need to have an attorney, and you can present your case, examine witnesses, and produce your documents on your own or with the help of a friend or lay advocate, as you prefer.

Arbitration procedures are more streamlined than court procedures. Document exchanges are handled informally, procedural hearings can be done over the phone, witnesses are often questioned informally, and the arbitrator will help focus the testimony and speed up the hearing. Even though the parties pay the arbitrator's fee (usually about the same as an experienced attorney's fee), the overall costs will often be less than for litigation. A two-day arbitration *with a lawyer* usually costs less than $10,000 and often less than $5,000. This is a bargain compared to litigation, since a courtroom trial of the same length can cost more than twice as much. If you are able to handle the arbitration without an attorney, your costs should be less than $1,000, as you'll only have to pay the arbitrator's fee and spend an hour or two with an attorney getting prepared.

Arbitrations are also over far more quickly than courthouse trials. You don't need to wait for months for an available judge, you know who is going to make the decision, and you select when and where the hearing will be. There is no waiting for a courtroom to free up, no stalling because of the interruptions of a judge's other cases or vacations, and no risk of facing an irascible and prejudiced judge.

Moreover, the public is not invited and there is no written record of the case or decision. Confidentiality is assured, the press won't be notified, your family may never learn about it, and your case will never serve as a precedent for future decisions. Often the outcome is based more on general rules of equity and fairness than on specific laws, and since you get to choose and pay for the arbitrator, you should be able to eliminate homophobic or hostile judges.

There are two kinds of arbitration, binding and nonbinding. Binding arbitration, which is more common by far, occurs when the parties agree they will be bound by the arbitrator's decision, whatever it may be. No appeal, no retrial, no rehearing. At the end of the hearing (which can last as long as the parties make it last, but usually only a day or two), the arbitrator makes a decision, and that is it. In most states the arbitrator's decision can be enforced through the legal system, just as if a county judge had made the decision.

Such finality can be either a lifesaver or a death sentence. If your ex will never allow a decision to rest, binding arbitration can be a blessing for you as there is a certain end; if you are the one who wins the first round, there is no fear of future hearings or subsequent reversals. On the other hand, losing a binding arbitration can be devastating. Ask anyone who has suffered a defeat he or she perceived as unfair and you will conclude that this approach is labeled arbitration because it feels so *arbitrary*. Not having any avenue of appeal can be very depressing. It's an all-or-nothing solution, and face it: that's a hefty price to pay for efficiency.

Nonbinding Arbitration

Some parties want to try arbitration but don't want to be bound by the arbitrator's decision. They want the right to have the dispute reconsidered in a courtroom if they are dissatisfied, or they want to try to resolve the case without being bound by the decision. This is called nonbinding arbitration.

Few people select this method, as it requires that both sides fully prepare and present their case and often spend thousands of dollars on a formal hearing only to have the decision tossed aside because one side rejects the results. If you have a mammoth dispute it may be useful to use this dry-run approach, but most attorneys suggest that if you want the right of appeal stick with the court system.

Litigation

If all attempts to resolve your disputes fail, there remains one final option: litigation. Litigation is the generic word for using the government's judicial system to resolve your conflicts by filing a lawsuit. Take note: even if you are able to settle the dispute before going to trial, you are said to be "in court" once formal papers are submitted to the court.

Why would anyone take his most intimate conflicts into the public arena of a courthouse? Because sometimes nothing else will get the job done. But try your hardest to avoid it, even if this means not taking any useful action for a few months while you try to talk settlement. Going to court should always be considered as the *last* resort for same-sex dissolutions, since while most lawsuits *eventually* settle, it can be very time-consuming to settle once a lawsuit is initiated. But if your negotiations have stalled and your ex won't talk to you or your attorney, filing a lawsuit may be necessary to force him or her to hire an attorney, which by itself can reopen discussions and lead to a settlement.

Litigation is a four-phase process: (1) pleadings, (2) discovery, (3) trial, and (4) appeal and enforcement. Once you understand each stage you will see why it is so expensive and so slow. You will also realize why it can also be extremely effective.

PLEADINGS

The first stage is the pleadings stage, in which you and your attorney frame your story in legal terms and submit a written summary of your claim to the court—which will be your local state court, not federal court. This requires a lengthy interview with your attorney, after which she or he translates your story and demands into "causes of action."

At this stage you will have to find out what kinds of legal claims are allowed in the state you live in, as each state has its own rules about what kinds of complaints same-sex couples can bring against each other. If the law disfavors a claim you want to bring, carefully consider whether you are willing to be a test case. You will also have to decide whether to describe your relationship as that of lovers, something you may *have* to do if your claim is dependent on enforcing an oral or implied agreement. If you live in a county that allows same-sex couples to file their claims in family courts, you may need to follow the particular rules of that court.

Your attorney also has to check out whether any of the time deadlines, called statutes of limitations, have expired. All states have rules that prevent people from waiting too long before filing a claim, on the grounds that memories fade so it is unfair for complaints to be filed years after the events have occurred. In California, for example, oral contract claims must be filed within two years of the time the contract is breached, whereas claims regarding written contracts, in which memories are less crucial, can be filed up to four years after a contract is breached. In many states personal injury complaints must be filed within a year.

If you are the one initiating the lawsuit, you are called the plain-

If you are brave enough to handle your case without an attorney you will need to generate the complaint, which should raise the following claims:

1. Disposition of the real estate and any personal property, either through a buyout between the parties or sale to a third party with a distribution of the proceeds (generally called a partition action), along with an accounting of the financial records of the parties.
2. Breach-of-contract claims, either for promised repayments of loans, sharing of assets, or promises of ongoing support.
3. Breach of fiduciary or confidential duties for mishandling of joint assets or the refusal to share the proceeds of joint efforts.
4. Partnership or joint-venture claims if a co-owned business is involved in the dispute.
5. Emotional distress or personal injury claims if things get really ugly or there are peripheral claims such as physical assaults, exposure to HIV, or destruction of personal property.

tiff, and the ex-lover you are suing is labeled the defendant. Either party can initiate the lawsuit. You may feel less in control and a bit angry if you are the defendant, simply because you have been caught off guard, but this initial impression rarely affects the outcome. Of course, if your ex is the plaintiff you won't be burdened with these initial strategies; your work begins only when you have to respond to the complaint.

Once you and your attorney (if you are using one) draw up the pleading, generally called a complaint, it is usual to try one last time to settle the matter. Lawyers often send the opposing side a copy of a complaint they are about to file to demonstrate their seriousness. If settlement seems imminent, don't jeopardize an informal solution by rushing into court, but if it is impossible to get your ex's attention or craft a reasonable settlement, filing the complaint with the court is your next step. This opens the lawsuit up formally and this is when you pay your court fees, which generally are less than $200. If you're worried about maintaining your privacy, in some states you can file your case using a pseudonym.

After the complaint is filed the next step is to have a copy of it delivered to your ex (or, with his consent, to his attorney), as he has a right to see what you are saying about him. This is called service of process, and, depending on how evasive your ex is, it can take several weeks—and you may need to hire a process server to locate your ex. The defendant generally has a month after receiving the complaint to file a response with the court. This is called an answer, and it sets forth in legal terms what she or he thinks about your allegations.

Answers come in several forms. Some defendants say, "No, I'm not guilty of the allegations. I did nothing, I owe nothing, and therefore I will pay nothing." This answer sets the stage for the rest of the litigation by telling the plaintiff what has to be proven. Sometimes defendants even deny things not seriously in dispute just to make the plaintiff's burden of proof more difficult. Other defendants admit some facts but deny others. For example, your partner might admit that you both own the residence but deny that you are entitled to anything extra for renovation expenses. She might admit you started a business together but assert that since the business never made a profit you aren't owed anything.

Other defendants admit all the facts but argue that there are no legal grounds on which you can prevail. This is a complicated sort of response, and it can often lead to extended court battles over what kind of a claim is allowed, and since the law is not very clear in the area of same-sex dissolutions, such arguments happen fairly often. Some courts prefer to resolve these battles before they hear any evidence. For instance, if you are living in a state that has never considered a claim for postseparation support by a same-sex couple, you may be forced to argue whether such a claim can even be filed. Only if you are successful in proving the legitimacy of the concept will you be able to argue over how much money you should receive.

DISCOVERY

Once the legal papers are filed and the dispute has been framed, the real battle begins. One of the most important features of litigation is the right to conduct discovery, through which you gather the facts before you start the trial. Generally, there are two means of doing this: through an exchange of documents and through a formal interview called a deposition. Document exchanges are critical, since in same-sex dissolutions one party may hold all the records, either because she was the one keeping track of them or because she grabbed them as she dashed out the door.

The records can be essential to proving your case. If you are asserting that you are entitled to a reimbursement, say, of your construction contributions, you'll need the receipts and construction records to prove your claim. If you say your partner promised you a portion of a business you helped start, you'll need to see how much money the business is earning. You may even find that you don't have a copy of that agreement you signed long ago.

A deposition is an interview conducted by one partner's attorney in front of a court reporter, who takes verbatim notes of the interview "for the record." In a deposition the questioning attorney has the right to ask a witness or a party any pertinent questions and he or she is under a sworn oath to tell the truth. The lawyer representing the partner being questioned is also present and can object to questions as improper or too invasive. If there's a disagreement over what questions are pertinent and who is an appropriate witness, either party can ask the judge to resolve the disagreement.

Even though the interview takes place in a private law office without a judge or jury, the truth usually comes out, for several reasons. First, the formality of the questioning has a way of focusing people's attention, and the formal oath puts most people on their best behavior. Second, if the attorney is well prepared and skilled in asking questions, it is easy to catch people in lies or exaggerations. Third, and perhaps most important, in most states the transcript can be read to the judge or jury if there is a trial, and if stories are changed an attorney can discredit the witness, which discourages most folks from lying.

Discovery serves several purposes. It enables you to get the information you need in order to put on a good presentation at a trial if the case doesn't settle. It's a dress rehearsal, where you can see how convincing your story sounds and how plausible your ex's version is going to be. A focused deposition can pin down a witness to a particular story and discourage her from changing it later on.

Discovery can have indirect benefits as well. It flushes out each side's version of the story and can lead the parties to a settlement of the dispute since once the parties and their lawyers hear the full story and see the documents, they may back off from extreme positions. Some witnesses actually make admissions that undermine their positions, and if so their lawyers can convince them to make compromises rather than lose at the trial. I've seen witnesses admit to lying or forging documents, or even change their story, and nothing works faster to encourage settlement than a confession of perjury.

The discovery process can also bring people to compromise simply because it is so painful and so expensive. Sitting across the table from the woman you loved for so many years and watching your attorney grill her about credit card expenses and business plans (or getting grilled yourself) can make both of you ill. When you add the hundreds of dollars per hour the process is costing each of you, compromising can begin to appear a lot more attractive.

In most states the document exchange and deposition process will be scheduled cooperatively, regardless of how contentious the monetary disputes may be. If one or both parties is recalcitrant and refuses to participate, you can ask the judge to order the other side to show up at a deposition and turn over key documents. If that person refuses, the judge can order him to pay your attorneys' fees or even declare you the winner of your case without having to go to trial.

TRIAL

If after all the facts have been compiled all attempts at a settlement have failed, then the third step is the trial. This is the central act in this drama, and it is an exhilarating but brutal experience.

As the trial approaches you and your attorney will spend more time getting prepared. If there's a dispute over the value of the house an appraiser will be hired; if there's an argument over the finances of a business an accountant may be retained. You'll spend every night going over diaries, notes, and conversations with friends, getting prepared for your testimony. The rest of your life will barely exist. You may miss work and be unable to concentrate on anything else, and you will likely be thoroughly anxious and depressed. Depending on the scale of the dispute and the way things work in your particular locale, years may have passed since you broke up and all of your past conflicts will be brought back before your eyes.

And then, just when you are all set to tell your story to the world, chances are there will be further delays. In many counties courts are overloaded with criminal cases or claims by dying people that have priority over yours. Judges also like to encourage settlements rather than host a trial and a possible appeal, and they have a clever method of encouraging settlement: they postpone the trial, forcing the parties to endure more delay and more costs, in the hope that some of them will give up and settle.

Judges in most courts do not look benignly on domestic disputes, and they resent it even more when homosexuals drag out their dirty laundry. They are uncomfortable with the emotions, they may hold you both in disdain, and they would rather deal with more pressing matters like million-dollar corporate affairs or criminal punishments.

But eventually you will have your day (or days) in court. You will each testify, and each attorney will have the chance to question each witness. Sometimes there is even a jury, though this is fairly rare in same-sex divorces (and almost never allowed in heterosexual divorces). You each present documents and witnesses and try to prove the legitimacy of your demands. The judge establishes the legal boundaries of the dispute, ruling on procedural arguments and disputes over legal principles.

After the trial has been completed the judge or jury will issue a ruling. One of you will win—in whole or in part—and the other will lose. Often the decision is a mixed bag, as one person may win on some points and the other prevail on others. But finally a decision adjudicating how to distribute the property and ruling on each person's demands will be issued. Most likely the reasons for the decision will appear logical and obvious to the winner and outrageous, subjective, and irrational to the loser.

APPEAL AND ENFORCEMENT

Having endured months or years of delay, discovery, and trial, everyone will feel exhausted, depressed, and relieved that the end has come—whatever the trial's outcome. In many instances the parties comply with the terms of the decision and the end has arrived, but often you are just beginning the fourth phase of litigation: appeal and enforcement.

One of the reasons people choose litigation, you will recall, is that it allows you to appeal to a higher court. In most states *any* decision can be appealed to at least one higher-level judge. On appeal generally there is no new trial; instead, each side's attorney presents a written (and maybe an oral) argument, and the record of the trial is typed up for the appeals judges to read. But this process alone can take as long as a year, and in complex cases the appellate briefs and transcripts can cost each side as much as $20,000—or more.

In most states the decision will only be overturned if the appellate justices determine there was not any evidence to support the winner or if the basic legal rules were not followed. For example, if your state doesn't have clear rules about the enforceability of oral contracts between lovers about real estate and the trial court threw out your oral contract claim, the appellate court may uphold that decision or decide to seize on your troubles and establish a precedent allowing oral contract claims. But reversals of domestic disputes are rare; most decisions are upheld, and thus an appeal only means more delay and higher costs.

Once the case is really over and all appeals have been exhausted, the winning side has the right to enforce its victory, one of the key reasons some people prefer the legal system. If you doubt whether your ex-lover will sign over the property or divide the bank account as the court has ordered, the legal system will be there to enforce your victory. The process can be time-consuming and expensive, especially if court orders are needed and assets hard to discover, but if you persist you will prevail. But remember: if you are seeking a monetary payment (rather than a share of property) the court cannot manufacture money if there is none to be found—or if your ex files for bankruptcy.

Enforcement is usually a multistep process. If the loser doesn't pay or sign documents as ordered, you need to serve legal papers, and, then, if he continues to refuse, you have to pay the sheriff a few hundred dollars to get your money or seize the property. The sheriff can impound bank accounts, go after wages, or even stand at a store's cash register and seize the cash each night to pay you. If your ex-lover refuses to sign over a deed to property the court ordered should be yours, the judge can sign the deed. It's a messy process, but in the end you will receive what you have won.

The Downsides of Litigation

While court action offers the finality of a judgment and the power of enforcement, it has a few very negative aspects. First, it is usually *very* expensive. It is unlikely any attorney will take a dissolution case on contingency (where you pay nothing up front but turn over a percentage of your financial recovery to the attorney), so you are stuck paying her or him on an hourly basis. Hourly fees for attorneys can range from $100 per hour on the low side in small towns and rural areas or for less-experienced attorneys to more than $300 per hour for top flight big-city lawyers.

In most instances this hourly rate applies only to the time the lawyer spends directly on your case, so you don't pay extra for secretarial time, office space, legal research, books, or computer time, but you may be required to pay out-of-pocket expenses such as copying, postage, and delivery services. Court fees are low, usually less than $250, since the taxpayers pick up the tab for the judges, clerks, and courtroom expenses (finally, here is something in return for all the taxes you have paid!).

A hotly contested case can take fifty to one hundred hours of an attorney's time. You spend five hours telling your story to your attorney and asking questions; your attorney spends five hours writing up pleadings and ten hours on the phone and writing letters trying to settle the case. Then she or he spends three days going through documents, researching legal issues, and dealing with outside experts, plus two days interviewing the key witnesses and organizing the facts. If your trial lasts three days, you'll quickly reach a total of one hundred hours of attorney time.

In nastier cases there may be prolonged arguments about the relevant legal concepts, with a lot of research to be done and many briefs to be written. There may be discovery battles, long sessions with accountants and appraisers, and repeated settlement meetings and mediation sessions that end in naught. Thus, even at the lower hourly rates it is not unusual to spend $10,000 to $20,000 or even more to resolve a relatively simple dispute.

Not only do you have to pay your lawyer's fees, but the legal system is unforgiving, so everything along the line is expensive. It can take hours to reschedule a hearing date. Papers need to be written, calls made, and someone needs to drive to the courthouse and submit a request. Your attorney may have to wait around for an hour or two while the judge considers the request and makes a ruling, and then written notices have to be prepared and sent out.

Another downside of the litigation process is that courthouses and the law are ill equipped to handle same-sex dissolutions. Unlike heterosexual divorces, which are handled in special family courts with trained counselors, specially written rules, detailed procedures, and judges who specialize in domestic cases, same-sex dissolutions are usually assigned to the regular court system. You get in line with the mega-corporate battles, personal injury claims, and small-business disputes. It's likely that the laws' vagueness is only worsened by the arena's coldness and the inexperience and brooding resentment of judges assigned to handle these cases.

You may think that since both parties are homosexual, homophobia won't hurt you—but it will. Some judges mistreat both sides equally, so neither side will have a fair chance to tell its story. Others will be inclined to deny whatever claim is being made, so the plaintiff is at the greatest disadvantage. In some towns the judge's displeasure at having to hear the gory details of a lover's quarrel will be so apparent as to motivate both sides to accept a compromise neither would have previously considered.

Don't deceive yourself into thinking that living in a big city or being openly gay exempts you from this problem! Judges can be the most conservative people in town, so you may find yourself encountering serious discrimination. I've seen straight sixty-year-old WASP male judges handle lesbian real estate divorces with a dignity, clarity, and calm that meets any standard of objectivity, fairness, and equity, and the professionalism and sophistication of many judges can lead to some refreshing surprises, but many experiences are extremely negative.

Putting your fate in the hands of the tax-supported court system also means you are coming out. I've seen lawyers try to conceal their client's homosexuality under the guise of a business conflict or real estate investment battle, and if the town gossips read only the official lawsuit listings the romantic undertones of the battle may not be recognized. But show up in court and start arguing over who owns the car or who should get the pets, and your closet door has been opened. And it's not just your closet door that's been opened: the most intimate stories of your breakup are on display. Courtrooms are public places where reporters and curious townspeople can sit and watch. If you've been keeping your personal life private and you want to continue to do so, litigation is going to cause you enormous problems.

Because of all these inconveniences and expenses, litigation just seems designed to make everyone miserable. It is adversarial, formal, contentious, and unpleasant. Lawyers litigate because it helps their clients if they win and it can be very lucrative, but there is no reason anyone else should get involved. Even if you win your case, you will be emotionally and financially drained and angry at your ex-lover. You may be encouraged to exaggerate your claims and inflate your demands, and you will be forced to sit by as your attorney attacks the person you used to love. You may think it will be pleasurable to inflict pain on someone who has rejected you, but the joy will soon fade. Every lashing of the legal whip will cost you a lot, and chances are you will suffer as much as your ex.

SELECTING THE RIGHT APPROACH

Here are the main factors to consider when selecting from the above approaches to resolve your dispute. Remember, though, for the most part you can always switch gears along the way, so long as you both are willing to do so.

1. Unless your partner is impossible to deal with, won't talk with you, or won't follow through on any of the promises he or she makes, avoid litigation. The formal court system is far too impersonal, too rigid, too slow, and, for most people, far too expensive for all but the nastiest of domestic battles.
2. If you think the two of you can work together on a solution, first try direct discussions or formal mediation without attorneys. You'll save thousands of dollars, and you may reach an amicable resolution. If you can't, little time or money has been lost.
3. If a solution is close at hand but you are having trouble getting yourself heard or finalizing things, bring in lawyers or professional mediators to help (one should work here), but establish a limited budget of time and money and commit to avoiding litigation. Don't allow the mediation process to de-

plete all your energies or exhaust your savings—you will need some of each later on if matters are not quickly resolved.

4. If mediation or negotiation has stalled, opt for binding arbitration. Appeals rarely lead to reversals in domestic matters, whereas arbitration allows you to pick the judge and have a hearing quickly. This should cost you less than a trial, the decisions are usually based on the same principles as they are in court, and the results are usually just as fair. You can select a gay-friendly arbitrator and keep the procedures confidential, and you may not need an attorney for the hearing. But if you do plan to handle it yourself, spend a few hours with an attorney beforehand to be sure you know how to present your case.

DEALING WITH THE STUCK SITUATION

In an ideal world the two of you would sit down together, present your points of view, and promptly compromise any disputed issues. You'd proceed to implement your settlement, transferring property and dividing up assets as you've agreed to do. There would be no need for attorneys, no need for protracted mediation sessions, no long, drawn-out delays as you argue and complain. But real life is rarely that simple! Some separations *are* amicable, and there are instances when there's nothing to fight over, either because the parties resolve everything promptly or because the couple has few possessions. But more frequently there are battles big and small.

The standard divorce proceeding isn't painless, but the process is mandatory, and it usually works quickly and relatively cheaply. The court issues forms that can be filled out without an attorney's help. Once the petitioner sets forth her claims and arguments, the other side (labeled the respondent) submits written answers. Designated judges hear disputes about possession of the house, payment of the bills, and custody of the kids. Many states mandate that the parties enter into counseling or mediation, which is often provided free of charge. If there are matters that can't be resolved amicably, a quick and efficiently run trial is held.

Same-sex couples who are unable to reach a resolution but won't agree to an alternative process such as arbitration usually are left with only two second-rate options: personal pressure by one party (or her attorney) or filing a full-scale lawsuit in civil court without any of the expedited forms or procedures of divorce court. There is no single solution for the stuck situation, but there are several ways to improve things. If you are persistent and pay close attention to the obstacles before you, one of the following methods may very well work.

What's the Problem?
Make a serious effort to understand why things are stuck. If disputes can't be readily resolved you may need an outside arbitrator for even just one issue. Take your ex's position seriously and attempt to understand why there's dissension, and, if the conflict is legal, try compromising or moving straight to arbitration. But if the problem is emotional—either anger at the separation or punishment for past misconduct—decide if you can deal with the feelings. If you can, put aside the practical battle and try to heal the emotional wounds, and, if that is impossible, be prepared to wait it out or turn to the legal system. If you are going to deal with the emotional issues, hire a counselor to help you.

The Passive-Aggressive Partner
If there is no genuine reason for the delays, your ex simply may not want to deal with the unpleasant realities of the situation. One of you may see prolonging the battle as a way to stay in touch with an ex, one may be overwhelmed by work and not want to face these unpleasantries, or, in some cases, the practical results of a resolution, such as having to move out of your house, will be a burden.

If this is what is happening you have two options: either accelerate the resolution by making it *more* difficult not to resolve things or yield to the resistance and embrace the delay. If you are eager to move forward, you may want to make more phone calls, write letters, and present legal arguments so your ex realizes there is no escape from the problems. You may wish to point out that delays will only force you to take legal action. If, on the other hand, postponing the battle makes sense, be sure to structure your living arrangements to avoid creating worse financial imbalances.

Listen to Me!

If you can't get your ex-partner to deal with you at all, create some less-threatening events to bring you together in order to open the door to discussion. Meet to talk about the pets, have a common friend invite you over to see what can be done, or write a letter proposing that you take a walk and *not* talk about the heavy stuff. Any of these suggestions should begin to loosen up the tension and, over time, make it possible to take on the more sensitive subjects.

Is There a Lawyer in the House?

Try using an attorney to push the process along. Most folks are *really* uncomfortable having to deal with lawyers and lawsuits. If you explain to your ex in writing that you are only using an attorney because she or he won't deal with you directly, and if your attorney, acting under your direction, makes it clear she will back off if there's any reasonable response to the threats of legal action, you may be able to cajole your ex back to the table.

Put It in Writing

If every attempt at a direct discussion of the hot issues blows up, put together your own written proposal that focuses on solutions rather than on justifications. Ask your ex to respond in writing, again focusing only on the practical solutions rather than arguing her points. A series of nonemotional letters that point to real solutions and avoid dogma or diatribe may eventually lead to a resolution.

Meet with an Expert

If the impasse appears totally irresolvable, try meeting with a skilled professional either on your own or with your ex. A few hours with an accountant, realtor, attorney, or even a therapist might unblock some of the sticking points and provide a fresh perspective on a frozen dilemma.

Organize Your Affairs

In order to avoid the cumulative impacts of getting stuck, try to protect yourself by avoiding situations that put you under severe time pressures. If you must close on a home or buy a car *now*, you are making yourself vulnerable to threats of delay. The more stable your situation the less incentive there is for others to take advantage of your predicament.

Part of the self-protection strategy means building up your own structure of support, both financial and personal. Have the courage to ask for loans from friends and relatives if you need them, find a place to live if you think it is going to take a few months to sort out your property conflicts, and get counseling for your anger at your ex. Self-destructive delays may feel empowering in the short run, but you will surely become a victim of your actions in the long run.

One of the most difficult decisions you will ever make is whether to give in to the demands of an unreasonable ex-lover. Before you reject a settlement you feel is unfair, think seriously about what it will cost to continue fighting. But if you offer a compromise, make sure it is not confused with giving in too early, which may only empower your partner to demand even more.

If you are considering getting tough—either by delaying a resolution or grabbing for more than you deserve—remember that your relationship (1) involves two people who once were in love and (2) involves two homosexuals. Bearing these inescapable premises in mind, think about these four points:

Remember the love you used to feel. This is not a stranger you are dealing with, it's your ex-lover, and whatever went wrong happened in the context of a relationship that, at least for a while, went right. Don't blame your ex for the loss of the love, as his or her friendship is worth more than any house or furniture.

Remember you are a member of a community. You are a member of a special community and have suffered discrimination and hardships. Chances are, the only reason you weren't legally married is because of this discrimination. Do not turn this comrade into your enemy! Be flexible, be cooperative, and see the big picture.

Display your nobler values. Lesbians and gay men have been fighting for years for equal rights, and if we respond to our own conflicts selfishly we provide justification for those who would like to deny us our rights.

End a relationship, but make a new friend. Especially for those without close ties to their families of origin, staying connected to ex-lovers is one of the most valuable ways that lesbians and gay men create extended families. Keep your eyes focused on retaining your ex-lover as a newfound friend, and try to allow this goal to steer you through the tough times.

DOCUMENTING YOUR SEPARATION

If your case is resolved by arbitration or litigation, the resolutions will be imposed in a decision issued by the arbitrator or judge. But most of you *eventually* will resolve your conflicts by agreement. The last thing you want to endure is future battles over what precisely was agreed to, so put it in writing. If one of you refuses to sign a legally binding agreement, then this so-called agreement doesn't deserve to be called such.

The agreement doesn't need to be notarized or witnessed (unless you think there will be subsequent charges or forgery or, in some states, if real estate is involved), but it must be clearly written and signed by both of you. If you've worked things out on your own or a lot of property is at stake, you should hire an attorney to write the agreement—or at least review what you've written—to be sure you haven't created any ambiguities or inconsistencies or forgotten to resolve some major issue.

Here is what should be included in every settlement agreement:

1. Describe which conflicts you are resolving now and which (if any) you are leaving for later resolution; if possible, agree on a procedure and a time line for resolving any unresolved matters.
2. State in clear terms who is getting what property (real and personal), how the assets and debts are going to be divided, and how the nonmonetary issues are going to be resolved.
3. Establish a time line and procedure for carrying out the terms of your agreement; be sure to include an allocation of any costs or duties, such as taxes on transferring property or the expense of moving your furniture.
4. If your agreement covers all your disputes, state that clearly so neither of you comes back later to reopen any arguments.
5. Decide who is paying the fees incurred in the resolution process, and include a mediation and/or arbitration provision to resolve any conflicts about the agreement that subsequently arise.

Don't forget the one essential last step: *carry out the provisions of your agreement*! If you set the tasks aside for too long, years may go by and you may then find it more difficult, more expensive, and, in some cases, even impossible to implement the agreement.

Property transfers are the most complex task to implement. In some states you will need to have an attorney or title company draft the transfer documents, and in some cities a hefty transfer tax is charged, even where heterosexual divorces are exempt from the tax. Visits to a notary will be required, and consultation with a tax accountant is frequently needed. All these steps take time and cost money, both of which you may be short of, but don't let things slide. Procrastination can be expensive. Ex-lovers who move away make it hard to get a deed signed. Documents get lost, and deadlines for implementation expire. When you try to sell the property you may have to recontact your ex and try to work things out. This is inevitably going to be a painful process, so get it done now and move on.

THE USE AND ABUSE OF LAWYERS

One of the most difficult decisions you will need to make is when to use a lawyer. Everyone has strong feelings on this subject and each situation presents it own challenges, but here are a few tips on how to approach this particular task.

1. If a significant amount of money or any real estate is involved in your dissolution or if either of you faces a large amount of debt, consult an attorney for at least an hour or so for advice. There are some terrible pitfalls that can await an unknowing couple, and you should be equipped with the basic knowledge before you make any substantive decisions. Select an attorney who has experience representing unmarried couples, gay or straight, and have a list of questions for him. This process should cost you less than $200, and it is definitely money well spent.

Sandra was about to buy out her lover Erika's half interest in their house without knowing that Sandra could face a recalling of the mortgage upon transfer and a reassessment for property tax purposes. Sandra was also going to pay a price that was quite excessive, given the property's serious defects. Sandra's lawyer was able to educate her about the financial consequences of the buyout and show her how to assess the real value of what she was buying. The settlement was delayed a bit as a result of Sandra's revised demands, but in the end she was able to refinance the property, split the costs of the refinancing with Erika, and negotiate a lower price by getting an appraisal that showed why the property had a lower value than was previously thought. Erika was convinced to accept this deal once Sandra pointed out what her lawyer had told her abut how she could force a sale if the dispute wasn't settled, to both women's financial detriment.

2. If you are facing serious disputes but feel able to handle the process emotionally, I still recommend you hire an attorney as a "consultant" and then continue to manage most of the process on your own. You may want your lawyer to advise you on strategies and review your letters, and she or he can also clarify at what point you have a decent argument and when you should settle your dispute because, legally speaking, your claim is a losing one. If you focus your questions and make efficient use of the lawyer's advice, the consultation process overall shouldn't cost much more than $1,000.

Peter had reached an informal agreement with Randy, his ex-lover, regarding reimbursement for contributions Peter had made to Randy's business. But the agreement got sidetracked by an angry disagreement about who was going to pay one of the business's biggest outstanding bills. Peter met with an attorney who pointed out the strengths of Peter's claims but also showed him the difficulty of going to court. She also reviewed Peter's letters to excise the diatribes and focus Peter on the key issues, and she convinced him to cover half the debt if he could get the reimbursement he felt he deserved. Peter had to compromise a bit, but soon an agreement was reached and his attorney helped him draft a binding settlement agreement, thus assuring him that Randy wouldn't come after him for any money later on.

3. If you think the dispute can be resolved by arbitration but you really aren't equipped, emotionally or skill-wise, to handle it alone, you should seriously evaluate the pros and cons of hiring an attorney. Even in a moderately simple case the attorney's fees can run as high as $5,000, so you will have to analyze whether you can afford this and whether it is worth

it. If you are fighting over the equity in a house or business and the amount at stake is significant, and if you have trouble articulating yourself or can't deal with your ex, you should definitely consider hiring an attorney to tell you the best way to frame your argument, make the written demands and propose a settlement, and give you candid advice as to when you should cut your losses and make a compromise settlement.

Leona was on title as a fifty-fifty owner of her house with her lover, Amanda, but Amanda had contributed 80 percent of the down payment. Leona considered herself a half owner since she had contributed months of labor for a renovation and because Amanda had always told her the house was theirs, equally. A binding arbitration was scheduled, and Leona felt totally unable to present her side of the story. Leona's lawyer, however, managed to win 40 percent of the sales proceeds for her. While it wasn't a total victory, Leona ended up with nearly $30,000 more than she feared she would get, even after she paid her attorney.

4. If litigation is necessary or if you have been sued, you must consult with an attorney for at least part of the process. This can become very expensive if you need the attorney to handle the entire procedure, often as much as or more than $10,000. If this is unacceptable, you need to give serious consideration to settling the case early on. Court procedures are far too intimidating to most people, and, if they are not handled correctly, serious damage can occur.

Carl had contributed half of the money to pay for the purchase of a house, but the title was put in Phil's name alone because of Carl's bad credit history. When they broke up Phil ordered Carl to leave "his" house, but Carl's attorney filed a lawsuit immediately and got an injunction preventing Phil from evicting him or selling the house. This one action forced

Phil to the bargaining table, and he came without an attorney. After one mediation session Phil agreed to pay Carl $30,000 for his contributions. If Carl hadn't used a skillful attorney to file immediate court action, the house could have been sold and he might never have received anything.

When deciding whom to hire as your attorney, make sure you select someone who knows the rules affecting unmarried couples—lawyers who handle traditional divorces often are not experienced in this area. A lesbian or gay attorney can make you feel comfortable during a difficult process, but experience and skill are more important than sexuality here. Be sure to think carefully about your goals when you hire an attorney: if you hope to reach a compromise settlement—as you should—choose an attorney who has a balanced disposition and is open to compromise instead of someone who sees the process as an opportunity to go to bat for every dollar. Make sure you get references, set a precise budget with your attorney, and give clear directions so he or she knows how best to help you.

You will also need to decide whether to hire a single lawyer jointly or whether you each need your own attorney. Usually each side will need her or his own attorney, but if you are basically in accord and only need your attorney to help you finalize your agreement and work out the details, a single lawyer will be fine. Keep in mind that if you hire a single attorney and you don't finalize the settlement, neither of you will be able to hire him to help you individually.

8

Home Is Where
the Heart *Was*

The Seven Commandments
of Resolving House Disputes

1. Know that this is going to be difficult. It always is.
2. Resolve your emotional conflicts elsewhere—the house dispute should be viewed primarily as a practical matter.
3. Renters' disputes are easier to resolve than homeowners'.
4. Living arrangements are part of your love affair, not a business deal, so don't feel inadequate if nothing is in writing and memories are vague.
5. The legal system is inappropriate for resolving housing conflicts, but if you have to use it, make it work for you.
6. If you co-own a house with your ex, prepare to:
   - Assess the financial realities before you start negotiating.
   - Learn what the law says about your particular situation.
   - Figure out what your goals are, and know your bottom line.
   - Select a resolution process that's appropriate to your needs.
   - Be prepared for a lengthy process, and set up a good support system.
   - Be prepared to compromise.
7. You're dealing with your ex-lover, so don't expect her or him to heal your hurt feelings. Make a deal, and move on!

EVERY HOME WEARS THREE HATS

Sorting through issues involving the apartment, condominium, or house you lived in together as a couple has the potential of becoming a fierce battle, regardless of who is initiating the separation. Only disputes over children are more contentious, so if there are no kids to fight over, the "battle of the house" can be *the* most brutal one.

This shouldn't be surprising. Whether you are renters or homeowners your residence has served three vital functions. First, it is the place you lived and where you shared your greatest joys. It's where you savored your romantic nights together, it's been the focus of many of your labors and talents, and it's the hearth where you stoked your domestic fires.

Second, whether you rent or own, your home is a major investment. Renters pour time and energy into improvements and moving out can be expensive, and if you're an owner your home probably represents your major financial asset. Salvaging your fair share of the equity is going to be vital to your financial well-being.

Third, your home may be a powerful symbol of your relationship, as moving in together is as close as many of us get to exchanging vows. To our families and friends it's what makes us a couple, it exemplifies stability, and our homes often become a repository of our love and commitment.

Whatever your feelings, put the soap opera on hold and focus on protecting your investment and making sensible and practical arrangements. The key to solving your housing conflicts is to accept the end of the relationship, acknowledge that one or both of you has got to find a new place to live, and admit that the breakup is going to be expensive for the two of you. If you both can accept these unavoidable facts and be flexible in the way you resolve the debates, you should be able to sort things out in a less painful and less costly way than if you do not.

RENTERS, REJOICE!

The legal and emotional conflicts for renters are usually easier to conquer than they are for homeowners. The financial consequences are usually more manageable, too. You should therefore try to settle your disputes quickly yet effectively.

Your first task is to determine your *joint* legal obligations to the landlord by reviewing your lease carefully. If it states that you are obligated to stay a certain length of time, that doesn't prevent you from moving out. It may, however, mean you could owe your landlord for lost rent while he or she finds a new tenant or that you may owe the landlord something for the reduced rental income if the only available new tenant negotiates a lower rent.

If both you and your lover are planning to move out, you will need to decide how to handle these potential liabilities. The best option is to find a replacement tenant willing to pay the same rent you paid or to make a deal with your landlord limiting your financial exposure. If neither of these options is possible and you both want to leave, you'll need to draft an agreement between yourselves that sets out who pays up if the landlord sues. If such an outcome looks likely, it's a good idea to obtain the advice of a landlord-tenant lawyer before you make any final decisions.

Another option is for one of you to stay put until the lease expires and even take a roommate to help pay the rent if necessary. *Assume* the landlord will come after you for unpaid rent if she doesn't find a replacement tenant, and *don't* simply pack up and move out without reaching an agreement on these issues. If there's a realistic prospect of financial liability to the landlord, decide which one of you is going to handle the demand for payment. A letter agreement is sufficient so long as both of you sign and date it.

If one of you wants to stay put, you need to decide whether the one who remains should pay anything to the one who departs for improvements you've made together or for any furniture that stays behind, and you'll need to make arrangements for distributing the security deposit when it's collected. The best solution is to get the lease rewritten so the departing one is taken off the lease and gets her deposit back and the remaining one signs a new lease and pays a new deposit. Change the names on the utility accounts, take care of the outstanding phone bills, and sort out who owes whom for what.

In some cities, like San Francisco and New York, you'll also need to think about any rights you might have under local rent control laws. Depending on your local ordinance, there may be a preliminary question of who is the *legal* tenant and, therefore, who is entitled to benefit from the rent control protections. If there's any doubt about how your local laws work, seek assistance from an attorney who knows them.

If one of you wants to remain in the apartment, you'll need to resolve whether to pay any compensation to the departing one for moving expenses, new utility hookups and phone service, and possibly the costs of new appliances and furniture. If the rent at the old place is high and you're both avoiding a lawsuit by having one of you stay put, the person who is departing should contribute something to those expenses. The amount at stake probably isn't that large, so try to reach a compromise.

If you are really stuck and can't reach a compromise, it's usually better for one or both of you to move out fairly soon, agree on a temporary arrangement, and argue about the money later on. Binding arbitration is a perfect way to handle this kind of dispute, so at the outset write up a letter of agreement committing yourselves to participating in binding arbitration. This will ease both partners' minds about the temporary arrangements, as they will know that the person who pays money up front isn't barred from seeking reimbursement later on.

When it comes to the move-out, decide on the furniture division ahead of time to avoid any scenes while the movers are there. Each of you should take a friend along to calm everyone down in case something gets out of control. If necessary, ask a friend to negotiate the arrangements. If it's going to take awhile to work out the details, make sure you've made arrangements to cover the interim costs and security. Be aware that the police will rarely intercede if a dispute arises unless it gets violent, but if violence appears imminent, by all means seek police assistance.

A Checklist for Separating Your Household If You're a Renter

1. Assess your options: decide if either of you wants to stay put.
2. Assess your legal situation to see if you face any major liabilities.
3. Make an agreement about the apartment, and arrange to cover moving costs if only one of you is moving on.
4. Agree in writing on the schedule of moving or staying put.
5. If there are areas of disagreement, itemize them and set up a method of resolving them after you've moved out.
6. Take care of the details with the landlord and the movers.
7. Organize the move-out so as to minimize the emotional dramas.
8. Pay the bills and balance the accounts so that you leave a clean slate.

YOUR HOUSE IS A HOME

Start by acknowledging that resolving co-ownership of your home is not going to be simple. Straight couples have the relatively efficient divorce court to help them solve their problems, but until lesbians and gay men can legally marry, the more cumbersome regular court system is all we have. Since it's not set up to handle domestic disputes like ours, it won't be of much help, and it's far too expensive, too adversarial, and too slow. Thus, we are left mostly to our own devices when it comes to implementing efficient solutions.

Who Gets to Live Where, Short-Term?

The first question you will face is who gets to live where while you resolve the larger ownership issues. Given your likely emotional state, securing decent and affordable housing may be of paramount importance. It is also easier to resolve the other disputes once both of you have secured temporary housing. If you have a written agreement covering this issue, if only one of you is the owner of the house, or if you can agree on what your oral agreement was, start there. If your agreement specifies who is assigned the first option to stay in the house, you can always jointly change that arrangement.

The next step is to figure out how to make financial sense of the interim arrangements. Decide who pays what until the ownership issues are settled and who has to take care of which tasks. The one staying in the house typically pays more than the one moving into an apartment, but since many of the housing costs cover your investment (the mortgage) rather than just the actual rental value, the one who has moved out probably should still contribute something. The fairest option is to combine the total housing costs of both of you and split that amount according to the relative rental value of the two places. Since it may take a year or more to reach a final resolution of these matters, be sure to put your interim arrangements in writing.

If the answers to these questions aren't covered in your preexisting agreement or if you don't have a preexisting agreement, you'll need to consider carefully a temporary arrangement. For example, is the house spacious enough to accommodate the two of you if you don't share a bed? Keep in mind that you can deal with the immediate needs on an interim basis without prejudicing the resolution of your long-term solutions. For some couples there is often a pressing circumstance, say, a new job, a heavy travel schedule, or a particular family or medical need, that may make it necessary for one of you to stay.

Be honest about your financial limitations. Unless you can handle the payments, either by yourself or with a housemate or new lover, it doesn't make sense for you to fight to stay in the house, unless you can negotiate a favorable deal with your ex. In some instances the long-term ownership outcomes are fairly predictable, and it only makes sense that they should affect the short term as it is expensive for anyone to move twice. Check into the tax consequences of moving out before you sell the house since doing so may jeopardize your right to shelter any profits from its sale.

When putting your interim plan in writing, make it clear that the short-term occupancy does *not* determine who gets the house long-term. Set a deadline for resolving the larger issues, and stick to it. Commit to meeting occasionally to discuss needed repairs and improvements, and agree that, except in an emergency, the one living in the house won't make major decisions without consulting the other one.

If you are going to sell the property jointly, you will want the one living in the house to be tidy and responsible to help market it. If significant renovation work is being done in connection with the marketing, you may want to reduce the remaining person's share of the monthly costs, depending on what the nonoccupant has to pay for his own housing. If money is *really* tight, prioritize which bills absolutely must get paid. It's usually okay to postpone the property taxes for a while, even though some small penalty may be incurred, but do not let the insurance lapse or the mortgage loan go into default.

If you can't reach an agreement, try informal mediation or have an outside decision maker, either an arbitrator, a mutual friend, or a counselor, determine the occupancy issue. You could even flip a coin or auction off the right to stay in the house, granting the privilege to whichever one of you is willing to pay more for the right to do so.

You could even agree that *neither* of you will stay in the house and try to rent it out to a third party. This can be tricky, as you're entering into a real estate business with your ex by jointly renting out property that used to be your home. If you choose this option, you should definitely see an attorney to draft up a detailed partnership agreement that covers the obligations for maintenance and the rights to the rental income. If the rental income is less than the monthly mortgage, you'll have to decide how to allocate this shortfall.

If all else fails and the emotional heat is rising to an unacceptable temperature, there are two legal last-resort options to consider. If one person has become violent or is threatening violence or physical harm to the property, the "nicer" one may be able to obtain a court restraining order requiring that the offending ex stay away from the property. This usually can be done without an attorney and is not very expensive, and in most states you can convene a very quick court hearing. Some judges, however, consider this a backdoor kind of eviction and may rebuff the effort, though often they can be sympathetic and helpful. In fact, serving papers seeking a restraining order has a magical ability to get everyone's attention, which quite often leads to a quick resolution of the possession debate.

The second option is to file a lawsuit and seek a preliminary injunction for possession while you await a trial on ownership, which can be more than a year away. While both parties legally have the right to remain in the house as long as they pay a fair share of the costs, a court proceeding usually forces each person to hire an attorney and show up in court, which alone almost always results in a settlement of the possession issue and an allocation of the costs pending trial.

Who Gets the House, Long-Term?

The more critical possession question to resolve is what is going to happen to the house long-term. If neither of you wants or is able to purchase it alone, then admit early on that selling it outright is your only option. Tougher conflicts arise when *both* of you want to and are able to buy out the other one and stay on. Practical as well as financial considerations should apply in deciding who is going to buy and who is going to sell since the buyer may have to obtain a new mortgage in his or her name alone. If one of you owned the house before the relationship began or one person owns most of the equity, it only makes sense for that person to stay put and buy out the other's lesser interest.

Consider as well who *needs* the house more. Depending on your emotional state, employment status, and financial capacity, one of you may be more or less able to move on. If one of you has custody of the children, it's likely you'll need a stable home environment. The school district may also be an important factor.

If one of you wants to stay on as sole owner, you may have to make some arrangements with your lender. Taking one person's name off the loan agreement may not be easy since the departing one may insist on being released from any future liability and the remaining one may not earn enough to qualify by himself. In some states homeowners are not really personally liable for most home loans, since the bank will seize the house if you don't pay, and won't come after your personal bank account. If this is so in your state, the departing one shouldn't worry about having to pay the mortgage, but staying on the loan agreement *may* give you a problem if you want to buy a new house or create credit problems for both of you if the mortgage isn't promptly paid. If getting a new loan is too difficult or expensive, you should at least consider staying on the loan agreement rather than having to sell the place. In this event you should definitely have an attorney alert you to the risks and draft an agreement allocating the potential liabilities.

You'll also need to be sure that the quitclaim or grant deed taking one of you off the title is properly recorded, and this may also cost you something. It's essential that you follow through on this, though, since you don't want to find yourself having to track down your ex years later to sign a deed. Since these expenses are inevitable when one partner wants to keep the house, it's essential that you get an estimate on them and agree on their allocation before making a final decision. You should split these separation costs equally, without trying to put them on the back of just one of you.

Carrying Out a Buyout Deal

If you've agreed that one of you is going to stay in the house and buy out the other's interest, you'll need to set a value for the interest purchased, and decide who pays any fees and whether the purchasing party is coming up with all cash or paying off the purchase over time. In setting the price for the buyout, you'll need to decide whether you are using a value based on an appraised value as of the date of separation or as reduced by the costs of sale the buyer may face in a few years if he wants to sell the property. Sales commissions and escrow fees can eat up 8 to 10 percent of the property's value, and at some point someone is going to have to pay them.

In addition to handling the paperwork of the deed transfer, you'll need to tackle the seemingly endless details of the move-out, deciding about furniture, utilities, and appliances. You'll need to decide who handles the interim payments, insurance, and prepaid property taxes and who pays the moving costs of the one who is moving on. Try to keep calm and stick to the business at hand here. If your ex won't cooperate, bring along a third person or deal through a neutral intermediary.

If you can't reach an agreement about the mechanics of a transfer, even when you've agreed in principle as to who is getting the house, try an interim housing solution while you set up a procedure for resolving the outstanding items and issues. Be clear about the terms of this bridge solution, and put it in writing. Be fair about who should pay the costs during the transition period. If the monthly costs exceed the property's fair rental value, the one moving out should probably contribute something extra. On the other hand, if the monthly costs are less than the reasonable rental value, the one staying behind should fork over part of that benefit to his ex to help cover *his* rental costs.

Partition procedures (the technical term for a real estate divorce in the civil courts) offer little immediate help on the interim aspects of a co-ownership dispute. You won't want to file a lawsuit just to resolve a few little details, especially if you've already agreed in principle on who is going to buy the other one out, though be prepared to take legal action if nothing else works. Since *both* co-owners have equal rights to occupy the property, neither owner has the right to kick the other one out unless *all* the questions of ownership are resolved. If you've signed an agreement that covers this situation or if the resident occupant isn't living up to her or his regular obligations, you might be able to "eject" (that's the legal term for evicting a co-owner, who, technically, is not a tenant) your co-owner.

Try to resolve the disputes through mediation, and, if that fails, propose a quickly scheduled arbitration hearing with a privately hired arbitrator to focus just on the disputed issues. You may even need to hire an attorney to help you straighten things out. If you use an outside representative, whether it's an attorney, therapist, or friend, and you tell her your bottom-line concerns, he or she should be able to work out a reasonable deal with your ex-lover's representative.

Why does this all get so difficult, even after you've resolved the basic issues? At times it's the result of underlying emotional conflicts, especially if one of the parties doesn't really want to move on. In other instances there will be genuine disputes about practical arrangements or finances. I've had clients resolve conflicts involving hundreds of thousands of dollars and then come to blows over the scheduling of the move-out or the blocking of the driveway by a parked car. Be patient, be practical, and try to compromise.

Here's a checklist of the most commonly recurring possession questions.

1. Who wants to and who can afford to stay put, either by herself or with a roommate?
2. What are the real costs of keeping the house, and do they exceed the property's fair rental value?
3. What housing options does the departing partner really have, and what help will she or he need to get settled in a new place?
4. Where are the kids or the pets going to live, and how does that affect the decisions about the house?
5. How do your interim decisions about the house affect the long-term questions about it?
6. How will possession decisions impact the sale of the house, and how can these matters be managed in your mutual best interests?

THE HOUSE AS YOUR INVESTMENT

The laws regarding same-sex dissolutions are particularly gray when it comes to the financial component of property disputes. Since few couples have written agreements and the legal questions can have significant financial ramifications, dividing up the funds is rarely easy.

What makes this situation particularly painful is that for most of us the house represents the primary—if not the *sole* asset—for one or both parties. In many San Francisco neighborhoods, for example, down payments can exceed $25,000 for a simple bungalow. Mortgage payments are sometimes high as well, often in excess of $2,000 a month, so house equity may be the only savings any of us have. Whether you've just bought a place or you've been living together in one for a long time, appreciation, one hopes, has led to a significant nest egg. The problem is that the "egg" is locked tightly in a *non*liquid nest called real estate. If the egg isn't "removed" carefully, it can break and much of your accumulated equity will drain away.

Compounding the dilemma is the astoundingly mercurial value of real estate. Couples breaking up in the middle of a renovation or during an economic crisis are bound to face problems selling their house, and, short of selling the place, it's hard to know exactly what it's really worth. Depending on what's happening in the real estate market when you break up and on the condition of the property, property values could drop as much as 20 percent in a year or two. Most people don't realize until it's too late that if your down payment was 15 percent and you have to pay a 6 percent commission to sell the place, a 20 percent drop in value will wipe out your entire investment.

Resolving the financial issues begins with following the trail of the law, starting with your deed and your agreement, if you have one. The deed states who owns the property and, if the parties thought about it ahead of time, what percentage each one owns. See if you're holding the property in joint tenancy, which means your ex will inherit it if you die before it's sold. If that's not what you'd prefer given the recent circumstances, you should immediately convert it to tenancy-in-common and then write a will naming someone else—perhaps your *new* favorite—as your beneficiary. The change-of-ownership form can usually be accomplished by simply filing a deed yourself, but if you're confused, check with a local attorney or a title company on the procedures.

A well-written cotenancy agreement will set forth who owns what portion of the house, how to sell it, how to reimburse each other for contributions, and how to divide up the proceeds of sale if it is sold. An agreement will also cover compensation for improvements, payment for debts or delinquencies, and a method of resolving disputes about the property's value and the sales procedures.

Here are some common real estate finance problems that recur whether or not you have an agreement and some suggestions on how to resolve them:

Who controls the process? In theory you are supposed to work together, but often that simply won't happen. Imagine trying to tell your real estate broker how to respond to a purchase offer when you can't even decide who gets to keep the VCR or trying to settle a dispute over the value of your home when you can't decide what the car is worth. In such cases I recommend you either appoint a neutral third party to handle these issues or each use an attorney or representative. If you don't settle things quickly you can often spend more in legal fees to resolve the disputes than they are really worth.

Who absorbs the losses? It's likely that a forced sale during difficult emotional times will result in a lower price than a sale during happier times. Some brokers can smell a divorce a mile away and may encourage buyers to bid low, knowing sellers are desperate. In sad times the house usually isn't at its best and maintenance problems often aren't getting taken care of. Beyond these woes, the costs of sale can be steep, especially if there are transfer or capital gains taxes or high brokerage fees. If you are selling in a downwardly moving market, your losses could be significant.

Fighting over losses can get very ugly. My advice is to abide by the rule that applies to straight divorces in nearly every state in the union: *no fault*. Renounce any attempts to put the blame on one person and split your losses equally or, if you own the property in unequal portions, pro rata. That's what most judges are going to order, so save your legal fees. But there is one exception: if your partner acts outrageously *after* you've broken up or causes your costs to soar, or if she or he jeopardizes a house sale, consider letting the sale go through but fight for an extra share of the proceeds afterward.

If the local real estate economy is heading south, or if you have refinanced your loan, or if you borrowed money for the down payment or closing costs, you may end up owing your lender more than you receive in a sale. You may want to ask for some partial forgiveness of the loan or an extended-repayment period; in some locales the banks are willing to do this, but don't be unrealistic or self-righteous about the situation. As with any other form of loss, this additional debt should be shouldered on a pro rata basis.

What's the property worth? Sometimes you'll agree that one person will buy out the other, but you can't agree on the value. Real estate appraisals sometimes can cost more than $500 and they can be unreliable—and without an actual sale no one can be sure of the value. Even the best appraiser makes judgment calls, and a clever appraiser can push the numbers up or down—if that's what the client wants. The same can be said for assessing the worth of any improvements that are in dispute.

For these reasons, I suggest you start with estimates by brokers, which can be obtained for free or at a low cost, but reduce their values by 5 percent, as brokers sometimes estimate on the high side. If you and your ex are within 5 or 10 percent of each other, split the difference and skip the professional appraisal. If you insist on a formal appraisal or the brokers' estimates vary a great deal, use one reliable appraiser rather than one for each of you, split the fee, and accept the single value. If you absolutely insist on each getting your own appraisal, don't waste your time arguing about whose expert is right.

How do you allocate unequal investments? If each of you contributed half of the down payment and half of each monthly mortgage payment, all you have to do is figure out the equity and divide it in half. But if one of you contributed more at the outset or at a later time and you have an agreement or understanding on the subject, apply the principles you agreed to and make a fair division.

But if there never was such a discussion or agreement and either one of you wants to divide the goods up other than fifty-fifty, it may be difficult to resolve the matter. The key is to try to compromise on a dollar amount rather than try to convince each other who is right. By the way, the same approach can be taken even if one person was never listed on the title, as she or he can claim an equitable ownership interest based on the value of her or his actual contribution to the property, and the value of that person's interest can be compromised based on its approximate value. This is the same approach you should take if you've agreed to sell the place to a third party and are arguing over how the proceeds of sale should be distributed.

Here are some suggested approaches you can take to reach a deal:

1. Estimate the current mortgage debt and costs of sale to calculate the likely proceeds of a sale, and estimate who will get what based on each one's claims. Do several versions of the distribution based on the different theories of recovery each one is presenting, as this will translate the conflicts into actual monetary terms and help focus the arguments.

2. Acknowledge how the legal presumptions in your state would decide each issue, lay out what each of your arguments will be, and establish a percentage likelihood of who you think will prevail for each of your claims. No one can be

certain about the outcomes, but you can probably agree on a *range* of likely results.

3. Take your estimated numbers and discount them according to the percentage likelihoods of success for each strategy, and you'll have a matrix of likely divisions. For example, you may be able to agree that there's only a 20 percent chance one of you will get more than 80 percent of the proceeds, a 50 percent chance the proceeds will be split equally, and a 30 percent chance the proceeds will be split sixty/forty or seventy/thirty. Then, eliminate the least likely outcomes (say, those with less than a 20 percent chance) on both ends, and the resulting middle range should be your settlement range. This is where you should focus your settlement discussions. If you've been realistic in this process, you'll probably discover that you're not all that far apart.

4. Try to split the difference between these narrowed amounts to reach a compromise. If one of you concedes the likelihood that the other will prevail in certain respects, factor that into the compromise split. If the gap between the compromise and your goal is less than the amount of attorneys' fees it will take to resolve the matter legally, accept the compromise.

5. Explore different options for financing the preferred solution. One of you should consider staying on the mortgage loan agreement or receiving your payment in a few years, so long as there's a legally enforceable agreement assuring you of your payment and protecting you from any loan complications.

Keep your eye on the prize. If fighting in court and paying the mortgage for a year will eat up 30 percent of your equity, don't reject a settlement offer just because it's 15 percent less than your goal. Even if you decide to spend the money to hire an attorney or even pursue the matter in court, eventually you will be forced to make compromises.

Where can I turn for help? Divorcing couples always encounter conflicts, even with the best of agreements and the noblest of intentions. Give serious consideration to hiring professionals to steer you through this process if you can afford it. In many instances you and your ex can hire a single professional to help you work together. In my opinion lawyers generally offer the best help, but in some instances a good therapist or a sensible real estate broker with a strong personality can do the job. If either of you is one of those lone cowboys who wants to do it all by yourself, spend at least one hour with an attorney and an accountant before making a final agreement.

What's the likely outcome to be? If you are like the vast majority of lesbian and gay couples and *don't* have a written agreement or a deed that says who owns what and if you can't reach an agreement early on, your options may be limited. Here are some suggestions for resolving these battles.

1. Honor the legal principle that oral and implied agreements are enforceable between lovers with regard to real property. Be honest about whether you had an oral or implied agreement. The truth has a way of leaking out, especially in a courtroom, and little is gained by trying to deny an agreement you know was made. Chances are your conduct during the relationship was consistent with whatever agreement you had, and thus there will be many trails of evidence supporting the agreement. Like any agreement that's unwritten, there are bound to be some unresolved issues, and there's nothing wrong with asserting that *certain* areas are vague and open to dispute, but don't deny the obvious. Be honest about what your agreement was, even if it doesn't operate in your favor now.

For example, if only one of you was on the title or you've moved into a house your lover already owned, figure out what the nonowner has been paying over and above what he would have paid as a renter. Compare that to the excess over the fair rental value paid by the house's owner and divide up the actual appreciation over the course of the relationship, pro rata. Don't try to take back your earlier generosity, however angry you are. There's one thing that Ann Landers *and* the courts of this country agree on: gifts can't be converted to loans retroactively, even when the love disappears.

2. If your former partner has a different understanding of your unwritten agreement, you'll need to talk out what each of you believes the basic terms of the agreement were. See if you can reach a compromise, and, if necessary, turn to an intermediary such as an attorney or friend. Real estate disputes that don't involve a lot of technicalities can often be resolved through mediation, and if the underlying conflicts are primarily emotional in nature, a couples' counselor might help. Create a safe environment where the truth can emerge.

3. Sort out the controversial from the uncontroversial. You may both agree that you each get your down-payment contributions back but disagree over how to divide up the appreciation. You might reach consensus about the appreciation but disagree about who pays for the not-quite-completed renovation work. Perhaps you agree on all these issues but disagree over who should pay the brokerage fees. The narrower you can focus your disagreements, the easier it is to find solutions.

4. Don't get confused between your hopes and dreams and the hard realities. Hoping your lover will one day forgive a loan he made to you for the down payment doesn't make it so, and dreaming that one day you'll inherit enough money to pay back the loan you took out to fix up the bathroom won't produce the needed funds. You may have expected that real estate values were going to rise high enough to cover the added debt, but if that hasn't happened, you've got to deal with the extra obligations.

5. If there truly was no agreement, not even an implied one, because you couldn't bear to discuss such nasty details, then you have only two options: fight it out legally and abide by what the judge or arbitrator orders or reach a settlement between yourselves. Obviously, a settlement (just like a marriage) takes two cooperative people, so start the ball rolling in the right direction by making a decent offer. Remember, being open to a settlement process

doesn't bind you to a particular result, but it may open the door to resolving the conflicts.

THE FOUR STAGES OF RESOLUTION

Now that you understand what's at stake and what the key issues are going to be, you'll need to ascertain the best method for handling these problems. Try to divide this task into four manageable projects: (1) assessing the facts, (2) learning the law, (3) setting your goals, and (4) settling on the best possible compromise.

Step One: Assessing the Facts

Your first job is to analyze the property, realistically, in financial terms. Sit down either with a savvy friend or a real estate professional and verify the amount of your current loan and the monthly payments. Figure out if just one of you can assume the loan. You may have to call the bank to get answers about an assumption, the process by which one person's name goes off the loan and the other one remains the sole borrower. Add up the other costs associated with the house and write down the dates they are due.

This information will help determine if you can afford to keep the house. It will also give you an estimate of the monthly costs you will face if you postpone resolution of the conflicts. At the same time, evaluate the house's condition with a critical eye, determining what will need to be done in order to sell it for a good price or what you will do if you buy it. If you are both owners, you both have the right to inspect the place, even if you're not currently living there.

Your next job is to estimate what the house would sell for on the open market. Talk with a local broker and evaluate what could be done to increase its value, such as postponing the sale until springtime or doing some repair work. Be realistic about how long it will take to sell it, and bear in mind that someone needs to make the payments while it's for sale.

Once you've made an estimate of the market value, subtract the likely costs of sale (broker's commission, closing costs, transfer taxes, and the like) and the remaining mortgage obligation and you'll see what the likely proceeds of sale, or the *equity*, will be. If you have a lot of variables in your equation use a range of amounts rather than a single figure. This is what you and your ex-lover are going to have to deal with.

Once you've gotten a good estimate of the likely equity, you can evaluate what's at stake in real-money terms and compare the benefits of selling the property to the burdens of buying out your partner. Doing this is essential, and you may be surprised to see how little this number changes using the different approaches. It amazes me how many couples argue over whether one of them is entitled to 45 percent or 50 percent of the proceeds or who should get the credit for painting the house, only to learn that less than $1,000 is actually at stake in the dispute.

Another element of your first task is to figure out—as clearly as you can in this difficult position—which *non*financial issues about the house are the most important to you and your ex-lover. Are you going to be able to handle a protracted conflict and keep on owning the property jointly while you decide things? Can either of you take calls about the house at work, and can you take off work if you're in charge of the selling process? How angry are you, how angry is your ex-partner, and how will this impact your actions? Are you more inclined just to sell out and move on, or do you desperately need more cash to find decent housing, even if the fight takes a while?

Even though your goal is to *de*emphasize the emotional aspects of this process, certain emotional realities cannot be ignored. There's a reason why you are in this mess, and in part it's because your hopes and dreams have been shattered. Be realistic about what this means for the house-division process for each of you, as only by recognizing the emotional roadblocks can you realistically avoid them!

As part of this first stage you should also try to discern which issues you and your partner are most likely to fight over and which of these are the most important to you. For some, timing is everything, and being able to move on quickly makes some monetary sacrifice worthwhile. Others care only about the bottom line and will hold out for the most money, no matter how long it takes. Some houses are truly special to one or both partners, so the property itself is going to be the prize each of you is reaching for. Try to figure out where you and your ex fit in this real estate landscape in order to be as prepared as possible for what will happen.

Step Two: Learning the Law
Once you've assessed the financial situation and your own personal needs, you'll need to do a bit of focused legal research. Some of you may need to hire a lawyer and let her or him tell you the news about your co-ownership situation, good or bad. If you do, find a lawyer who has expertise regarding property owned by unmarried couples, straight or gay, as most family lawyers who handle traditional divorces don't know these rules—and you can't afford to pay for their education. You may be able to do some research on your own, but in any case don't delude yourself into thinking the law doesn't matter.

Even in the more than twenty states where homosexuality is illegal, *real estate law still applies to gays and lesbians.* As we've seen, the law concerning real estate owned by unmarrieds is, for the most part, based on the general contractual rules for unmarried couples. You and your ex-lover are treated by the law like real estate business partners, and general real estate law and procedures, not family law, apply. Look at the deed and review any agreements you have signed, and if the deed's language is inadequate to resolve an ownership dispute and there's no written agreement, the law will enforce the parties' agreement. In many states agreements regarding real estate between lovers (unlike agreements between competitors or business partners) need *not* be in writing.

Implied agreements about houses are notoriously vague. A client of mine was house hunting with her lover, and they were looking at a serious fixer-upper. My client said she couldn't afford the renovations this place needed, and her well-to-do girlfriend said, "Don't worry, I have enough to cover those costs." The richer girlfriend paid for everything, and they later broke up. When she tried to argue that my client owed her for half the costs, we cited this comment to establish that there was an implied agreement to make a gift of the costs. We won the case, in part because my client testified so clearly as to the overall setting of the relationship and the implied meaning of her partner's assurances.

Develop a clear recollection of what happened in the better days, and be prepared to articulate *your* version of what the implied agreement was—if there was one. An implied agreement is a set of ideas and beliefs that *both* parties reasonably held in their minds when they acted the way they did, not your personal fantasy of what was supposed to happen.

If one of you paid *all* of the down payment and otherwise kept your money separate, chances are your implied agreement was that you'd get your down-payment money back out of the proceeds of a sale. By contrast, if you always shared *all* your money and pooled all your resources, the implied agreement may have been that all proceeds would be split equally, even if the initial contributions were far from equal.

And what if there was no implied agreement because you each had different concepts about what was going to happen with the house or because neither of you gave it any real thought? Judges usually impose one of two solutions on adversary partners. Most try to follow the rules of title presumption and impose a solution neither of you may have considered possible, such as selling the property and splitting the proceeds equally. Other judges take a more subtle approach and attempt to guess what your agreement would have been *had* you given it much thought. Unfortunately, neither is a very attractive or precise approach. A few judges will be inclined to apply family law rules, whether or not the codes authorize this.

Legal presumptions are useful from the law's perspective, as they take care of messy situations in which no one has reached an agreement. For example, tenancy-in-common ownership means a fifty-fifty split if there is no agreement to the contrary. If that's what's on the deed it's what the court might impose on you if neither of you can prove a contrary agreement. But if your name was never on the deed because you didn't want the bank to know about your bad credit, the legal presumption may say that without a proven agreement, the one on the title gets it all.

The second approach, in which the judge may impose what he or she thinks the parties would *likely* have agreed on had they talked about it, is creative but extremely unpredictable. It sometimes leads to an absolutely right decision, but it can also be a debacle, especially if the judge considers your relationship more like a business deal than a love affair or if one of you makes a more attractive or sympathetic witness.

I served as an arbitrator for a couple who had overinvested in a house they rented out by remodeling it during a declining market. When it came to selling the place they were faced with a loss and had no agreement about what to do. I followed California law and ruled that an agreement to share profits *implies* an agreement to share losses by the same percentages. Given the difficult circumstances, that seemed as fair as fair could be. I'm not sure, though, that this is what the parties would have decided if they'd actually thought about it back when they were buying the place. Chances are that had they seriously thought about the possible losses, the poorer partner wouldn't have been willing to go ahead with the remodeling in the first place.

Learning the law means being realistic about these glaring unpredictabilities. A seasoned attorney can describe the rules to you and give you a sense of what evidence the court will consider, but it is difficult for *anyone* to predict what the actual outcome will be.

The rules in this area of real estate law are just too vague for that kind of certainty.

In summary, the most important legal questions for real estate disputes are (1) what your agreement was and (2) if there wasn't one, what presumptions the law will apply. The key evidence is likely to be whose name is on the deed, who paid the down payment, and who made the monthly payments; what monetary obligations you shared when you were together; whether anyone promised to take care of the other one or cover her or his debts; and if either of you invested significantly more money in the house and, if so, under what arrangements.

Step Three: Setting Your Goals

In order to figure out what *you* want to do with the property, you should first choose the most effective method for solving the problems and then focus on your goals.

In attempting to solve real estate disputes, begin by talking directly with your ex-lover. To make your discussions most productive, gather your factual information about the property before you sit down to talk. Keep your discussions focused on the subject, and limit them to practical issues: What does the house cost to keep up, can either of you afford to keep it, what are the improvements really worth? Make every effort to avoid demonstrations of anger or blame.

The second approach, and one that everyone should try for at least a few sessions, is mediation. Real estate mediation works best with an appropriately trained professional since the financial and legal issues can be so complicated. Compare your lists of hot topics to be sure you are working with someone who is comfortable with you, not only as a gay couple but also with the particular topics on your list. If you are using a nonattorney as your mediator, save some time to meet separately with an attorney for an hour or two to verify that your proposed solution doesn't create any legal or tax problems.

If you need to hire an attorney to handle the negotiations instead of talking directly with your ex, make sure you choose one who knows real estate law and, ideally, has experience working with same-sex couples. Real estate knowledge is the most important skill, as the laws and the procedures about property are critical features of your dispute. Your sexual preference won't be so important so long as your attorney is aware that this was a love affair and not a business deal. Real estate negotiations between attorneys can take a long time because of the complexity of the deals and the endless details that arise. If you are using attorneys, consider limiting them to a few key issues, such as buyout rights and property values, and leave the remaining, minor issues for a broker to deal with.

Legal arbitration, your next option, is a private system in which an individual, usually a lawyer or a retired judge, acts as the judge and issues a ruling after hearing the evidence from both sides. If the parties arrange the exchange of documents informally, attorneys may not be needed. As long as the arbitrator's decision is followed, there are no court records or court action, and in most states you can petition the local court to enforce the decision if your opponent refuses to comply.

Since the carrying costs for property can be so high, reaching a quick resolution through arbitration is very attractive. If you are using arbitration you will need to sign a written agreement consenting to arbitration, and, when you do this, include in your agreement the list of topics the arbitrator is going to decide. Make arrangements as to who will live in the house and pay the bills during the process, and if you aren't living in the house make sure you have the right to conduct inspections, as you will need to do this to confirm the property's value.

If a lot is at stake and your opponent won't agree to mediation or arbitration, you can always use the court system. Ambrose Bierce described litigation as the process by which a pig ends up as sausage, and he was right. The legal system for resolving real estate disputes is, for the most part, slow, cruel, and expensive.

In most states there are special procedures for adjudicating real estate disputes, and you should be aware of these rules, in detail, before you decide to use the court system. In these states, there is a preliminary hearing at which the judge selects the best solution, which usually involves listing the property for sale to a third party. The judge then appoints a referee to manage the sale. After the property is sold there is a second hearing, at which each side presents its demands for distribution of the proceeds. On paper this is an efficient system, but it can take more than a year to get a hearing and all the procedures are expensive. If you and your ex don't reach a settlement early on in the process, you may find yourself waiting years, with hardly any proceeds left to argue over after the lawyers have been paid.

It's also quite likely that the court won't be compassionate to you as a gay couple. In some towns the judges will be outright homophobic and blame and punish both of you for your distress. In other places the judges might be less hostile, but they may have no idea about or patience with the sensitivity of your dispute. Since you aren't going to be in front of a judge who regularly handles divorces of any sexual persuasion, he or she may also be uncomfortable with the emotional dynamics of this sort of case.

Depending on your particular situation, however, a courtroom might be the best place for you. If you need the court's protection just to manage the property during the sale process or if your partner is impossible to deal with, the formality and enforcement powers of the court system can be a lifesaver. If you are looking for a strict interpretation of the law to win you your rights, a courtroom also might be the best place for you. If there's an enormous amount of money at stake, you may want the right to file an appeal if the judge rules against you.

Court action also may be needed if you've contributed to the property's acquisition or maintenance but aren't listed on the title. In this situation, you can file a lawsuit under the constructive trust or equitable ownership theory, and in most states you can block your ex-lover from selling the house while your claim is being adjudicated. Be cautious, however, if your contributions are less than what you would have paid in rent and you don't have anything in writing to back up your claims, as it will be difficult to convince a judge to anoint you as an owner.

The other important part of this educational phase is figuring out what you want. You need to determine what your financial and domestic goals are and what you will settle for. You should have your wish list well thought out, and then be realistic and make note of where you can afford to be flexible. Considering these issues will keep you focused on your goals so that you don't just react to what your ex-lover demands or offers, and it will also allow you to negotiate financially rather than over principles.

Developing your own version of your history is part of the process of moving on, and it is essential in coming to terms with the breakup itself. This is true for both of you, so disagreeing about what happened is actually part of the individuation process. Your ticket to freedom, however, is to be able to talk numbers, not principles. Stop arguing over who is right and start negotiating.

Step Four: Reaching a Compromise
Having assessed the facts, scoped out the law, and set your goals, you are ready to tackle the task of getting results. This may be a lengthy process. You're not only dealing with your own emotions and the uncertainties of the law; you have to deal with another person's emotional agenda and personal quirks. This alone can entail long conversations, lengthy exchanges of letters, and a hefty attorney's bill.

Here are some suggestions on how to get the best results:

Develop your own personal support system. If a substantial amount of money is involved, find a good lawyer who knows this area of law, can relate to your personal situation, and is capable of negotiating without blasting everyone in sight. Seek out a "best friend" you can talk to for free. Your lawyer will warn you that conversations with others can be "discovered" by your ex if the case goes to trial, which could therefore be used against you later on, so pick out some warm and cuddly friends who will distract you and comfort you—without asking to hear about all the gory details.

Stay in touch with your personal goals and financial needs, but stay flexible as well. Your needs will change as your case progresses, which may force a reexamination of your goals. Keep focused on your primary needs, pay close attention to the new information coming your way, and be ready to revise your game plan if necessary. At the same time, if you know you are right and the issue is really important to you, stick to your guns and don't cave in out of fear or confusion.

Stay cool. This is hard advice to follow, especially if your ex doesn't seem to know how to behave. But for the most part deal with your emotions in the proper arena: with your new lover, your therapist, your friends, or by yourself. When you are with your attorney or, more important, dealing with your ex or in front of a judge or arbitrator, stay calm. You'll do a much better job, your claims will be taken more seriously, and you'll feel better about yourself.

Marshal your resources and use them carefully. If you see a major court battle coming up, don't spend a lot of time or money on mediation that isn't going to work. If you know you can't afford a litigation fight, make the best settlement you can early on. Remember, unlike a lawsuit over a random car accident or an industrial injury, this situation is deliberate: you actually picked that lover of yours. Accept a degree of responsibility for the mess you are in, and pace yourself to be there for the long haul if that becomes necessary.

Stay open to compromise, and don't fight beyond reason over principles. My clients always ask if the proposed compromise is fair. I tell them that's not the right question to ask. Better to ask whether you will regret it later if you *don't* accept the compromise, since fairness may be a luxury you cannot afford. If the attorney's fee is going to exceed your likely recovery, don't fight on endlessly.

For example, consider taking a secured IOU rather than all cash in a buyout deal if that will resolve the dispute. Consider accepting 75 percent of what you're aiming for rather than spending more than the difference on legal fees. Consider staying on the loan for a while. Of course, if the proffered deal is *way* below what is reasonable and you can afford to fight on, don't settle for less than what you feel is right. But if you're looking for a way to prove your worth and stand up for what is right, focus on your job—or, if you can afford to, take on yet another worthy social cause. You'll accomplish far more and feel far better than if you spend your next five years fighting with your ex.

Be efficient in implementing your resolution. Once you have reached a compromise, implement its provisions quickly. Transfers can be tricky and may require professional assistance. You may be able to retain a broker to handle an internal buyout for a set fee, or you may prefer to use a title company or a real estate attorney. Even if you are going to handle things by yourselves, spend an hour with a professional to verify that you are doing it right. It's best to write up a summary of your agreement before you set out to implement it; then, if the process takes a bit longer or costs a bit more than you thought it would, neither of you will be tempted to rewrite your agreement retroactively.

Transfers may be expensive, depending on the laws in your state. Figure out ahead of time what the costs will be and include them in your negotiations, and try to follow my "no fault" rule and split these expenses equally. Be realistic about how much time it is going to take to effectuate the transfer.

If you are selling the property be efficient about it. Choose a broker who can relate to both of you without taking sides. Make sure he understands he is dealing with a gay divorce so he knows what to ask—and what *not* to ask. You may not want a buyer to know the details, but work together as a team to make the best presentation. Organize the logistics of getting approvals and signatures on offers and counteroffers, and ask your broker to serve as a go-between if necessary.

If you are selling the house to a third party and can't agree on how to divvy up the proceeds, complete the sale and hold them in an escrow account while you resolve your disputes. This way you won't hold up the sale while you are fighting over money and you'll transform your battle into a dispute over a fixed sum. Doing this will make it much easier to reach a compromise, and, if you have to arbitrate or litigate the dispute, you'll have a fixed amount at stake.

THE HOUSE AS A SYMBOL

When your love is strong your house is an embodiment of your passion and the setting for your domestic delights, but if you break up it can become the symbol of everything *wrong* with the relationship. As such it can become a perilously attractive arena for playing out the dramas of your separation. As good a symbol as a house may be when things go well, it functions terribly as an arena for acting out the emotions of a breakup. Trying to settle emotional scores by arguing over the proceeds engages you in a painful competition over whose version of reality is correct, and neither of you will ever win that argument.

Focus your efforts on addressing practical concerns, and resist the temptation to argue over the house as a symbol of who is going to win the dissolution wars. Avoiding such symbolic battles will speed your emotional recovery and also probably help enable you to find a new home and salvage more of your investment as well.

9

These Are a Few
of My Favorite Things

The rules for dividing up everything else you've accumulated—including debts—are not complex, but the practical tasks can be a challenge. Follow the same procedures you've already learned: assess the facts, review the law, be honest about your bottom line, and make reasonable compromises.

ITEMS OF MONETARY VALUE

For unmarried couples, the legal doctrines regarding real estate other than your home are generally the same as those determining ownership of residential property, and the rules in most states regulating the disposition of your personal property are just about the same as the real property rules.

Bear in mind that oral or implied agreements about real property that is not your home probably will be given less weight, as these properties are viewed primarily as business investments and are thus analyzed along strictly business terms. In most states oral contracts are given greater deference when they involve personal property than when real estate is involved because the doctrines mandating a written contract for real estate deals don't apply. In most such instances there won't be any formal deeds to non–real estate assets (other than cars, bank, and stock accounts), so the legal presumptions of ownership will be based primarily upon possession and the source of payments, not title.

The issues that regularly come up concerning such assets are:

1. What is owned solely by one person and by whom, and what is jointly owned?
2. What is each person's percentage of ownership for jointly owned property and items, and does either partner have any right of reimbursement for his or her contributions to the purchase?
3. What is the easiest and fairest method of distributing jointly owned property?

There are six basic methods you can use to resolve such property conflicts:

1. Return everything to the person who paid for it. Your separate finances are your own, as are things you brought into the relationship that were not gifts to your partner.
2. Distribute the nondisputed items; auction off any items in dispute between yourselves; sell them to whichever one of you is willing to pay more for them, and then split the proceeds of the auction equally between yourselves.
3. Each of you choose a series of objects by flipping a coin to see who picks first and then each select one item in turn until everything is gone.
4. Divide everything into two piles, then each of you select one of the piles, either by flipping a coin to see who gets to make the first selection or by letting one person do the division and the other one make the first selection.
5. Sell everything, and divide the proceeds equally.
6. Hire a neutral arbitrator to hear each side's claims and let her or him make all the decisions of ownership and compensation.

The rules applying to these joint assets are similar, but each type of asset has its own peculiar features and practical challenges.

While the financial ramifications of property battles usually do not warrant large-scale conflict, the interpersonal dimensions can make such disagreements tortuous. At least once a month I spend several hours helping clients sort out who is going to get the curtains, bicycles, rug, or souvenirs from last year's vacation, and rarely is the amount at stake worth the size of my bill.

Vacation Homes

If you have been smart or fortunate enough to acquire a lakeside cabin or cottage by the sea, one of the more delicate debates you will face will be over ownership of this second parcel of real property. You'll need to decide who is going to keep it if either of you can afford to, as well as how much the unlucky one is going to be reimbursed for his or her investment. In order to resolve these questions you must trace the very same steps you took when you dealt with your primary residence.

Solving a dispute about a vacation house should be relatively easy. You don't need to make decisions so quickly, and if the resolution gets delayed a bit, each of you can still use the house on alternate weeks or weekends. Usually there isn't as much money involved as there is in your primary property, although the sentimental value and the property's uniqueness can make the process difficult if both of you want to hold on to it. If an irresolvable conflict arises because you both want the place or can't agree on its value, there are a few special methods of resolving the dispute:

- Add a set premium to the market value and see which one of you is willing to pay that premium, or hold a private auction at which you award the property to whichever one of you is willing to pay the other one the most money above the market value for his share.
- Select an assortment of especially valued personal property as extra compensation on top of the fair market value payment, and flip a coin to decide who gets what. Then, the feelings of

disappointment will at least be mutual as you will each be deprived of something extraspecial.

- Continue co-owning the vacation home for a year or two as an interim solution. Make reasonable plans for sharing costs, and alternate using it yourselves or rent it out as a business venture. If you can weather a few years of co-ownership as ex-lovers, you may be able to work out a buyout in less volatile times—or your temporary solution may become permanent.
- Once you've made your agreement, speak with a broker or attorney to learn how to transfer ownership and what fees will be incurred. You may need to register the transfer with a homeowner's association, as well as with the county recorder.

Here is a caution for those who co-own vacation property with other friends or investors: keep your private battles private, and don't drag your friends or partners into your drama. Sort out your personal disputes between yourselves first, keep up with your joint-payment obligations, and then present your solution to the rest of the group. If emotions are really tense, appoint one of you as the "liaison" to the rest of the group so the others don't need to sit through your private arguments!

Time-Shares

Remember that luxurious free breakfast they fed you in Puerto Vallarta or Maui, seducing you to sign up for a specially priced opportunity to spend a week each year at a beautiful oceanside condo? With any luck you've enjoyed that garden paradise for at least a few seasons before the breakup has converted the time-share into just one more thing to fight over.

Allocating your time-share investment can be tricky. Often there is no open market for your interest, so selling it for cash simply isn't an available option. You will therefore either have to continue sharing it or one of you will have to buy out the other's interest. If you are going to share it, write up an agreement between yourselves establishing who will pay what for annual maintenance and loan obligations and precisely how you will share the place.

If you are doing a buyout between yourselves, you will need to set a market value for the time-share as a whole and assign a relative value to each person's contributions. Chances are that similar units are still on the market, so setting the current value should not be difficult, but if you can't agree just use the original purchase price. Time-shares rarely change much in value, so it probably isn't worth spending money on a professional appraiser.

Once you've determined the value, verify whether you still owe anything on the original purchase loan, if there was one, and inquire whether there are any past-due payments. Deduct these amounts from the value and you've determined the equity. If you are both on the title, the law will presume that you own it in fifty-fifty shares, even if one of you paid more for it at the outset, unless the one who paid more can prove there was an agreement for reimbursement or an excess ownership share. Divide the equity by the percentage interests and you'll know how much the selling partner should be getting for his share.

The procedures for transferring a time-share can be tricky, so be sure you know what they, as well as any transfer fees, are before signing documents. In some cases you just send a letter to the operator of the homeowner's association or fill out a form it will provide. In other locations, however, you need to draw up a deed and have it filed with the local recorder's office. The fees will differ from state to state, and if your time-share is overseas the transfer rules may be more convoluted.

You may belong to an exchange club that allows you to trade your time for another season or a different location. If so, you may need to fill out a separate form with the club to transfer your account and pay another fee to transfer your membership. If you have accumulated credits for use elsewhere, make sure you verify what they are worth and decide who gets to use them. Some clubs only allow you to retain credits for a year or two, so make sure you don't forfeit them.

Investment Real Property

Real estate is real estate, and the basic property rules will apply to any investment property you own. When it comes to nonresidential property, however, oral agreements are rarely honored. Judges accept the fact that people are informal about their personal residence, but you probably won't be given such slack when it comes to an investment property.

As you did with your residence, you will need to analyze what your investment property is worth, iron out what percentage each of you owns, try to put a dollar figure on each party's investment, and decide whether you are going to have to sell it on the open market or arrange a buyout between the two of you. Holding on to the property jointly should not be difficult so long as you can make management decisions together or agree to hire a management company to handle the task for you. If it's a bad time to sell and the whole process seems too overwhelming, consider staying on as co-investors for a year or two while you sort out other things in your lives.

Once you've reached an agreement in principle, you should document it and then move forward to implement it. If you are selling the place, make sure you pick the right broker, and explain to her or him the delicate nature of the co-ownership structure. If you are able to make a quick sale before you resolve your ownership percentage dispute, remember that you can close on the sale and divide up the proceeds later on.

If you've earned a profit from your investment, speak with a tax expert ahead of time about the tax ramifications of a sale. Generally, you will have to pay taxes on your profit on investment property unless you promptly buy another investment property. Be aware that an agreement to share profits implies a willingness to shoulder losses in the same percentage if you don't have an agreement to the contrary.

Furniture and Appliances

Major appliances and built-in furniture should remain with the residence as fixtures, and whoever ends up with the house is likely to be entitled to them. If one of you feels you should be reimbursed for excess contributions to the purchase of any appliances or fixtures, resolve this in connection with the real estate resolution. You also should separate any items you both agree only one of you owns, either because you had them before the romance began, because only one of you purchased them, or because they were a gift to just one of you.

The two most preferred methods for dividing such property are the equal value division and the you-choose/I-choose alternating method. Under the equal value division method you first work together to assign a market value for each disputed item and settle on what percentage of the total assets each of you is entitled to. Then you each select a set of items from the list you have made that are equal in value to your percentage share by making a separate list of the items you want most and distribute them by alternating order of preference. If you hit a snag over an item you both really want, you may need to flip a coin to see who gets it. You may also need to exchange a few items at the end to balance the books and ensure that you each are ending up with the appropriate value from the items you want.

The alternating selection method can work very easily since you don't have to argue over market values for each item. With this method you flip a coin to decide who goes first and then each of you claims one item in turn. Each of you thus gets to decide whether you prefer a sentimental object over an expensive one. And, other than deciding who starts the selection process, neither party has any significant advantage over the other one. So that neither of you tries to grab clusters of items rather than one item per selection, jointly decide ahead of time what constitutes an "item" (for example, is the dining room set one item or five items?) before you know where you are going to land on the picking order.

Automobiles/RVs/Cycles

Vehicles constitute an area where practical compromises should be possible. Use the midrange "blue book" value (the published guide for car values) to set a market value for the jointly owned cars, and don't try to argue that *your* car is really special. Decide if either of you wants to buy out the other one or if you are going to sell the car to a third party. Split the value (after subtracting any outstanding loans), and make the transfer. If you both really feel your wheels have special value, then choose one of the enhanced auction methods described above. Whoever is willing to pay the most above the blue-book value should take the car.

If you owe a significant amount on the auto loan, especially if it is more than the car is worth, you may need to adjust another area of your property distribution or pay off the excess loan amount out of joint savings to avoid burdening the purchasing partner with more debt than is fair. The same may apply to a leased automobile.

Once you've reached an agreement, you need to carry it out. In some states you simply sign the pink slip, or title, and file it with the motor vehicles department. In other states you may need to fill out a bill of sale, and you may have to pay a sales tax or registration fees when you transfer the car. Don't forget to change the name and the billing address on the insurance policy, and *don't* be tempted to stay on as co-owners of a vehicle just because it seems like too much trouble to arrange the transfer. If the car gets stolen or someone gets into an accident, it is going to be a bloody mess sorting out the liabilities, and given the likelihood of a theft or a crash in most cities these days, this is one risk too many.

Businesses

If you co-own a business you will need to decide whether this arrangement can continue or whether one or both of you will have to find an outside job. This probably will require that you hire a replacement employee and decide how to cover the costs of paying her or him.

If both of you have been directly involved in the management of the business and the tensions are too great for any sharing to continue, it's vital that you set up an arrangement to keep the business operational while you sort out the ownership issues. It is inevitable that many jointly owned businesses suffer terribly when the co-owners break up. Make every possible effort to set up a management system that will accommodate your internal conflicts.

Once you've established a method for handling immediate operations, you can move on to the more difficult chore of allocating ownership. As with any asset, you have three choices: continue to own it together, sell it outright, or negotiate an internal buyout between yourselves. Selling it outright may be difficult, as there is rarely a market for a small, owner-operated business.

If you are going to try to continue with the co-ownership, one of you must act as managing partner. Draft a written agreement as soon as practically possible because now you will need to operate more like business investors than spouses. You will also need to decide how to compensate the one who is putting in more time, and it's a good idea to establish a method for a future buyout with an arbitration provision, to resolve disputes if the co-ownership approach just doesn't work long-term.

An internal buyout often makes the most financial sense. The major hurdles are agreeing on a value and finding a way for the buying partner to come up with the cash for the buyout. Once you resolve these issues, it should be simple to document the transfer. Setting a value can be done by a negotiation process between the two of you, but if that doesn't produce results, you should consider hiring a business appraiser. If you are in a personal service business that is tough to evaluate or if it's a new enterprise, you may each need to hire your own appraiser and average the two estimates, as doing so probably will cost far less than litigation. The value of a business consists of the assets (a lease, equipment, accounts receivables, and so forth) and the present value of anticipated future profits. If future-profit values are uncertain or if there's been a magic that derived from the two of you working together that may not survive the separation, setting this value can be extremely difficult.

Coming up with the cash for a buyout can be hard, as small business owners are rarely flush and it's difficult to get a loan in such instances. If you are the one selling your interest and your ex doesn't have the cash, you should seriously consider taking a promissory note paid over time. If you insist on cash, you may be faced with having to close the business and thereby receive nothing at all.

The final hurdle is a matter of paperwork and taxes. While in theory this should not be difficult, if your business is of any significant size, you definitely should see an attorney to draw up the papers and advise you of any special tax consequences. You will need to address the issues of accounts receivable and unpaid bills, possible future payments based on the future performance of the business, and the handling of liabilities for unknown claims. If your business is a corporation or registered partnership, it may be necessary to file papers with the secretary of state, and special filings may be required by county offices or licensing agencies as well. Assign any leases or service contracts to the buying partner, and be sure to change the names on the bank accounts.

Either mediation or binding arbitration is the way to go with disputes regarding co-owned businesses. First, you will want to keep your conflicts as private as possible so your clients and customers don't get wind of your problems. Second, you'll want to keep the costs as low as possible so you don't eat up all the profits on the nuances of the resolution process. And third, chances are you will need some degree of ongoing interaction to keep the information flowing and the products selling, so it's in your mutual best interest to have the resolution process be as amicable as possible. If you are going to use mediation or arbitration, make sure you hire someone who has experience working with businesses so he can help you hammer out a realistic and workable solution.

Savings/Pensions/Retirement Funds

The law in most states regarding financial assets is similar to the one that applies to real property: whoever's name is on the account is presumed to be the legal owner. If either party wants to claim an interest greater than what the title says, he will have to show a written, oral, or implied agreement in support of his claim. Be sure to scrutinize your accounts carefully, as some accounts have a second name listed as a "death beneficiary" only. In this situation you inherit the account if your partner dies, but you are not a half owner of the account while your partner is alive.

This is an important distinction, and it has parallels throughout the ownership debates. A willingness to turn over an account to a partner at the time of death does *not* constitute an agreement to share its bounties while both partners are alive but separated. Unfortunately, unlike a married person, neither of you has any automatic rights to each other's savings accounts, pension funds, or private retirement accounts unless you can prove an agreement to share them. But if both your names are listed on the account, then you are each presumed to be half owners, even if only one of you has contributed to the account. For this reason, if you don't intend to make a gift of half your savings to your lover, don't put money into a joint account without having an agreement clarifying who really owns it.

Gay couples often select joint-tenancy accounts with a right of survivorship as informal will substitutes because they believe it's cheaper and easier to put all the money in one account rather than keeping the funds separate and signing wills. It may be easier, but in effect you've each just gifted half your funds to your partner. If this isn't what you intended to do, say so immediately and make the appropriate changes to the account or have your partner sign a letter clarifying who owns what. You may create some hurt feelings and some sense of distrust, but this is far better than creating legally binding arrangements that don't match your feelings.

Royalties/Copyrights

Those of you with special talents in creative areas may face the chore of dividing up royalties or copyright benefits. The law here is the same as it is for most other assets: whoever has her name on the benefit is presumed to be its legal owner if there is no proof of a written, oral, or implied agreement to the contrary. Even if you have both worked together at length on the disputed project, it is going to be very difficult for you, as an unmarried partner, to win an interest in your partner's professional or creative work if your name isn't on the product. So unless the evidence is very strong and a lot of money is at stake, don't put much hope in recovering anything in this area.

If you do hold a joint copyright or are receiving royalties jointly—or if the two of you agree certain benefits will be shared—be certain to put your agreement in writing. You may need to contact the publisher or other company to instruct it where to send the checks in the future, and if the amount of money at stake is large, you should consult with an attorney to have a formal agreement written up.

Debts/Contractual Liabilities

If you've been looking around for a haven where unmarried couples are favored, this is it. Unless your name is on your partner's credit card or you are listed as a coborrower on the contract or loan, most likely you can never be held liable for your partner's debts. Any funds in a joint bank account, however, are usually fair game for either one's creditors. And if both of you are listed as borrowers, debtors, or cardholders, there is a good chance each of you will be *fully* liable for the debt, even if you didn't get any benefit from the loan. Thus, it's essential that you cancel any joint credit cards immediately on word of a dissolution—or on the day before you announce your departure if you are the departing one.

Since you are both equally liable for any debts that were incurred in both your names, you should arrange a clear (and preferably written) agreement between the two of you covering the debts. I strongly encourage you to make every possible effort to pay off your joint debts as part of the separation process rather than agree to each cover half of them over time. The last thing you want to face is an ongoing creditor's demand or a bad credit rating when you've already paid your half of the obligation since, as you will recall, you're still legally liable to the bank even if your ex has told you he'll make the payments. Get the debt paid off soon, and don't pay your portion unless you're certain your ex is paying as well. If your ex fails to pay his or her share, consider filing legal action before you fork over more than you are supposed to.

Even though you aren't liable for your unmarried partner's debts, your credit rating certainly can be affected by the way your partner handles her or his financial affairs. For this reason, a bankruptcy filing by either of you can have a negative credit effect on both of you. This will usually happen when there are loans on property held in both names, but be careful. You may have signed a guarantee or agreed to be a cosigner long ago and since forgotten about it, so even if you think the debt isn't yours the bank may know otherwise.

If you are faced with potential credit problems as a result of your ex's defaults, you will have to make the hard choice of either paying off her debts or suffering the bad credit. Writing to the bank explaining that it really isn't your fault probably won't work. And, if you are the defaulting one, be conscious of what you are doing to your ex, and either try your damnedest to avoid the problem or at least give your ex fair warning of the likely consequences.

ITEMS OF NONMONETARY VALUE

Sentimental and Irreplaceable Items

Distributing the sentimental or irreplaceable items and the family pets can be a very difficult point of contention. Photographs can be copied, but priceless crafts from foreign travels and works of art are one of a kind. The longer you have been together, the more mementos you've probably acquired.

There are two ways to distribute sentimental objects. First, if there are presumptive reasons why certain items should stay with one of you rather than the other, admit this and let go of what is not really yours. Heirlooms should go to the person whose family they came from, and gifts should remain with the person who received them. Second, anything else that remains in dispute should be allocated according to an alternating selection process. Flip a coin to see who goes first, and then each one of you should select one item, in turn, from the pile of disputed objects. Alternate your selections until you each end up with at least half of what you really want, and in the end neither one will be any happier than the other.

Pets May Be Our Best Friends

Our pets are like our children in many ways. They comfort us in our sad times, distract us in our difficult times, and are the recipients of our love and attention for years on end. Resolving where the pets are going to live should start with deciding who can give them the best home. If the dogs need a big play yard, then the one with the biggest backyard should have first rights. If one of you travels constantly, it doesn't make much sense for you to keep dogs who need daily care, and if one of you has been the primary caretaker, you should have first rights.

After one of you has given up custody of the pets, work out an arrangement for regular visitation privileges by the noncustodial "parent." If you really want to keep the pets, be prepared to give up something else of great importance to you. Chances are that if you are willing to pay a sufficiently high price, your partner will accede to your wishes. But try to keep the bargaining in terms of other valuable things, not money.

Mediation can work well for pet disputes. The issues are always going to be emotional rather than economic, and there are rarely any legal grounds for favoring one person over another. Talking it out and reaching an equitable compromise is the *only* way to solve the dispute, and mediation will bring you together with an unbiased party who should be able to help you reach one.

MONETARY CLAIMS

In addition to claims regarding jointly owned property, assets, debts, and businesses, one or both of you may feel your ex-partner owes you money. If a promissory note was signed it should be enforceable, regardless of the nature of your relationship. But more frequently the debt was never formally acknowledged and the borrower may feel that it was a gift and not a loan. In addition, one partner may have incurred significant expenses for a forced relocation or business development. When the love turns sour, the partner may want to be reimbursed for these expenses.

In a traditional heterosexual marriage a financially dependent spouse who makes such trade-offs is protected if the relationship falls apart by retaining a financial interest in any accumulated property, even if it is derived from the other spouse's earnings. Nonmarital partners generally have no such rights unless there is clear evidence of an agreement for *post*separation support, and an agreement for support during the course of a relationship says *nothing* about support after the love dies.

Without a formal agreement it will be very difficult, if not impossible, to win any recovery in this arena. Only in a few extreme cases, where there is a clear pattern of one party giving up a lucrative career based on a direct reliance of assurances of support from the higher-earning partner or when there are strong indications of a promise to repay a loan, have a few courts in a few states awarded financial compensation to the dependent one based on an implied or oral contract claim. In most cases, therefore, I recommend that you save your money, move on with your life, and don't pursue such a claim in court.

But bear in mind that fighting for lesbian and gay rights and for the right for gay marriage is hollow hypocrisy if you are unwilling to abide by the property laws that would apply to you if you were a married couple. If both of you agree at the outset to keep your property separate, that is fine—every heterosexual married couple is allowed to sign a prenuptial agreement. But if you're the richer one and you've allowed your partner to become financially dependent on you, don't walk away and hide behind the lack of legal protections for your dependent nonmarital spouse.

ALTERNATIVE DISPUTE-RESOLUTION METHODS

If you are using mediation or arbitration to resolve a real estate dispute, include the other disputes in the same process. If your only disputes are non–real estate in nature, mediation and arbitration will work best, as the amount at stake is usually small, the legal issues are not likely to be highly technical, and the evidence each of you needs to present should be fairly simple.

If the disputes involve valuation, you can probably hire a joint appraiser—for art objects, businesses, or vacation homes—without the need for an attorney. Once you resolve the valuation disputes the other battles will probably appear more manageable and you won't need an attorney to represent you in these areas. Consider using a local dispute-resolution service, such as a neighborhood conflict-resolution board, a local lesbian/gay mediation service, or even your local American Arbitration Association or a conciliation forum.

10

Public Affairs
in the Hard Times

In times of discord, it is inevitable that the social and legal rules of the outside world will have a powerful impact on your lives, for better or for worse.

Every separation is played out on a public stage. Those who claim to care about us want to know what is happening and often are happy to tell us how to manage the demise of our affairs. The practical logistics of a breakup inevitably shove each of us up against the opinions, regulations, and resistance of bankers, real estate brokers, tax authorities, and meddling in-laws. It's an unavoidable problem, and if you aren't strategic in your separation planning, the clash between the public and the private realms can have disastrous consequences.

THE SOCIAL REALM

When your relationship is going well, you cherish the public's interest in your life. Your commitment ceremony is joyous, you delight in opening your home to your friends and family, and you fight for the right to be treated equally in your business and financial affairs. But if things turn sour, most likely you will want to hide from any outside intrusion. Unfortunately, you cannot.

Breaking the News

As hard as it is to face your breakup in the privacy of your own home, telling others can be even more brutal. Just when your parents come to love your partner, you have to tell them you no longer want her in your life. Breaking the news to friends isn't so easy either. Everyone knows how difficult a breakup is, and it can be painful to spread bad news, especially with all the hoopla surrounding long-term relationships.

There is always tension between wanting to keep your private life private and wanting to share your story. You will find yourself oscillating between wanting to tell the whole world what is happening to you and, moments later, not wanting a soul to know a thing. Just as same-sex couples lack any vocabulary or ritual for a marriage, we also are deprived of the official words or events to demarcate our divorce.

To minimize the injuries, don't tell many others about an impending breakup until you've told your partner. We are each entitled to a best friend or confessor, and it may be necessary to confide in this friend early on, but limit your broadcasts. You need time to sort things out between the two of you before either of you has to deal with others' inquiries, and telling too many others can cause everyone pain. When you do tell your tale, try to agree on an official story for all but the most intimate friends, so that you aren't tempted to push your perspective on everyone.

Make every effort to keep the financial details of your separation to yourself. Other people's views can vary wildly on this subject, and you don't want to endure the judgments of those who don't know what you're going through. Most important, if your partner hasn't been public about his homosexuality, don't use the breakup as an opportunity to out him. Respect your partner's privacy, and fight out your personal battles where they belong, in private.

The Ritual of Divorce

Our culture lacks rituals for the *end* of important passages in our lives, and so I recommend some kind of separation event as without any ritual there is no sense of farewell. This event can be as simple as the burning of a letter or the return of the commitment rings. We all remember that painful moment when an ex-lover drove away, plants and pets in tow—the last good-bye. Our dissolutions deserve greater ceremony.

Some traditional cultures have developed divorce rituals. Even if you aren't the type to engage in primal ceremonies and sacred dances, you may want to create an event based on the way straight couples do it. Married couples have the legal rituals of divorce, and, as cold and dry as these can be, they do provide some benefit. You file papers, show up in court, and, then, as the judge's gavel comes down on the bench, you are declared divorced. This, of course, is not a very spiritual way of cleansing your soul emotionally, but at least you know your life has officially changed. A simple private ceremony might actually be of some psychological benefit for you.

THE LEGAL/FINANCIAL REALM

Compared to the legal quagmires of most traditional divorces, the logistics of ending a same-sex relationship can be simple once you sort out the distribution of any jointly owned property. Unless you have major financial or property arguments, you won't have to go to court at all, and if your disputes are minor, you may not even have to see an attorney. The same-sex dissolution generally is a do-it-yourself job.

Property Records
If you are transferring ownership of any real estate—or any personal property that has a title or deed—you will need to fill out a special form, get it notarized, and take it to the appropriate government office for filing. For real estate transfers you generally record a grant deed or quitclaim deed at the local county recorder's office; you may need to fill out a recordation document as well, and in many counties you will need to pay a transfer or deed tax at the

time of filing. Make sure you figure out these fees ahead of time, so you can resolve who is going to pay them.

If you co-own real estate that has a mortgage, the transfer process can be tricky. Most banks like to keep as many people on the hook as possible, and often the only way around this is to sign an enforceable private agreement between the two of you that states that the remaining partner won't fall behind on the payments (and then honor it) or have the remaining one get a new loan or formally assume the existing loan in his or her name alone.

Automobiles, RVs, and boats are generally transferred by signing the title over to the new owner and filing the title or bill of sale with the state motor vehicles office, which will then send out a new title with the new owner's name listed. Again, in some states there may be a tax on transfer of ownership of vehicles, equivalent to the sales tax. You should also remember to change the names on corresponding insurance policies, which may require proof of the title change. Make sure you keep copies of all the documents for anyone who requests them.

If you have valuable possessions that don't have titles or deeds, you can transfer ownership simply by delivering them to the new owner. But to avoid future conflicts, it's wise to draft a bill of sale or transfer agreement stating that you've agreed to transfer to one another the items on the attached list for the specified payments or mutually exchanged objects. This prevents either of you from coming back later to "reclaim" something you thought was supposed to be yours.

Domestic-Partnership Termination

If you have registered as domestic partners, either with your local government or with an employer, make sure to file a termination of the domestic partnership with them, as this will help you avoid any subsequent confusion. This task is usually done free of charge. Most cities only allow you to have one domestic partner at a time, so if you don't file a termination neither of you will be able to sign up with a new partner.

Notifying Your Creditors

Be sure to cancel any joint cards and pay off any joint debts. In most instances you can't just withdraw one person's name from a joint debt since the bank will be reluctant to let that debtor out of its grasp. If getting new cards in your name alone and closing out the old account is going to be difficult, write up a valid agreement between yourselves as to who is going to pay the debt.

Court Records

Even though same-sex couples don't participate in the judicial divorce system, there are a few instances when you will need to visit your county courthouse. If either of you has filed a lawsuit over the dispute, you or your attorneys will need to file a formal dismissal once everything is resolved. If either of you has changed your name, now is the time to reclaim your "maiden" name officially.

Tax Issues on Separation

The tax problems for same-sex divorces are quite similar to those that arise at the outset of a relationship. If either of you is transferring real estate or personal property to the other one in exchange for a money payment, the seller may be liable for capital gains taxes if there is a profit on the sale and you aren't able to use the residential sale exemption. In order to determine if there is a profit on sale of real property, you need to calculate your portion of the "basis," which is roughly equal to what you originally paid for your portion of the property plus your share of the capital improvements, and then figure out the profit on your portion of the sale.

If either of you is making a gift of any property (real or personal) to your partner in connection with the dissolution, the generous one may be liable for a gift tax if any year's total gift is valued more than $10,000. Again, that tax is usually handled by reducing the donor's lifetime exemption from estate tax rather than paying it at the time of the gift, so the tax bite isn't really felt until the donor dies. According to the IRS, payments between unmarried couples based on claims of oral or implied contracts, including ongoing financial support for an ex-lover, are considered taxable income to the recipient and are *not* tax-deductible to the one making the payments. This is yet another form of discrimination since married couples usually can transfer property to each other tax-free during a divorce and claim support payments as a tax deduction. If a significant amount of money is involved, check with an accountant before you implement your transfer.

In most instances it may be possible to reduce or even eliminate the tax liabilities of separation by characterizing the transfer in certain ways. You may be able to construe the payment as an exchange for other property given to the one making the payment so that no profit or gift is being made to anyone. You also may be able to characterize a payment as compensation for potential claims that aren't subject to any tax, or you may be able to stagger the payments over several years to keep them below any taxable limit.

Covering the Costs

Depending on your individual situation, breaking up may not be cheap. The commission on selling jointly owned real estate is usually your biggest cost, but there may be fees connected with transferring the car and one of you may not be able to avoid paying some taxes on one transfer or another. It is essential that you familiarize yourself with these costs, sit down with your ex, and decide how you are going to handle them.

Afterword

Creating the New
Same-Sex Marriage

And so we have arrived at the end of our story. You can now fashion your partnership using a variety of prescribed models, or you can create an arrangement of your own design. Working out your options will require a level of self-awareness and honesty that presupposes strenuous self-analysis and reflection. It demands a degree of open communication that carries great risks, and some budding relationships will not survive the unveiling and examination. Compromises and flexibility will be key to your partnership, even while some elements of disappointment, doubt, and risk taking will linger throughout the process.

As each of us works with our partner to articulate and formalize this new kind of partnership, we are also working as a community to foster a new model of relationship. You see it in the absence of gender roles in the domestic lives of your lesbian and gay friends. You see it in the conscious openness with which your women friends handle their birthing choices and in the rationality with which so many of your gay male friends have coped with the challenges and confusions surrounding terminal illnesses. You see it in the way you and your partner have learned to talk openly about money, house buying, and retirement plans.

Amid all the individual varieties of partnerships in our community, certain distinct characteristics are beginning to appear that point the way to a new kind of "gay marriage," one that combines the stability and social validity of traditional marriage with the flexibility, openness, and equality that our sexuality has taught us to value.

Your relationship is secular, not sacred. As powerful as our individual connections may be and as spiritual as our private moments of love may be, the legal nature of our relationship in the public realm is secular, not religious. Our contracts exist in the realm of the law, whatever our particular relationship to gods, goddesses, and spirits may be. Many of us may seek—and hopefully gain—the blessings of our churches, but they are not the arbiters of our legal and financial relationships.

Your relationship is gender-neutral and mutually caring. Our relationships are partnerships of two equal participants; the social roles will emerge from the individual needs and capacities of our unique personalities and the conditions of our lives; they are not based upon any predetermined genetic assignments. There are no husbands and no wives in a same-sex household.

Be together for now, though the future is unknown. While each of us hopes our relationship will endure, we know that many relationships do not. A breakup need not be seen as a failure, and being single should never be perceived as a punishment for one's inadequacies. We can incorporate the possibility of a dissolution into the formation of our relationships, and we will make every effort to orchestrate our dissolutions rationally and equitably, if and when they occur.

Yours is a partnership, not a merger, of two. The traditional model of marriage as a union of two individuals into a single united entity—with the accompanying disappearance of the two individuals—is no longer our model of commitment. We will campaign to preserve regions of autonomy and independence even while we work together to create our expansive realms of joint effort and shared obligations.

Children are a blessing, not an obligation. Families need not consist solely of two parents and their children but may include former partners, close friends, and the children of other parents— or perhaps no children at all. The rights and privileges of family life—including the public benefits of insurance, pensions, housing, and employment—should be bestowed to all families, regardless of composition.

Public benefits are universal, private relations are unique. Public benefits and obligations should no longer be available only to those who structure their relationships on one particular format. As full members of our civil society, we are just as entitled to those benefits, regardless of how we choose to arrange our particular relationships.

Equal. Voluntary. Unique. Realistic. Open communication. Willing to accept the possibility of dissolution. These are the watchwords of our way of marrying, as they offer the maturity and social stability that everyone—straight or gay—is looking for, without sacrificing the valuable lessons we have learned from the centuries of exclusion we have endured and the decades of liberation we have celebrated.

Glossary

Accounting: In the event of a dispute between co-owners of real estate, an accounting is done to determine who owes whom money or what percentage of the property each co-owner is entitled to. The accounting usually is done by an independent auditor or accountant based on documents provided by each party.

Alimony (spousal support): Money paid by one spouse to another after the termination of a legal marriage, either as temporary support between separation and divorce or long-term support after the marriage is legally ended. Most eastern states use the term alimony, while most western states use the term spousal support.

Appraisal: An evaluation of the fair market value of an item of property, usually real estate, but an appraisal may also be obtained for personal property or a business. It is usually based on sales of comparable properties in the area. The value is based on what a willing buyer is likely to pay a willing seller before costs of sale and mortgages are paid off. An appraisal is usually done by a licensed appraiser and is different from a market value opinion done by a real-estate broker or the assessment done by the county to set property taxes.

Arbitration: The resolution of a dispute by a neutral third person, either an attorney or a retired judge. Arbitration can only occur when the parties have previously agreed to it or when they agree to it after a conflict has arisen. An arbitration is usually conducted informally, but the arbitrator's decision can generally be enforced by a local court, just as if a court judge had issued the decision.

Bill of sale: A written document, signed by both parties, setting forth items of personal property that are being sold or transferred. A bill of sale is generally used for items that don't have a title or deed.

Burden of proof: The legal doctrine that establishes which party has the obligation to prove a certain fact when it is disputed by the other party. If the evidence is inconclusive, the party bearing the burden of proof will not prevail.

Capital gain: The profit made in the sale of property, usually real estate, on which federal (and perhaps state) tax will be assessed. The capital gain for real estate is generally the difference between the sales price and the original purchase price, as reduced by depreciation if the property is held for investment. For purposes of calculating capital gain, the amount of a cash down payment or the mortgage loan is irrelevant. Capital gain on residential real estate is generally no longer taxable.

Child support: Money paid by one spouse to another to cover the expenses of caring for a child who is the legal offspring of both parents; unlike spousal support, child support can be awarded even if the parents are not legally married to each other.

Cohabitation agreement: An agreement, generally in writing, between two unmarried partners specifying financial obligations and rights between the parties.

Common-law marriage: In several states heterosexual couples who live together for more than seven years can assert a common-law marriage and thus seek the legal protections of marriage and divorce, such as spousal support or allocation of marital property.

Community property: In the western United States, property or income acquired by either spouse (other than by inheritance or gift) after marriage and before separation by either spouse is community property and is generally divided equally between the spouses upon dissolution. In most other states, such property is called marital property and can be divided in any proportions upon a divorce, based on the judge's decision.

Consideration: In order for a contract to be legally enforceable, the party receiving some benefit must give something in return, called consideration, or the promise will be considered a promise of a gift and not legally enforceable.

Cotenancy agreement: An agreement, generally in writing, between co-owners of real property stating the percentage each party owns and how financial obligations are to be allocated. The agreement can also include provisions on how to resolve conflicts and how to handle the sale of the property, and it frequently includes an agreement to mediate and arbitrate any disputes.

Custody and visitation: These rights occur between coparents of a child. Legal custody determines who has legal authority to make decisions regarding the child, physical custody establishes where and with whom the child resides, and visitation sets the guidelines for a coparent's right to spend time with the child. Custody and visitation orders must be signed by a judge, although the parties can agree on a plan and submit it to the judge for approval.

Discovery: The process of obtaining information from an opposing party in court litigation. Discovery can include interviews of the opposing party (called a deposition), submittal of questions to the opposing party (called interrogatories), request for documents, request for inspection of property, and requests for admissions of certain allegations. While the discovery process generally occurs without court supervision, if the opposing party does not respond to a request a court order compelling responses can be obtained.

Equitable owners: The official term where someone has the rights of ownership of a property but is not listed on the recorded title or deed. The parties listed on the deed are known as legal owners.

Family law: The body of law and, in most states, the area of practice and the court division that handles disputes between legally married parties. In some nonwestern states this area is known as marital law.

Family Leave Act: A federal statute that allows employees to take unpaid leave from their jobs to care for family members without the risk of losing their jobs. As currently written, the act does not cover nonlegal partners who need care.

Fiduciary relationship: A fiduciary relationship exists between unmarried partners and co-owners of real estate (as well as between attorneys and clients). In such situations, each party owes the other a duty to care for that other person and not just him- or herself. Oral and implied agreements between fiduciaries are generally enforceable if proven, even if they involve real estate. If one party actually has control over jointly owned property, this is called a confidential relationship and similar rules apply.

Full faith and credit: A federal doctrine that establishes that court judgments issued in one state regarding marriage, divorce, or adoption are generally honored by other states unless a judge in *that* state determines that doing so would violate a fundamental state policy.

Grant deed/quitclaim deed: A document signed by one party transferring all or partial interest in real property to another person. The deed is generally valid even if it is not recorded with a public official, although the grant can be superseded by a subsequent deed if it is not recorded. A grant deed specifies what the transferor has to convey to the receiving party, while a quitclaim deed transfers whatever the transferor has, which could be nothing or everything.

Implied agreement: A course of action that reasonably leads another party to reasonably believe that a contract or agreement has been made. If proven, implied agreements often can be enforced, even with regard to real property, if the parties are in a fiduciary relationship with one another.

Insurable interest: A legal or financial relationship between two people that justifies the purchase of insurance on the other person's life or the naming of the other person as an insurance beneficiary. Unmarried partners generally do not have an insurable interest in each other's lives unless they own property together, and for that reason it can be difficult for them to buy life insurance for each other's benefit.

Joint tenancy: Equal co-ownership of real estate (as opposed to unequal shares of ownership) in which the surviving co-owner inherits the other person's share if he or she dies while they co-own the property. In most states it is not necessary to go through a court probate to confirm a joint tenancy inheritance, but the value of the property will still be included in the decedent's estate for inheritance tax purposes. By contrast, property owned in tenancy-in-common can be owned in any proportion, and if one owner dies, his or her share passes to his or her heirs, who may not include that person's co-owner.

Lease: An agreement, usually in writing, that grants a non-owner the right to use and occupy property in exchange for payment of money to the owner.

Litigation: Resolution of disputes by court action, commencing with the filing of a formal complaint and lasting until the conflict is resolved, even if there is no trial.

Mediation: This is a valuable method of resolving conflict in which the disputing parties meet with a mediator (and/or with their attorneys) to reach a mutually agreeable settlement. The mediator can be an attorney but could also be a therapist. The parties must agree ahead of time to enter mediation, and the mediator does not render a judgment as to the merits of each argument and cannot compel the parties to accept any proposed settlement. Instead, the parties work together to try to reach agreement, and if they do, they sign a contract which is legally enforceable.

No-fault divorce: The dominant rule in most states of this country providing that the allocation of marital property is unaffected by who terminated the marriage and who may have been guilty of extramarital affairs or cruelty to the spouse.

Palimony: The nontechnical term for a claim for postdissolution support by one unmarried partner against the other partner. While many states allow the filing of such claims, in fact they are rarely granted unless there was a written agreement.

Partition: The legal procedure by which a co-owned property is sold by the court, with the proceeds of sale distributed to the co-owners. If there is a dispute between the parties regarding allocation, the judge will often hold a hearing after the property is sold at which he or she will adjudicate the conflicting claims. In most states, co-owners have the right to demand partition unless they have waived that right in writing.

Pleadings: The generic name for formal demands, responses, and arguments submitted to a court in the litigation process.

Powers of attorney: Authority given by one person to another person in writing. Powers of attorney can cover medical or financial decisions or both, and they can either be general or limited to specific types of actions (i.e., the sale of a particular piece of property or access to a specific bank account). In most states, powers of attorney can either lapse upon a party's disability or survive disability or incompetence (this is called a durable power of attorney).

Prenuptial agreement: An agreement, usually in writing, between two parties who are about to be married in which the general rules of marital property are waived and both parties agree that specific property is to be owned separately by one party. If the agreement is signed after marriage it is generally known as a marital agreement; if the parties are not married the agreement is often referred to as a cohabitation agreement. In most states it is required that each party have his or her own attorney review the agreement in order for it to be valid.

Promissory estoppel: A legal doctrine that holds that if a person reasonably relies to her or his detriment on the express assurances of another person, those assurances can be binding upon the person making the assurances. This doctrine can be used to overcome the doctrine that states that promises made without consideration generally are not considered binding contracts.

Promissory note: A written agreement, generally signed only by the borrower, which states that he or she has received a specified amount of money from the lender and establishes the timing of repayment and the interest to be paid. If the borrower is putting up collateral for the note, it is considered a secured note and must be accompanied by a mortgage or deed of trust, which generally is recorded.

Recordation: The submittal of an agreement to a local county official, usually known as the clerk or recorder, who will copy and register it in the local property records. Once a document is recorded, it can be located and read by the general public. While a document need not be recorded to be valid, if it isn't it can be superseded by a later recorded document. Property transfers and some property agreements are generally recorded, and in most states the signatures must be notarized prior to any recordation.

Second-parent adoption: The legal adoption of a child by an adoptive parent, in which the court order states that the birth parent remains the other legal parent. Some states specifically allow second-parent adoptions, some states ban them, and other states have no firm rules on the subject. A joint adoption takes place when two parents adopt a child from a third person, who then ceases to be a legal parent.

Standing: The legal doctrine that determines who has a right to file a particular claim in court. A nonlegal parent, for example, in many states lacks standing to seek custody or even visitation of his or her partner's child.

Statute of frauds: The legal doctrine that states that contracts regarding certain items, such as transfers of real estate or other valuable possessions, must be in writing and signed by the person giving or transferring them. Agreements between unmarried couples in many states—but not in all states—are exempt from these doctrines and thus need not be in writing.

Statute of limitations: The legal doctrine that establishes time deadlines for filing claims in court. Many claims must be filed within one year of the event giving rise to the claim, whereas other claims need not be filed for two or even four years later.

Trusts (constructive, living and testamentary): An agreement by which one person assigns ownership or future use of property to another person. A constructive trust is said to exist when one person holds title to property but another person has an equitable ownership interest in that property. A living trust is a document signed by someone who transfers certain rights to property to another person during (and/or after) his or her lifetime. A testamentary trust is like a will in that it states who will receive property upon the transferor's death, except no probate is necessary at time of death.

Further Reading

Basic Concerns

Hayden Curry and Denis Clifford. *Legal Guide for Lesbian & Gay Couples.* Berkeley, Calif.: Nolo Press, 1996.

Eric Marcus. The Male Couple's Guide: Finding a Man, Making a Home, Building a Life. New York: HarperCollins, 1992.

Kath Weston. *Families We Choose*. New York: Columbia University Press, 1991.

Parenting Issues

Laura Benkov. *Reinventing the Family: Lesbian and Gay Parents*. New York: Crown Books, 1994.

April Martin. *The Lesbian and Gay Parenting Book: Creating and Raising Our Families*. New York: HarperCollins, 1993.

Lesbians Choosing Motherhood. National Center for Lesbian Rights. San Francisco: 870 Market Street, 94102.

Financial Issues

Peter Berkery, Jr. *Personal Financial Planning for Gays and Lesbians: Our Guide to Prudent Decision Making*. Burr Ridge, Ill.: Irwin, 1996.

Larry M. Elkin. *Financial Self-Defense for Unmarried Couples: How to Gain Financial Financial Protection Denied by Law*. New York: Doubleday, 1994.

Political Matters

Matthew Coles. *Try This at Home, A Do-It-Yourself Guide to Winning Lesbian and Gay Civil Rights Policy*. ACLU Handbook Series. New York: The New Press, 1996.

Counseling and Emotional Issues

Lois Gold. *Between Love & Hate: A Guide to Civilized Divorce.* New York: NAL/Dalton, Plume, 1992.

Index